Mind Your Manners

Mind Your Manners

Managing Business Cultures in the New Global Europe

Third edition

John Mole

NICHOLAS BREALEY
PUBLISHING

LONDON
YARMOUTH, MAINE

This new edition first published in Great Britain by
Nicholas Brealey Publishing in 2003

3–5 Spafield Street
Clerkenwell, London
EC1R 4QB, UK
Tel: +44 (0)20 7239 0360
Fax: +44 (0)20 7239 0370

PO Box 700
Yarmouth
Maine 04096, USA
Tel: (888) BREALEY
Fax: (207) 846 5181

http://www.nbrealey-books.com

First published in paperback in 1992

ISBN 1-85788-314-4

British Library Cataloguing in Publication Data
A catalogue record for this book is available from the British Library.

Library of Congress Cataloging-in-Publication Data

Mole, John. 1945-
    Mind your manners : managing business cultures in Europe / John Mole.– 3rd ed.
    p. cm.
    ISBN 1-85788-314-4 (alk. paper)
    1. Industrial management--Europe. 2. Business etiquette--Europe. 3. Corporate
culture--Europe. I. Title.

HD70.E8 M653 2003
395.5'2'094--dc21

2002038396

Printed in Finland by WS Bookwell.

Contents

Introduction

This book answers the following question:

**What do I need to know about people from European countries that will
help us work successfully together?**

The first edition of this book was published in 1990. At that time there were 12
members of the European Union. In the decade or so since then there have been
extraordinary changes. Communism collapsed, the Berlin Wall came down, and the
two Germanys united. Three more countries joined the EU and the applications for
membership of a further 13 countries have been accepted and are at various stages
of implementation. Twelve countries replaced their currencies with the euro. The
political, economic, and social environments of all the member states have

---

EUROPE AND THE EUROPEAN UNION

Euroland	EU not euro	EU applicant	Non-EU
Austria	Denmark	Bulgaria	Norway
Belgium	Sweden	Cyprus	Russia
Finland	UK	Czechia	Switzerland
France		Estonia	
Germany		Hungary	
Greece		Latvia	
Ireland		Lithuania	
Italy		Malta	
Luxembourg		Poland	
Netherlands		Romania	
Portugal		Slovakia	
Spain		Slovenia	
		Turkey	

The Helsinki European Council declared in December 1999 that, provided the necessary institutional
reform is in place, the Union "should be in a position to welcome new member states from the end of
2002 as soon as they have demonstrated their ability to assume the obligations of membership, and
once the negotiating process has been successfully completed." Countries are expected to become full
members by participating in European Parliament elections between 2004 and 2007.

changed, none more dramatically than Ireland, Spain, and Italy. Privatization and deregulation have transformed sectors such as air transportation and telecommunications. The personal computer, the mobile phone, and the internet have revolutionized how we work together. By the time you read this there will doubtless have been more developments, a few of which may make some facts in this book out of date. Unless these changes are cataclysmic, however, I am confident that the underlying arguments will remain valid.

Change will surely continue to accelerate in ways that we cannot predict. Enlargement of the EU will open up new markets with well-educated, younger populations. However, this will come at a price—political strains on EU institutions and the economic strains of absorbing undercapitalized, unreformed, and underperforming economies. Developments outside Europe will also have a material effect on the personal and working lives of Europeans. The events of September 11, 2001 brought into focus many issues that had previously been ignored: the need to combat terrorism directly, of course, but also to address the political and economic conditions that give rise to it.

The great migrations and colonizations of the nineteenth and twentieth centuries continue unabated into the twenty-first. It is estimated that at any one time there are 12 million migrants on the move, uprooted by economic and social injustice. Some of them seek their fortunes in Europe. How they are welcomed and assimilated is a perennial social and political issue. We can choose to address the causes and management of migration or raise the walls of fortress Europe around our aging and affluent citizens. Globalization, especially terms of trade, environmental policies, and oil politics, whether managed wisely or not, will also lead to shifts in the European business environment.

IN YOUR BUSINESS

- ❐ Do you use first names or last names?
- ❐ Do you make jokes at meetings and presentations?
- ❐ Do people pay more attention to what you say or to what you write?
- ❐ Can you do business before developing good personal relationships?
- ❐ How important are socializing and hospitality?
- ❐ How important is punctuality? Does everything start exactly on time?
- ❐ Where do the most important conversations take place? In the office or somewhere else?
- ❐ At meetings is there a detailed agenda or spontaneous discussion?
- ❐ Does everyone contribute equally or does the boss dominate?
- ❐ Does everyone have to agree on a decision or does the boss decide?

Will people from other cultures give the same answers?

What do the answers tell you about deeply held values and expectations and beliefs?

How do you create and manage a team whose members give different answers?

In this changing world individual people carry on getting up and going to work and doing the best they can for themselves and their families. This book is not about European geopolitics. It is about the values and behavior of people within their organizations. In the following pages I have tried to reflect the changes that affect people's working lives while not losing sight of those fundamental values and behavior.

The book is based on interviews with managers working in countries other than their own, seminars and workshops I have conducted throughout Europe and the US, web-based attitude surveys, and my own experience of 15 years with an American bank. It is not meant to be a book for scholars but for people who deal with cultural differences in their working day. I have excluded anything that the people I spoke to think is irrelevant. The country chapters, for example, are not written to a formula. This is because in some countries aspects of history or geography or behavior are more relevant to understanding people than in others.

In addition, I have a company that markets Russian biotechnology in several western countries and have revised this edition in the light of my experience, so I am confident that it is practical and relevant.

Managing diversity and change

For working people the challenge remains to manage diversity and change simultaneously. The European Union will continue to foster partnerships and joint ventures, mergers and acquisitions, within its territory and across its borders. It has prompted multinationals to convert national subsidiaries into product groups managed by multinational teams. Their effectiveness depends on how well managers of different nationalities work together. Global markets demand a global corporate culture that does not impose uniformity but capitalizes on diversity.

Creating a global business culture takes place on many levels and in several timeframes. At senior executive level there may be a need to create a strategy for developing a business culture appropriate to global goals with measurable objectives and benchmarks. In the short term there may be an immediate problem with dysfunctional multicultural teams. In between these two extremes are skills such as negotiating across cultures and managing project teams. Your culture is changing all the time and will do so ever more quickly with the impacts of globalization and technological development. The question is not whether you want culture change but whether you want to *manage* it.

Working together is different from doing business together as buyer and seller. It requires a deeper understanding of why people from different backgrounds behave the way they do.

A frequent reaction to the different ways that other people do things is judgmental and condescending—"typical German/Italian/Brit"—or something much ruder. Our reactions derive as much from our own attitudes and values as from those underlying the behavior of others. When people pick up this book their first inclination is to look up their own country. They usually want to check if I have got it right, but I hope it has a positive effect too. Understanding one's own culture is a prerequisite for understanding other people's. If this book is an encouragement to suspend judgment and ask why we act in the way we do, it will have succeeded.

About this book

The book is in two parts. The first examines the fundamental differences between European organizational cultures from the point of view of individual managers working within them. It looks at the behavior, values, and beliefs that have most influence on our working relationships with colleagues, bosses, subordinates, and the outside world, within the framework of the Culture Triangle of communication, leadership, and organization. It suggests a simple tool, the Mole Map, for examining different ways in which organizations work.

The second part consists of brief and generalized portraits of the countries of Europe, concentrating on aspects that most affect the national way of doing business. They provide the overall context in which individual organizations operate. The principle was to talk to people of at least three different nationalities about each country, so the result is an amalgam of different national viewpoints. These chapters should be read in addition to more technical books and websites on business practice, taxation, legislation, accounting, and so on, as well as general guides.

There are sound arguments for thinking about European culture on a regional rather than a national basis. A French person living on the North Sea coast may have more in common with a Belgian or a Brit than with a compatriot from the Mediterranean. I have stuck with nation states because in the area of business and organizational cul-

COUNTRY CLUSTERS (FROM NORTH TO SOUTH)

Nordic	Denmark, Finland, Norway, Sweden
Baltic	Estonia, Latvia, Lithuania
British Isles	Ireland, United Kingdom
Low Countries	Belgium, Luxembourg, Netherlands
German-speaking	Austria, Germany, Switzerland
Central Europe	Czechia, Hungary, Poland, Slovakia, Slovenia
Latin	France, Italy, Malta, Portugal, Spain
Balkan	Bulgaria, Cyprus, Greece, Romania
Turkey	
Russia	
Americans in Europe	
Japanese in Europe	

ture people of the same country are likely to adopt a standard way of working together. When the northerner and the southerner meet in Paris on business or work for the same company they are likely to leave their regional behavior at the office door and adopt a standard French way of doing things. If there are differences they are more likely to be associated with the industry or generation. Belgium is the only notable exception.

The countries are grouped in clusters based on a subjective assessment of their cultural similarity. The countries are different from each other and may not have a common language, but in their business cultures they are more similar to each other than to countries in other groups. An outsider with cross-cultural skills in Denmark, for example, will be able to transfer them more easily to another Nordic country than to France or Greece. For countries like Switzerland and Belgium that could be split between two groups, I have plumped for the dominant one.

Euroquiz

Scattered through the book are some quiz questions. The only basis of selection is that I found the answers entertaining. The sources are the web, *Eurostat 2000*, and the *Economist Pocket Europe in Figures*. The answers are at the back of the book.

COFFEE
Which country's citizens drink the most coffee per capita?

Italy

Germany

Finland

The Mole Map Survey

Over three months in 2001 I conducted a web-based attitude survey about the business cultures of European and Asian countries. It was targeted at business school graduates, mostly from INSEAD, but also incorporating those of other business schools in Europe, including Russia. It was also sent to anyone in my email address book whom I knew worked with foreigners. There was a deliberate bias toward people who had graduated after 1985 in order to capture the impressions of a younger generation of business people.

There were 1,100 respondents from 35 countries and 40 nationalities, 30 percent of whom were women.

The survey did not purport to describe the business cultures of the countries concerned. The sample is heavily biased to those whose email addresses I could find and who were willing to respond. Although some simple statistical tools were applied to order the results, the survey has no statistical validity and should not be used in any form of academic research or policy making unless its basis is made clear. Its sole purpose was to substantiate the anecdotal evidence collected in interviews for this book.

That said, the results were pleasantly surprising in that they closely mirrored the ideas outlined in previous editions. There were definite and predictable differences between the results for each country. I am confident that while they do not stand up to statistical scrutiny, they are not misleading.

Above all, the survey results and everything else in this book should be tested against your experience. Please ask your own questions.

If you would like to see the questions and the reason for them, please go to www.johnmole.com/survey.

MURDER

Which EU country has the highest and which the lowest official murder rate?

> Italy
> Luxembourg
> Portugal

PART ONE

ORGANIZATIONAL CULTURES IN EUROPE

The Culture Triangle

Culture is a system that enables individuals and groups to deal with each other and the outside world. Think of it as a spiral. At the heart of the system are shared values and beliefs and assumptions of who and what we are. They manifest themselves in our behavior and language, the groups we belong to, the nature of our society. They are further externalized in our artifacts, our art and technology, the way we deal with and change the physical world. The system also works from outside in. Our physical environment conditions our technology and art, our behavior and language, and so on to the heart of our identity.

Culture is a living, changing system that embraces our personal and social life. Everything we do or say is a manifestation of culture. There is no aspect of human life, from the way we say good morning to the rockets we build to go into space—or bomb our neighbor—that is not culturally conditioned.

There are three points to make about this model:

❏ Whatever culture they belong to, everyone does what works best for themselves and their group. American, German, and Japanese companies make cars that are virtually indistinguishable, yet the cultures that produce them are very different. The only success criterion of a culture is how effective it is in ensuring its survival and prosperity. No culture is intrinsically "better" than any other.

❏ No culture is static. It turns like our spiral. As the rim of a wheel turns faster than its axle, the values at the heart of a culture change more slowly than the technology at the edge, but they still change. And if something changes it can be directed.

❏ The way people behave is not accidental or arbitrary. The external characteristics of culture, from its superficial etiquette to its architecture, are rooted in its hidden values and beliefs. If the externals need to change then so must the values, and vice versa.

As well as debating what culture *is*, it is also interesting to look at what culture *does*. Whether it is national or corporate, culture is a mechanism for uniting people in a common purpose with a common language and with common values and ideas. It can liberate and empower individuals with a sense of self that tran-

Communicates	common language, symbols	*conceals*
Unites	creates groups, societies	*excludes*
Legitimizes	defines good, bad, right, wrong	*represses*
Teaches	shares values and beliefs	*misleads*
Unifies	creates common identity	*marginalizes*
Regulates	maintains order	*oppresses*
Entertains	facilitates play	*trivializes*
Secures	protects against outside forces	*threatens*

scends their own singularity. Or it can create prisoners of a culture no longer appropriate for its time and circumstance, which isolates its members and threatens those outside it.

Corporate cultures are determined by the interaction of parent culture, technology, and the external environment. Again, these are never static and can therefore be directed; there is no "right" culture, only a successful one; and the externals are rooted in deep underlying values.

When people from different nationalities or cultures come together in teams, meetings, negotiations, or as employees of the same company, they bring with them different expectations and beliefs of how they should work together. They have different concepts of what an organization is, how it should be managed, and how they should behave within it.

Cultures of all kinds are invisible until they encounter others, when the differences become apparent. The least dangerous differences are the obvious ones—we notice them and can make adjustments. The dangerous ones are those that lie beneath the surface. In a corporate environment beliefs about the role of the boss, the function of meetings, the relevance of planning, the importance of teamwork, or the very purpose of an organization are often taken for granted among colleagues. Yet they can be very different even among close neighbors. Outward similarities between European business goals can conceal real differences in how they should be realized.

The way others do things is not different out of stupidity or carelessness or incompetence or malice, although it may appear so. Most people do what seems right at the time. The judgment of what is right is rooted in habit, tradition, beliefs, values, attitudes, and accepted norms; in other words, the culture to which that person belongs.

The purpose of this book is not simply to identify cultural differences. It is to identify which of those differences have a serious impact on the way we work together. It is based on a large number of anecdotes and impressions and judgments, ranging from the trivial to the profound. Not that the trivial is unimportant: It can be a source of constant irritation as well as a focus for much deeper frustration. Etiquette may appear trivial—whether to use first or last names, what to wear, how to behave at lunch or at meetings. However, if you get stuck on this superficial level of interaction it is hard to penetrate to a more satisfying level of understanding and cooperation.

> "We are meeting to decide on an investment proposal. I put a lot of time into studying the reports before the meeting. It is evident that my British colleagues at the meeting are examining the papers for the first time. It wastes all our time but it doesn't stop them giving their opinions."
> (Dutch engineer)
> "My staff meetings are very annoying. It is hard to get them to stick to the agenda. And they insist on discussing every point until everyone has had their say."
> (French manager of an Italian company)
> "You have the impression that the French don't realize that they are at a meeting. They don't pay attention or they interrupt or they get up and make a phone call."
> (English director of a Franco-British company)

In researching this book among managers, business issues like objectives or strategy or technology were rarely mentioned as areas of cultural difference; difference of opinion maybe, but not misunderstanding. Most of the difficulties occurred in day-to-day interaction between bosses and subordinates, members of the same work group, other colleagues. By interaction I do not mean the degree of formality or friendliness or other aspects of personal relationships, I mean the way people behave and relate to each other in a business context.

So what determines how people behave and how they interact? In what way do they differ from company to company and country to country? And, most important, which differences get in the way of working effectively together?

Three categories of behavior predominate: communication, organization, and leadership—the Culture Triangle.

Communication is centered on language, although it extends into nonverbal communication and other behavior that gives messages about our expectations and beliefs.

The other two categories relate to values. The first is a set of values about

communication

leadership   organization

organization and the role of individuals within it. How is work organized? How do you forecast and plan? How is information gathered and disseminated? How do you measure results?

The second is a set of values about leadership. Who has power? How do they get it? How do they exercise it? What is authority based on? Who takes decisions? What makes a good boss?

There is a spectrum of belief in each of these dimensions and these combine to influence how people behave toward each other.

There are many other ways of classifying corporate culture and it is possible to break communication, organization, and leadership down into a number of elements. If the human brain were capable of assimilating them in a coherent picture I would bring them all together. Like any other oversimplified theory—and I have never come across a model of human behavior that is not oversimplified—this draws attention to what is omitted as much as what is included. It would be fatuous to claim that this, or any other model, is anything more than an aid to understanding. It is a working tool rather than an explanation.

> **BIRTH RATE**
> Which country has the highest and which the lowest birth rate?
> Ireland
> Turkey
> Latvia

Communication

Language

The single most important competence in international business is the ability to make yourself understood and understand what others are trying to tell you. The rest is important, but not as important as this.

Language is the most obvious and immediate characteristic of another culture and the first barrier to overcome in understanding it. Almost everyone I have interviewed recommended that anyone embarking on a business or any other kind of relationship with someone from another culture should learn something about the language. This applies even if the other person speaks your language fluently or you are working in a third language. It is unlikely that you will ever be good enough to do business in the language or have a serious conversation. And if you do business in several countries those are impossible tasks. So why bother, especially if you speak English?

First of all, it is a courtesy to know at least some of the essential politeness words. Most people, especially if they speak a minority language, are pleased and flattered that foreigners make the effort, even if it is only a phrase or two. It is a sign that you do not take it for granted that they should speak your language and you appreciate the fact that they do. This is especially important if you are a native English speaker.

Secondly, an acquaintance with someone else's home language helps you to understand them when they are speaking yours. If French speakers say "actually" or "delay" or "interesting" when they are speaking English, they may be using the words in the French and not the different English sense. When a Russian or a Chinese speaker answers "yes" in their own language to a negative question they are reinforcing the negative. For example, "Are you not going to sign the contract today?"—"yes" means that they are not going to sign it. "Are you not going to sign it?"—"no" means that they are going to sign it. When they are speaking English or another European language it is possible that they are keeping to their own usage. Such nuances are useful to know.

Thirdly, language is not only a vehicle for communication but gives an insight into a people's ways of thinking, attitudes, and behavior. Much of our culture is handed down and disseminated through language. Look up "anglais" in a French slang dictionary and "French" in a similar English dictionary and you will sense the historical relationship of the two countries and the origin of the stereotypes that they have of each other. (In short, the English language associates the French with pleasure and sophistication, the French language associates the British with violence and boring food.) Knowing that Finnish does not distinguish between genders, that it has the same word for he and she, explains why Finns sometimes mix up pronouns when they speak English. Knowing that Chinese has no tenses, that verbs make no distinction between past, present, and future, may help understand Chinese concepts of time.

International English...

Some years ago I was hired by an American bank. I received a letter from the head of human resources that started, "Dear John, I was quite pleased that you have decided to join us." That "quite" depressed me. I thought he was saying, "We're kinda pleased but wish we had hired someone else." A few weeks after I started work I discovered that in American English "quite" does not mean "fairly," as it does in British English, but "very." At about this time my American boss told me to "table" an idea I had. So I brought it up at the next staff meeting, to his extreme displeasure. In British English "table" means put *on* the agenda, while in American English it means take *off* the agenda.

The concept of the boss as "coach" is still in vogue. An analogy taken from sport, it is originally American training speak and has been adopted extensively in Europe. However, the role of the coach in American sport is very different from that in Europe. The team coach in the US is what in Europe is called the team manager, an authoritarian figure who is solely responsible for selecting and managing the

WORD	INTERNATIONAL ENGLISH MEANING	POSSIBLE OTHER MEANING	EXAMPLE
Coach	Manager	Trainer, tutor (UK)	My boss is a good coach
Delay	Period of lateness	Period of time (F)	A delivery delay of three weeks
Eventually	After a time	Perhaps (F, D)	She will arrive eventually
Interesting	Holding the attention	Profitable (F) Stupid (UK)	An interesting idea
Motivate	Stimulate, urge	Justify (F)	The choice was motivated by…
Qualified	Partial, conditional	Total (F)	A qualified success, statement
Quite	Very (US, trad. UK)	Not very (UK)	Our product is quite reliable
Table	Put on the agenda	Take off the agenda (US)	Table a proposal
Luck out	Have good luck (US)	Have bad luck (SA)	We lucked out
Actually	In fact, but	At present (F)	Actually she's in Rome
Look at	Read	Revise, rewrite (UK)	(Take a) look at this report
Hear	Listen to	Disagree (UK)	I hear what you say

team and frequently dictates the play. A coach in the UK has an entirely different role, that of trainer or tutor. I have seen an American boss and his British staff in complete agreement about the nomenclature of his role as coach but at permanent loggerheads as to how he executed it.

The potential for misunderstanding increases with people who speak English as a second language. The English that they learn in the classroom as children is not the same colloquial language that native speakers use. International English has a simple vocabulary and a standard pronunciation. Native English speakers have a variety of accents, colloquialisms, and slang that foreigners find as difficult to understand as a Cockney does Glaswegian. At international meetings and conferences in English it is most often the native English speakers who are criticized for being unintelligible.

It is not an exaggeration that native English speakers should make a conscious effort to learn international English, perhaps by listening hard to their foreign colleagues. A first step is deliberately to try to avoid slang, jargon, and figures of speech like "what's the bottom line" and "it's all above board." Phrases like "I wonder if you wouldn't mind…" and "it's not worth…" can be mystifying. The result may be a bland Eurospeak, but at least everyone will understand it.

The problem is compounded by the reluctance of most people in any culture to admit that they have not understood what has been said, whether out of politeness or embarrassment. When I started to do multinational seminars I distributed yellow cards for people to hold up if anyone said anything they did not understand. No one ever waved one, so I abandoned the idea. Instead, we have comprehension checks every 15 minutes or so. Whatever the circumstances, I strongly recommend some routine measure to make sure that everyone understands what is going on.

Nobody can be expected to know all the ambiguities, "false friends," and traps. What is essential is that you check and check again that everyone has really understood what has been communicated.

. . .and how you use it

Survey

"Do they say clearly what they think?"

Cyprus Austria Spain Estonia Poland Norway
Hungary Ukraine Greece N Am. Germany
Bulgaria Portugal France Belgium Denmark
Romania UK Italy Slovakia Czech Sweden Finland
Japan Turkey Ireland China Austria Russia Switz N'lands

unclear   clear

Language is not only the words we speak. It is body language, dress, manners, attitudes, and conventions of behavior. The way language is used varies from culture to culture. Scandinavians and Dutch, for example, are very explicit. They try to say exactly what they mean and use facts and figures to back it up. The British are more vague. They are fond of allusion and understatement, hints and hedging, which many foreigners find confusing or even hypocritical. Conversely, allusive speakers can be shocked by blunter speakers.

Humor

In some cultures, Britain and Ireland for example, humor is widely used to create a relaxed atmosphere, lighten tedium, and defuse tension when things get difficult. It is also employed to disguise

Survey
"Do they use humor in business?"
Romania Bulgaria Finland Russia Italy Cyprus N.Am Estonia Portugal Poland Slovakia Norway Greece N'lands Germany Japan Czech France Ukraine Hungary Spain UK Turkey China Switz Belgium Sweden Austria Denmark Ireland
rarely   *sometimes*   *often*

aggression. In North America a speech or a presentation almost invariably starts with a joke, frequently an irrelevant one. But in other cultures humor has no place at work. To make a joke in the middle of a meeting, for example, is interpreted as frivolous or cynical.

What is more, humor travels badly, as a glance at foreign cartoons will demonstrate. So much depends on a subtle use of language—understatement, word play, innuendo, and so on—which gets lost in translation or in international English. The country humor rating from the survey applies only to the business context. As anyone who knows Germany or Japan or Turkey will confirm, outside the business environment a sense of humor is as well developed and as frequently exercised as anywhere else.

Oral styles

Direct speakers appear rude and overbearing to indirect speakers. Indirect speakers appear evasive and unclear to direct speakers. Those who use humor appear flippant to those who do not. There are many other ways in which different communication styles can lead to misunderstanding.

Oral Styles		
Direct	. . . .	Indirect
Rude		*Unclear*
Loud	. . . .	Soft
Domineering		*Uncommitted*
Expressive	. . . .	Inexpressive
Aggressive		*Secretive*
Humorous	. . . .	Serious
Flippant		*Unfriendly*
Simultaneous	. . . .	Serial
Shallow		*Critical*

In some cultures (France, for instance) people speak more loudly than in others. They may appear domineering to soft speakers (Turkey), who in turn seem uncommitted and unenthusiastic. People who use expansive gestures and emphatic facial expressions (Greece) may seem aggressive to people whose body language is restrained (Germany). Simultaneous speakers (Ireland) are those who like to interrupt, encourage, interject, finish sentences, and may appear shallow and rude to serial speakers (Finland). Serial speakers listen intently often without any verbal or body language except for a disconcerting stare, wait until the other person has finished, stay silent for a moment while they digest what has been said, and then reply without any expectation of being interrupted themselves.

It is difficult to change your communication style deliberately, partly because everyone sees themselves as "normal." It is more important to avoid drawing wrong conclusions from other people's styles.

Oral, literal, and visual

Survey

"Is important communication oral or written?"

Ukraine Ireland Portugal Czech Poland Denmark
Turkey Greece Romania Slovakia N.Am Sweden Switz
Cyprus Italy Russia Belgium Hungary UK Austria Finland
Bulgaria Spain China N'lands Japan France Norway Germany

oral   written

In all cultures people use a mix of oral, literal, and visual communication. You can tell someone you love them or write a love letter or draw a heart with an arrow through it—but different cultures use these in different proportions. They trust one more than the others.

Northern cultures are more literal and southern Europeans more oral. Most if not all of the examinations that Italians take to get a university degree are oral. They are brought up to acquire and impart information through the spoken word, while their German colleagues are trained to read and write what is important. People from oral cultures have longer concentration spans, better memories, and are prepared to act on the spoken word.

People from literal cultures will not usually take the spoken word seriously unless it is confirmed in writing, so it is a good idea to confirm conversations with a letter or a fax. For those from oral cultures, written communication is primarily for the record and not a vehicle for conveying information. Their first reaction to a written communication is not "What does this say?" but "Why is this being written down?" This does not mean that they create less paperwork than the others—they just don't pay as much attention to it. It is therefore a good idea to confirm letters and faxes with a covering phone call, if only to make sure that the document has been read. In North America communication is primarily literal but at the same time more visual than in Europe, incorporating graphics, diagrams, and highlighted bullet points.

Business or personal

If you are in the middle of a negotiation and it is time for lunch, northern Europeans and Americans may order in sandwiches and coffee while everyone gets on with business. This is an indication that they are taking the matter seriously. Breaking off to go to a restaurant may be seen as an unnecessary interruption. However, for southern Europeans the signals are opposite. Food and drink figure higher in their value system. Going to a good restaurant is an indication of seriousness as well as an opportunity to take the discussion further.

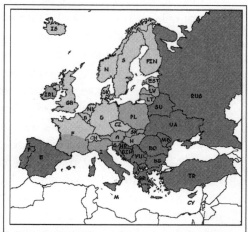

Personal relationships in business   irrelevant / important / essential

Wining and dining are more important the further south one goes in Europe, not because southerners are more sybaritic but because of different concepts of the role of personal relationships within a business relationship. In northern Europe and even more so in North America, it is possible to walk into the office of a complete stranger with a proposal and begin to talk business. A business relationship is seen as independent from a personal relationship. It is not that personal relationships don't develop, they are independent of the business relationship.

The further south you go in Europe and the further east around the world, the more important it is to cement social and personal relationships before you can even start to work together. Potential partners look for reassurance that the others are good people to do business with before they look at the deal itself. You need introductions, references, and time to develop personal relationships before getting down to business. Hospitality and gift giving are an integral part of the courtship period, unlike in

Survey

"Are good personal relationships essential to do business?"

Ukraine Italy Portugal Estonia UK N'lands
Bulgaria Greece France Czech Finland Denmark
Turkey China Spain Austria N.Am Switz Sweden
Russia Romania Slovakia Poland Germany
Japan Hungary Belgium Cyprus Ireland Norway

yes   _no_

northern countries where they belong to the honeymoon—is the Christmas gift in appreciation of last year's business or in anticipation of next year's?

Northerners find it difficult to understand not only the importance of personal relationships but also their nature. This does not mean getting on well with others or even liking them. Trust and confidence are important factors, but that is true among northerners too. The essential element of a personal relationship in this context is mutual obligation. People in "relationship cultures" grow up in networks of mutual obligation, starting with family and extending to religious affiliation, school and university, home town or region, intake into the company, or common work experience. These are enhanced and enlarged by favors, gift giving, hospitality, and other intangible exchanges. There is an expectation that people linked by such ties are bound to give first preference to each other in whatever social or business context they interact. To people outside these cultures this sounds like nepotism and cronyism, even corruption. To those inside them it is the foundation of social and business organization.

When employees of different companies do business with each other in non-relationship cultures, they are seen primarily as representatives of their companies. The companies are primarily responsible for carrying out the terms of the contract between them. If the people who did the deal leave or get transferred the business stays with the companies. In relationship cultures business is seen to be done primarily between individuals. They have a personal as well as a corporate responsibility to ensure that the terms are met. This obligation remains even if they get transferred. If they leave the company the business will go with them. If the business ceases for any reason the relationship will continue.

It takes much longer to start business in relationship cultures than in non-relationship cultures. People invest more time and effort in the personal relationship because of its importance and relative permanence. A short cut is to be introduced and recommended by someone already in the network. This in turn creates debt on the newcomer, which one day will be called in, although it is still up to the newcomer to build up their own credit.

Body language

Although language is the single most important element in communication, it is by no means the only one. It has been said that communication is only 20 percent verbal while the rest is intonation, body language, and so on. You may wonder how the percentage can be calculated, but the fact remains that mastering vocabulary and grammar is only the beginning of effective communication.

There are several types of body language. First are deliberate gestures meant to communicate something specific. Most of them are not universal and can be misinterpreted. For example, make a circle by putting the tip of your middle finger on top of your thumb. In English-speaking countries this usually means OK, good. In France it means zero, bad. In the eastern Mediterranean it is obscene. In Japan it means money. Who could forget seeing President Clinton giving the thumbs up to a mass rally in Nigeria and being greeted by a roar from the audience? It was as if a foreign dignitary had given the finger to those in the White House Rose Garden.

Even the simple handshake is different from country to country. Anglo-Saxons are taught to look the other person in the eye and use a firm grip. However, to many people that can feel like a challenge, an invitation to arm-wrestle. In central Europe and parts of Scandinavia you nod the head in respect, a gesture that can appear to others as a head-butt. In Mediterranean countries the handshake can be accompanied by an arm squeeze with the other hand, a vestigial embrace. Many other gestures and signals, whether deliberate or unconscious, have different meanings across borders.

Body language also means the involuntary postures that express our feelings toward others. Sometimes they contradict the feelings that we communicate verbally or that others expect. From an early age we are taught how to modify, channel, and suppress instinctive physical interaction with others. For example, cultures that favor indirect communication and the repression of outward displays of feeling, like those of Japan or England, encourage impassive facial features and rigid deportment. The physical space between people, eye contact, touching, the angle of the head and the torso are loaded with meanings that can be misinterpreted by outsiders.

While they may manifest themselves in different ways and with different emphasis, there are some general principles of body language that are common to most cultures.

There are two basic groups of body language postures: **open/closed** and **forward/back**. Open/closed is the most obvious. People with arms folded, legs crossed, and bodies turned away are signaling that they are rejecting messages. People showing open hands, fully facing you and both feet planted on the ground, are accepting them.

Forward/back indicates whether people are actively or passively reacting to communication. When they are leaning forward they are actively accepting or rejecting the message. When they are leaning back, looking up at the ceiling, doodling on a pad, cleaning their glasses, they are either passively absorbing or ignoring it.

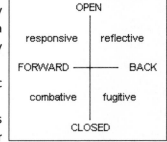

The posture groups combine to create four basic modes: responsive, reflective, fugitive, and combative.

In responsive mode, **open/forward**, the person is actively accepting. This is the time to close the sale, ask for

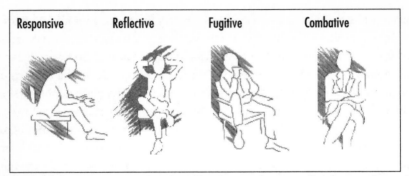

| Responsive | Reflective | Fugitive | Combative |

agreement, demand a concession. In reflective mode, **open/back**, people are interested and receptive but not actively accepting. Trying to close the sale or asking for
agreement now may drive them away into fugitive mode. This is the time to present
further facts and incentives. It may also be a good time to keep quiet and let them
think.

In fugitive mode, **closed/back**, people are trying to escape physically through
the door or mentally into boredom. This is the time to spark interest in any way you
can, even if it is irrelevant to the message. Finally, in combative mode, **closed/
forward**, there is active resistance. This is the time to defuse anger, avoid contradiction and outright argument, and steer the other person into reflective mode.

While there are cultural variations in how people express these modes, they are usually easily recognizable in any European country.

RELIGION
In which of these countries is Orthodox
Christianity an official religion?
> Finland
> Greece
> Romania

The geography of thinking

How do you teach children arithmetic? By counting beads and playing with rods or by teaching them multiplication tables? People in different cultures are taught to think differently.

At the beginning of the seventeenth century the English philosopher Francis Bacon formulated the "scientific method." The essence is that one gathers observable facts from which a general conclusion or hypothesis can be drawn. This is known as induction, the inferring of a general law from particular instances. A few years later the French philosopher René Descartes formulated a theory of knowledge derived from the single indisputable premise that he was thinking, therefore he existed, *Cogito ergo sum*. This is known as deduction, the inferring of particular instances from a general law.

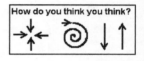

Since the Renaissance, Europe has been divided between the pragmatic, empirical, inductive thinking of Anglo-Saxon and North Sea cultures and the rationalist, deductive thinking of the rest of the continent. Anglo-Saxons are uncomfortable with theories, generalizations, and concepts. They prefer to deal with data. Other Europeans are uncomfortable with dealing with data unless it is in the context of an idea or a system. The difference is reflected in the history of European philosophy and the way our children are taught in schools, the way football teams are managed, and how we structure memos, reports, and presentations. In Britain public debates about the European Union, the euro, transport policy, and public services are notable for their lack of theoretical content, while in France they are driven by concept more than pragmatism.

What these modes of thinking have in common is that they are linear. They are based on logical reasoning, categorization, and a belief in cause and effect. Other ways of thinking—intuition, emotional intelligence, lateral thinking, free association, and flashes of insight from nowhere—are mistrusted unless they can be logically substantiated.

Within these broad categories of thinking, different cultures may use different intellectual tools to arrive at a conclusion. They can be misunderstood or misinterpreted as socially inappropriate. The Socratic irony often encountered in Hispanic culture, in which humility or pretended ignorance is a device for questioning, can seem like stupidity to others. Germanic skepticism, in which arguments are habitually doubted, can seem aggressive and rude to those who associate ideas with the people who voice them. The dialectic taught to French people from an early age, in which a thesis is instinctively countered by antithesis to arrive eventually at a synthesis, can seem like deliberate obstructiveness. Middle Eastern discursiveness that explores every aspect of a proposition from all possible angles can seem like obfuscation—and so on.

In reality we use all of these ways of thinking. Pragmatists need some kind of hypothesis or intuition in order to select data on which to work. Rationalists require some data to germinate ideas. Even Descartes needed an observable premise, that he was thinking. Nevertheless, different cultures give different emphasis to different modes or do not admit them at all.

Whenever people of different cultures work together there is a possibility that different ways of thinking will create barriers to understanding and communication. For example, at a management meeting or presentation, if you belong to the Anglo-Saxon tradition your contribution will probably be fact based, nontheoretical, and based on linear logic. You will have arrived at your conclusions by investigation and analysis and you will expect others to ask questions. It is possible that in some or all of these respects you will not connect with your audience. Throw in jokes, slang and jargon, and stick to summarizing the issues you expound in the written material you distribute, and you may lose them completely.

TENNIS

Which country has won the Davis cup most often?

France

Germany

Czechia

Organization and leadership

Organization

The organization dimension of the Culture Triangle is based on the balance between personal relationships and rational order in human affairs.

At one end of the spectrum people believe that an organization is like a machine, designed and built to certain specifications to achieve a precise objective. For the purposes of this book I have called this approach *systematic*. At the other end of the spectrum is the belief that an organization is a social organism growing out of the needs and relationships of its members. I have called this *organic*. In reality most people hold a mix of these views. However, different cultures have a different mix, tending to one end or the other.

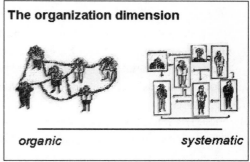

The organization dimension

organic   *systematic*

You could also call the dimension mechanistic–social or task–people or formal–informal or whatever description you find most meaningful. These are all jargon words whose meaning is loaded with bias, depending on which part of the spectrum you belong to. What is important is to identify the ways of doing things that are associated with each end of the spectrum.

Systematic organizations

Toward the systematic end is the belief that the basic elements of organization are functions that are coordinated by well-defined, logical relationships. The effectiveness of a systematic organization depends on how well its functions have been designed to meet its goal. Relations between people are primarily determined by the function they carry out.

A systematic organization exists independently of its members and its needs are more important than the needs of individuals. If there is a clash between order and the individual, then it is accepted that order prevails over loyalty to individuals.

What you do matters more than who you are. The relationship between the individual and the organization is rational. It is based on a contract, explicit or implicit. There is a clear distinction between an individual's identity and their organizational function. The individual contributes skills to the organization but is never absorbed by it. If what you do does not meet the needs of the organization, then you have no reason to belong to it.

Organic organizations

Toward the organic end of the dimension is the belief that organizations are like living organisms growing out of the needs of their members, their environment, and the circumstances of the moment. Functions change, as do the relationships between them. There is order—otherwise there would be no organization at all—but it is based on personal relationships and social hierarchy rather than being a functional system.

The effectiveness of an organic organization depends on how well its members work together to reach their common goals. If there is a clash between order and the individual, then the individual prevails or there is a compromise. This does not necessarily mean anarchy (see below), although it may mean that the order is re-examined.

The relationship between the individual and the organization is blurred, not because it is irrational or emotive but because the distinction between them is not perceived. It is inconceivable that an organization can exist independently of its members. It is not that who you are matters more than what you do; there is no distinction between these. Every member of an organization has a part to play in it simply by virtue of belonging. Company loyalty means loyalty to individuals.

The extremes: Anarchy and automatism

The organic end of the dimension can be extended to anarchy, where organizations, if they exist at all, are spontaneous and ephemeral. At the systematic end is automatism, in which the organization is seen purely in terms of functionality. Most European businessess fall well within these two extremes.

Making assumptions visible

The assumptions that people hold about the nature of organizations are for the most part invisible to those who hold them. They are more recognizable when they are translated into attitudes toward specific organizational processes.

The table opposite illustrates some of the features of systematic and organic cultures. They are examples rather than an exhaustive list. As you skim through the list, mentally tick off which statements you agree with most. This will give you an idea of where you come in the spectrum. The division will rarely be clear-cut, but there will probably be a consistent bias.

ORGANIZATION	SYSTEMATIC	ORGANIC
When decisions are made, do they include detailed action plans?	Yes	No
Do people have to be chased to carry them out?	No	Yes
Do you have procedure manuals?	Yes	No
Do people rigorously follow procedures?	Yes	No
Do you have an accurate written job description?	Yes	No
Do you have specific goals and targets?	Yes	No
Do you have regular appraisals?	Yes	No
Is analysis more respected than experience in decision making?	Yes	No
Are contacts more important than achievement in getting promoted?	No	Yes
At a meeting, do people stick closely to the agenda?	Yes	No
Are flexibility and last-minute improvisation common?	No	Yes
Are important decisions made informally, even outside the office?	No	Yes
Is it very important to be organized and punctual?	Yes	No
Are home life and office life rigorously separated?	Yes	No
Are personal relationships vital in getting things done?	No	Yes

Punctuality

A Litmus test for where a company lies on the organization dimension is the value given to time keeping. The more punctual people are, the more they will tend toward the systematic end of the dimension and its mechanistic view of organization. People toward the organic end of the dimension are not deliberately unpunctual or inefficient. If they are late an apology is called for, but sticking to a timetable is not an end in itself.

Survey		
	"How punctual are they?"	
Turkey Italy Russia UK		Sweden
Portugal Bulgaria Ireland Latvia Estonia Hungary Norway		
Greece China Ukraine Slovenia N.Am Slovakia Denmark		
Romania Cyprus Belgium Austria N'lands Germany Finland		
Spain France Lithuania Czech Poland Japan Switz		
over 15 mins late	*up to 15 mins late*	*on time*

The agenda (diary in British English)

In systematic organizations, unless there is a real emergency, it is difficult to see anyone or arrange a meeting at short notice. Schedules and agendas are arranged long in advance, kept by secretaries and adhered to. This takes a lot of the stress out of

life, but also removes the excitement and the potential for creativity. In such organizations I was given an appointment days or weeks in advance, conducted my
interview within a set time, and left.

> **Survey**
> *"Are they flexible or do they stick to procedures?"*
> China Turkey Portugal Russia Belgium Latvia Austria
> Estonia Ukraine Hungary Slovakia N.Am Lithuania Czech
> Greece Italy Belg W Cyprus Norway Slovenia Japan
> Bulgaria Romania Poland UK N'lands Finland Switz
> Ireland Spain France Denmark Belg F Sweden Germany
>
> flexible   procedures

In organic organizations appointments are scheduled and rescheduled at short notice and the timetable is fluid. The agenda is a guide known only to its holder-secretaries and assistants may not know anything about their bosses' whereabouts. You can hold a meeting or get to see someone at short notice even if it means canceling something less important. In really flexible cultures nothing will be canceled and everyone will turn up at the same time.

To those from systematic cultures this sounds chaotic, but those who live within it are adept at managing the conventions to everyone's advantage. This book, for example, was much easier to research in such organizations. If it sounded interesting to the person I contacted, he or she saw me immediately, passed me on to others, invited me to sit in on meetings, and so on.

Leadership

The leadership dimension of the Culture Triangle is based on the extent to which it is believed that groups give power to individuals.

This form of words was carefully chosen to reflect the fact that a leader's authority, at least in a European business organization, can only be exercised with the consent of the people who are being led. The values associated with followership are identical to those associated with leadership.

> **The leadership dimension**
>
> individual
>
> group

The spectrum of belief about leadership ranges from individual to group. You could also call it directive–participative, autocratic–democratic, top-down–bottom-up, authoritarian–egalitarian, or whatever description you find most meaningful. These words are themselves loaded with bias and ambiguity. What is important is to identify the attitudes and behavior associated with different parts of the dimension.

Individual leadership

Toward the individual end is the belief that individuals are intrinsically unequal and that the most effective, knowledgeable, or competent take decisions on behalf of the others. Power is a right to be exercised by superiors over inferiors.

Group leadership

Toward the group end of the dimension is the belief that while individuals may be unequal in ability and performance, everyone has a right to be heard and to contribute to all the decisions that affect them. For the sake of convenience leaders are so designated for as long as they embody the interests and the voice of those they represent.

The extremes: Collectivism and absolutism

The group end of the dimension can be extended to collectivist and the individual end to absolutist. The collectivist belief is that power should be shared and exercised equally, since all individuals are of equal value and take equal part and have equal weight in everything. The absolutist belief is that power is concentrated in the top person, who acts as he or she sees fit whether other people like it or not. Most European business organizations fall between these two extremes.

Again, it should be emphasized that these are attitudes shared by everybody in the organization, not merely the bosses. For example, an individual leadership culture implies not only that bosses take decisions and give orders on their own responsibility, but also that their subordinates expect them to do so and willingly execute the orders without question.

It is tempting to use the word "democratic" in this context. Unfortunately this has several meanings, most of them emotive and loaded with bias. For example, a boss in an individual leadership culture can go to great lengths to consult with subordinates about a decision. What he or she is looking for is information on which to base a judgment. The boss in a group culture is looking not only for information but also for participation in the responsibility for a decision. Both would regard themselves as "democratic."

It should also be remembered that the dimension deals with the role of individuals in the organizational process and not with their personal style. It is possible to be unassuming and empathic and still believe that you are the boss and the responsibility falls on your shoulders alone, just as it is possible to be macho and assertive and still believe that the only way to get things done is through the participation of a group.

LEADERSHIP	INDIVIDUAL	GROUP
Who makes important decisions?	Individual managers	Groups or teams
Who develops the strategic plan?	Top management	Everyone concerned
Who knows what the strategy is?	Top management	Everyone in the company
Do decisions need everyone's agreement before they are implemented?	No	Yes
Are decisions made after full consultation with everyone they affect?	No	Yes
Do managers keep their distance from subordinates?	Yes	No
Do managers make an effort to be participative and good listeners?	No	Yes
Who sets your goals and targets?	My manager	My manager and I together
When achievement is publicly recognized, who are singled out?	Individuals	Teams or departments
Does competition between individuals get in the way of teamwork?	Yes	No
If you have a work-related problem, who do you go to first?	My manager	A colleague
What are most of the meetings you go to for?	Briefing and instruction	Problem solving
Are most of your meetings firmly managed by the chair or round-table discussions?	Controlled by chair	Round table
If you want something done do you see people individually or call a meeting?	See people individually	Call a meeting
Are meetings an efficient way to get things done?	No	Yes

Teams

The concept of working in teams is common to most organizations. An organization is in itself a team. Nevertheless, the team's structure and purpose and how its members interact are different according to the prevailing culture. In a systematic culture a team is an assembly of specialists, each with a recognized contribution to make. In an organic culture the composition and purpose of the

Survey

"Do they work well in teams?"

Japan N.Am Finland Austria Lithuania
Sweden Estonia Poland Czech Ukraine Slovakia China
Norway Ireland Belgium Portugal Russia France Cyprus
Denmark Switz Spain Slovenia Italy Bulgaria Romania
N'lands UK Germany Latvia Hungary Greece Turkey

yes   *no*

team will be more loosely framed. Its members will see the goals of the team and their individual responsibilities as less clearly defined.

In group leadership cultures teams—taskforces,

Survey
"Are bosses one of the team or do they keep a distance?"
Ireland Norway   Italy Latvia Turkey
Sweden N'lands   UK Slovakia Lithuania Russia Czech
Denmark Finland Spain   Cyprus Slovenia Austria Japan
Estonia Poland Belgium Greece France Ukraine Romania
N.Am   Switz   China Hungary Germany Bulgaria Portugal
team   *distance*

SWAT teams, project teams—can cut across hierarchical lines, a concept that may be permanently enshrined in the organization with formal matrix management. This will be more difficult in individual leadership cultures in which organizational clarity and reporting lines are given a high value.

The role of the team leader will be different. In individual cultures leaders keep a distance from those they manage. In return for deference they are expected to set the

Survey
"Who takes decisions?"
Japan   Ireland   Poland   Spain   Russia
Sweden   Czech   N.Am   Greece Bulgaria Slovenia Romania
Norway   Estonia Germany   Austria   China Latvia Slovakia
Denmark Finland Belgium Italy   Cyprus   Portugal Turkey
N'lands   UK   Switz   France Hungary Lithuania Ukraine
team   *team leader*

team's goals and take the key decisions, with or without the consensus of the other team members.

In group cultures the leader's role is primarily coordination. All the team members, including the leader, have more or less equal status. According to the survey results this team model is primarily associated with Japanese, Nordic, and North Sea cultures. In every other culture it was reported that teams work best with strong leadership, including responsibility for decisions.

GEOGRAPHY
How far south does the European Union extend?
Tropic of Cancer
Equator
Tropic of Capricorn

Culture clash

From the tables on the previous pages you can get an idea of how the organization and leadership dimensions can combine to create four very different cultural archetypes. To make discussion of them clearer, I have borrowed images from Wild West mythology. (The company type is for alliteration, not nationality.)

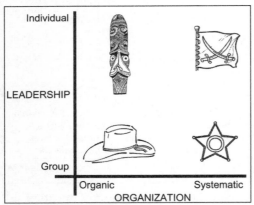

Indians Inc. combines organic organization with individual leadership. It is led by a hereditary chief sanctioned by the spirits of the tribe. Organization depends on tradition, precedent, folk memory, and an intricate network of tribal relationships. Its logo is the totem pole. The archetype is a family company.

Cavalry Corp. combines systematic organization with individual leadership. It is led by a commander who has worked his way up through an orderly system of ranks to a position of legally sanctioned and centralized authority. Organization is based on procedures, manuals, and a formal system of training and qualifications. Its logo is crossed swords on a flag. The archetype is a multinational company.

Posse plc combines systematic organization with group leadership. It is a well-organized and legally sanctioned group of specialists with well-defined targets. They elect a sheriff whose tenure depends on their support and his (or her) performance. He may appoint deputies among the group as long as they are willing to serve. Its logo is the sheriff's badge. The archetype is a large accounting or consulting firm.

Outlaws SA combines organic organization with group leadership. It acts on collective authority, decision making, and equal sharing of the spoils. Organization is fluid, spontaneous, expedient, and based on personal relationships between the members, who act as they see fit. A leader may emerge for the moment but is in danger of being shot in the back. It has no logo but its members wear various types of black hat. The archetype is a new creative or high-tech partnership.

Take the example of forecasting.

Indians Inc.

If it is done at all, forecasting is the expression of a general strategy based on the experience, business sense, and flair of the chief executive. He (or she) is prepared to change it if circumstances change. Only a few key people know what is in his mind, which gives him the opportunity of changing it without embarrassment and does not undermine his position if he gets it wrong. He does not have the tools to translate his plan into budgets and forecasts, but concentrates instead on a few key indicators such as sales, market share, or cash flow.

Cavalry Corp.

Forecasting and planning are regarded as very important. They are still the preserve of senior management, but are much more systematic. The chief executive has perhaps engaged a firm of strategy consultants, even if he (or she) has his own strategic planning staff. When the plan is drawn up and approved by the board, it is broken down into quarterly forecasts and monthly operating plans and presented to middle management. Adherence to the operating plan is closely monitored, with a sophisticated pyramidal management information system culminating in the chief executive.

Posse plc

The planning process is just as systematic as in Cavalry Corp. but many more people are involved. It starts at a low operating level with line management teams drafting their own plans and budgets during a series of planning conferences and meetings with their colleagues and staff advisers. Plans are centralized, consolidated, sent back for revision, redrafted, and finally accepted. The sophisticated management information system is designed to give the line manager as much feedback as possible.

Outlaws SA

There is probably no actual plan, but everyone has their own idea of what it is. There are interminable discussions about where the company should be going and what it should be doing. Although there is no formal plan, so much debate and discussion about it leads to a consensus through the organization of what the right direction should be. Attempts to formalize the consensus in a detailed forecast fail because people would not adhere to it, and in any case the information and techniques are not available.

No single one of these four cultures is intrinsically superior to the others. Each is a product of its environment and the generally accepted values of its members. Decision making in Posse plc is not necessarily superior or inferior to an entrepreneurial individual's flair in Indians Inc., for example. An organization can be paralyzed by rules and procedures or flounder because it has none. The position of the four hypothetical organizations on the map is no indication of their effectiveness.

However, what happens when they get together?

FOOD
In which countries do people spend the largest amount of their domestic budget on food? The smallest?
>   Greece
>   France
>   Netherlands

Merger mania

Let us imagine that each of our four companies has decided that it needs to join forces with one of the others...

Cavalry Corp. and Indians Inc.

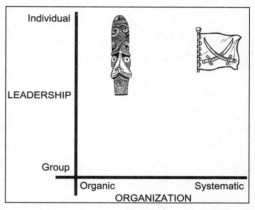

The first two to get together are Cavalry Corp. and Indians Inc. They both have individual leadership cultures, but one is more systematic than the other. It looks like a good match. They are about the same size, have a complementary product range, and are strong in different markets. Their chief executives hit it off on their first meeting. Both of them have strong, forceful personalities and they control their companies with vision and a firm hand. Each of them secretly looks forward to the duel that will eventually result in one of them coming out on top. They finally agree on a joint statement of intent.

When their professional advisers get to work there are some obstacles to overcome. Cavalry Corp.'s lawyers prepare an agreement an inch thick while Indians Inc.'s draft a one-page letter of intent. The chief executive of Indian Inc. is happy to sign Cavalry Corp.'s document as its essentials are in line with his letter and he can always renegotiate, he thinks, if circumstances change. Cavalry Corp.'s boss is happy too as he had expected arduous negotiations on the fine print that ties Indians Inc. up in permanent knots.

Cavalry Corp.'s accountants are less happy. They are appalled by the state of Indians Inc.'s books. Then they are shown, in confidence, Indians Inc.'s real books. (The real, real books are elsewhere.) Cavalry Corp.'s accountants are also dubious about the complicated structure of shareholdings among Indians Inc.'s shareholders and their relatives and friends.

Meanwhile, Indians Inc.'s accountants are appalled by what will be divulged. How can they continue to play their banks off against each other if everyone has the same information? And what about the tax authorities?

The marketing managers are having misgivings too. Cavalry Corp. is insisting on a swingeing rationalization of the joint product range, concentration on a narrow market segment, and reduction of the salesforce. Indians Inc.'s marketing manager thought that the idea of the merger was to increase the product range and expand the customer base. The company needs to keep a foot in as many markets and with as many products as possible in case new opportunities open up. However, he only has gut feeling to counter Cavalry Corp.'s color slides and printouts in fancy bindings with five-year projections and simulations, market research, demographic charts, and competitive studies.

Cavalry Corp.'s marketing manager is nervous about associating himself with Indians Inc.'s lack of delivery and quality systems. He wonders how anything at all comes out of its apparently disorganized factory. Indians Inc.'s manager is impressed by Cavalry Corp.'s highly efficient and automated production line, but nervous about its high prices and lack of responsiveness to design changes and individual customer requirements.

These differences over basic issues are compounded by growing friction in the day-to-day relationships between managers. The biggest source of irritation for Cavalry Corp.'s managers is Indians Inc.'s inability to keep to deadlines. Information promised by a certain date arrives late, and when it does it is incomplete. People are never at meetings on time. They sometimes cancel them at the last minute or expect to set one up at the drop of a hat, and they never come properly prepared.

Indians Inc.'s managers are irritated by Cavalry Corp.'s pedantic attention to detail. The latter's people want to do everything by the book. Meetings are frustrating because they never give enough time to the important issues. They often break off a discussion just as it is beginning to be interesting simply because they have another meeting to go to or a plane to catch. They are not very sociable either. Lunch is always rushed and unless there is a prearranged formal dinner they go straight home at the end of the day instead of going out for a drink and getting to know each other.

Eventually the chief executives break off the deal, both with relief. Indians Inc. would prefer a more flexible partner, Cavalry Corp. a more professional one.

Indians Inc. and Outlaws SA

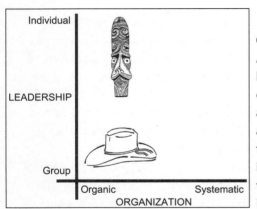

Outlaws SA approach Indians Inc. Although Indians Inc. is larger than Outlaws SA, it looks a good fit. Both have an organic organizational culture, but Indians Inc. has an individual and Outlaws SA a group leadership one. More wary this time, Indians Inc.'s chief executive enters into discussions. He is encouraged to find that Outlaws SA's approach to the market, its business philosophy, and the way it is organized are very similar. Indians Inc. will be able to keep its identity and relative independence in Outlaws SA's loose and pragmatic organization.

Indians Inc.'s boss thinks that he might do well out of the deal. Outlaws SA needs some strong leadership. The chief executive is not very impressive. For a start, he has only one secretary and drives his own car. More important, he is indecisive and always looking over his shoulder at his deputy and his finance director. He will never commit to anything on his own authority.

Negotiations are fruitful but agonizingly slow. At least with Cavalry Corp. you could thrash things out with your opposite number. With Outlaws SA there are constant meetings and debates and discussions that include all sorts of people, some of whom have no apparent responsibility in the area at all and some of whom are very junior. You think you have finally agreed something and on the next day more people make their appearance and it starts all over again. It is hard to pin down exactly who are the decision makers. And with so many people involved it is impossible to keep things confidential. Indians Inc.'s boss contains his impatience until a meeting in which someone from Outlaws SA says that they could not go further until they were sure the workforce would go along with it. He gives them all a much-needed lecture on the right of managers to manage.

Meanwhile, Outlaws SA's management is having misgivings too. Indians Inc.'s managers seem more concerned with scoring points and establishing their position in the pecking order than with achieving a proper level of cooperation. Outlaws SA's people are not used to their assertive style at meetings and grumble about their arrogance. Outlaws SA is also concerned that Indians Inc. will not fit into the management team. It is run like a personal fiefdom. All the decisions are passed up to the top and when the leader is not available the others will not take responsibility.

Cavalry Corp. and Posse plc

In the meantime, Cavalry Corp., having failed with Indians Inc., is having similar problems in its negotiations with Posse plc. At first it is a relief to deal with people who are serious and professional. They are punctual, predictable, and systematic. Quality permeates both companies.

Nevertheless, negotiations drag on interminably. No one in Posse plc can make their mind up. Cavalry Corp.'s organization is streamlined so that no one goes to more than two regular meetings a

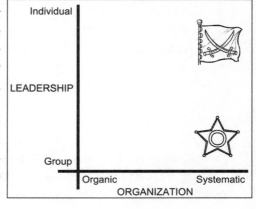

week, everyone knows what they have to do and gets on with it. But Posse plc is bogged down in bureaucracy and time wasting. You can never get hold of anyone, they are always in meetings. And, in Cavalry Corp.'s view, the management of Posse plc is at the beck and call of the unions. (Admittedly they have not had a strike in 40 years.)

Meanwhile, Posse plc is having doubts about how exactly its decentralized, divisional structure will be able to work with Cavalry Corp.'s centralized, top-heavy organization. Their operating units have little independent authority and refer everything back to head office...

The effect of cultural differences

This fictional account illustrates the kind of culture clash that can arise when people of different organizational backgrounds try to work together. The greater the distance between them, the more dramatic the collision. The worst case would be if Indians Inc. tried to work with Posse plc. The only association likely to work would be an acquisition followed by replacement of the acquired company's entire management.

Organizations do not have to go abroad to experience culture clash. The spread represented by our fictional companies exists in some form within every country in Europe. The size of the company, its recent growth, its industry, and its region all have an impact on its culture. Small and medium-sized family businesses will tend to be at the upper end of the leadership dimension, especially if they are still managed by their founders, as will traditional heavy industries such as engineering and steel making. Large companies and multinational subsidiaries will tend to be toward the systematic end of the organization dimension. High-tech companies tend to be systematic–group, while media and entertainment companies tend toward organic–group.

Differences within a given country or industrial sector tend to be along the organization dimension. In many ways these are the easiest to fix. Imposing common standards of performance, reporting, budgeting, forecasting, planning, quality, systems, rules, procedures, codes of ethics, even punctuality and dress is a question of education, communication, or simple enforcement. These are the tangible elements of management.

The elements on the organization dimension are what business schools mainly teach. They are the subject of most books on business and bread-and-butter training courses. They may not come naturally to people. At first they may be evaded, bureaucratized, and manipulated, but constant usage, compliance, and reinforcement will eventually create systematic uniformity.

The leadership dimension encompasses mainly the intangible, people-oriented elements of management: leadership, followership, people skills. These are much harder to impose. They are the stuff of books and courses on such topics as leadership, team building, listening, presentation, assertiveness, conducting meetings, and motivation. They are based on fundamental beliefs that individuals hold about themselves and other people. These beliefs are grounded much more deeply than the technical aspects of management in the social, political, and religious context in which people have been brought up. They are more likely to be uniformly held by those who share those backgrounds. And for the same reason, they are much harder to change.

However much organizational cultures differ within a country, the wider cultural background remains the same. There are common points of reference. It is when the organizations are seen against different national contexts that the differences between them are shown in sharp relief.

Transplants

Management styles, techniques, or tools evolve to meet the needs of specific types of organization. Theories about management are determined by the type of culture to which the researchers belong and in which the research was carried out. Because they work well in certain types of company, they become fashionable, disseminated by consultants and academics and grafted on to organizations of widely different types.

Several things may happen to these grafts. They may succeed because they are suited to the new host culture. They may be rejected out of hand. They may be adapted by the culture out of all recognition. Or they may, in rare circumstances, change the culture itself. What is certain is that they will not survive independently from the way everything else is done in the organization.

Take, for example, performance appraisal. In some companies it is laid down that at regular intervals employees meet with their bosses and discuss their performance. Both sides come to an agreement about the subordinate's job description, targets, and standards of performance, which are incorporated in a standard document. The appraisal is based on an objective review of the targets. The meeting with the boss is about what is necessary to improve performance: training, for instance, expansion of the job, or getting promotion.

This works well in Posse plc, a systematic–group culture. The underlying belief is that people take part in decisions that affect them, that they make the major contribution to their own performance, that it can be evaluated dispassionately and independently from their personal identity, that functions can be analyzed and systematized, even that the appraisal process itself can be enshrined in forms and procedures.

However, what happens when Cavalry Corp. thinks that it's a good idea? The system remains the same, the forms are sent out by Human Resources, goals and targets are set, and so on. But superiors and subordinates do not easily meet on common ground. It is unrealistic to state blandly in the manual that for the purposes of the annual appraisal interview you should both sit on the same side of the desk and the boss should listen and ask questions and not impose his or her ideas. Both sides expect the boss to give clear directions, to deliver judgments and encouragement and praise, to reward with pay rises and promotion. The appraisal is an end-of term report with grades and comments rather than a mechanism for sharing and negotiation.

In organic organizations it is difficult to set standards of performance because the underlying mechanisms do not exist. Performance is closely associated with personal qualities, so an objective discussion becomes embarrassing.

OBESITY
Which country has the fattest population measured by average body mass index?
> Greece
> Belgium
> Slovenia

The Mole Map

This is the bravest part of the book, positioning the countries of Europe along the two dimensions of the organization and leadership grid to make the Mole Map—Multicultural Organization and Leadership in Europe. The book would contain considerably more pages if every other statement were qualified with the warning that they were generalizations, but the generalization represented by the Mole Map is so enormous that it begs to be underlined.

Even the use of countries is suspect. There are arguments for using linguistic or racial or geographic regions instead of nation states, for example putting northern France and Francophone Belgium together, while separating regions such as northern and southern Italy.

The map looks only at business culture. It is tempting to toy with these ideas in the context of political systems, social structures, and national character, but these are outside the scope of this book. In most countries the world of work is a sub-culture within a much larger context. When

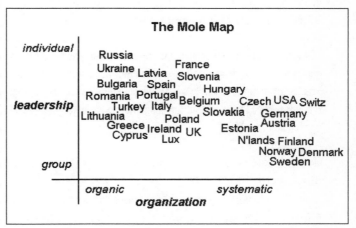

you go through the door of the office or the factory you enter a different sort of society from the one outside.

Reading the map

The relative position of the various countries on the map is more meaningful than their absolute position on the axes. Countries that are close together have such similar cultures that some companies within each may be interchangeable on the map. The further away from each other the countries are, the more unlikely there is to be this overlap. For example, the experience of working in a German, American, or Danish company may be similar, but you are unlikely to find many German and Italian companies that are alike.

There are no absolute standards of behavior. Somewhere in the world there are people who think that Germans are messy and unpunctual. (The chances are that they're in Switzerland.) There are countries where Greece is regarded as a model of efficiency. There are some in which French bosses would seem absurdly egalitarian and others where Italian company life would seem oppressively regulated.

"They are so inefficient. It is hard to get them to do things. At home I ask for something to be done, politely of course, and it gets done on time without any fuss. Here there are always problems, reasons why it can't be done the way I want it. If it gets done at all. Sometimes they just ignore me. You have to follow up much more here. Set deadlines. They always want to discuss things instead of doing them. Punctuality? Meetings never start on time. And they always drag on. You invite a customer to lunch at one o'clock and he arrives three-quarters of an hour late and thinks nothing of it. It is very frustrating. I get very irritated and I don't know how to handle it."

Was this said by a Danish manager about working with British employees or by a British manager about working with Italians?

"They are so arrogant. They think that every meeting, whether it's one-to-one or several people, is a chance to show off, to dominate everyone else. They always try to score points. But as soon as the boss puts his foot down they hardly say anything. Except 'yes sir.' There's rigid hierarchy, everyone in boxes. The boss takes all the decisions. Anything of importance gets passed up to him. He thinks he has to be right about everything."

Was this said by a Dutch person working with Germans or a German working with the French?

The answer to the two questions is "both." Danes and Germans think that the British are inefficient and unpunctual, while the British think the same about Italians and Greeks. The Dutch think that the Germans are authoritarian and high-handed, and the Germans think the same about the French. Our value judgments derive from perceptions about the ways others do things filtered through our own working practices and beliefs.

The attitudes that we express tend to be those that we would like to have, or that reflect well on us. Many people believe that they are more efficient and participative than they really are. The values that we incorporate in what we actually do may be different, like the man who spent an uninterrupted half-hour telling me what a good listener he was. However accurate self-perception is, almost everyone thinks that their way of doing things is the right way. We take pride in things that others may find incomprehensible, ludicrous, or even immoral. The British are proud of what they call "muddling through," Germans of what to others is obsessive thoroughness, Italians of compulsive improvisation.

We find it hard to recognize the truth of criticism of the way we do things. If we can, we try to explain away the criticism. Conversely, we think that the way others do things is inferior, even on the rare occasions when they are acknowledged to be more effective. Wherever people are on the map, those on the left of them can be seen as inefficient and disorganized, and those on the right as cold, clinical, and hair-splitting. Those beneath them are indecisive and uncompetitive and those above them are domineering and egotistical.

If you are from a systematic culture you might regard organic attitudes to decision making as based on snap decisions, gut feel, and what worked well last time. If you are from an organic culture you might see systematic decision making as unimaginative, overconservative, and hidebound by procedures and too much analysis.

E is for Europe

The Mole Map is based on leadership and organization, because they are the main source of culture-related issues in Europe and North America. Other important sets of values, for example those related to concepts of individualism, can be ignored because we hold them in common. The map is not so useful when looking at business cultures in other parts of the world because there are other dimensions that are equally if not more important. Japan is not on the map, despite its importance in Europe, because it is misleading to interpret Japanese behavior within a western frame of reference.

EURO	
Where is the euro the official currency?	
Guinea	West African republic
Guyana	South American republic
Guyane	French *département* in S America

Meetings

A litmus test for gauging where an organization lies on the Mole Map is the importance of meetings. The more significant meetings are for decision making and implementation, the lower down the leadership scale the organizational culture is likely to be. The number of meetings or how long they take is not important. What does matter is how necessary they are in getting things done.

In systematic organizations there is a regular schedule of different sorts of meeting. Apart from regular briefing and information meetings, there will be specialized taskforces, committees, and groups, all with specified purposes, agendas, and meticulous minutes. They start and end on time, even on the rare occasions when the business of the meeting is not finished.

In organic organizations the distinction between a meeting and a get-together is much more blurred. Meetings continue until all of the business is dealt with and, if this is not possible, take up again at the next opportunity.

In individual leadership cultures people complain about the number of meetings, however few there are. The senior person is in the chair and the point of the meeting is briefing, direction, and information gathering. In group leadership cultures meetings are for sharing information, decisions, and responsibility. They are taken seriously as an important tool for getting things done. A high value is placed on listening skills. Consensus is the overriding goal.

The range of meetings in which readers may come across a culture clash is vast, from an annual visit to a trade fair to implementing a multinational merger. As a practical example of a culture-sensitive approach in a frequent situation, let us take a monthly coordination meeting between representatives of companies from different countries involved in some kind of joint venture.

Let us also assume that each representative is a stereotypical example of their national culture. How can we predict from the Mole Map, and the other generalizations in this book, how they might behave? And what can be done to make their meeting as productive as possible?

Language

The first problem is language. It is most likely to be English, which will suit the north Europeans, or French, which may suit the south Europeans more.

Whichever language is chosen, there will be some participants who feel at a disadvantage because they do not speak it as fluently as others at the meeting.

There is a risk that those who are linguists will dominate those who are less fluent.

The language problem should be brought into the open by making the working language or languages the first item of discussion. It may be advisable to make arrangements for preparatory papers and minutes to be translated. At the meeting itself it may be decided that people may speak in any language they choose if the rest understand it. Some members may wish to bring along to the meeting *chuchoteurs* or "whisperers," in other words personal simultaneous translators. Whatever is decided, the rules should be made clear.

Expectations

Participants will have different expectations of the function and outcome of the meeting. For those toward the individual end of the leadership dimension—French, Belgians, Spanish, Portuguese, Germans—the purpose will be to brief the others with information. If it is clear that the meeting has to result in an agreement or a joint proposal, they will come armed with a detailed plan that they will attempt to impose on the others with as little amendment as possible.

Those toward the group end—Dutch, Danes, British, Irish—will expect the meeting to pool information or problems and take steps to resolve them on a basis of consensus and compromise. If they have developed a plan of their own, it will be a working hypothesis to be negotiated and amended, rather than a position to be defended.

For those at the organic end of the organization dimension—Italians, Greeks, Spanish—informal networking in the bar or over coffee or during lunch is as important as what goes on at the meeting itself. The meeting will give formal sanction to what has been discussed or agreed elsewhere. For those at the systematic end the extracurricular socializing, while it oils the wheels, counts a lot less than what happens at the meeting proper.

Time might, therefore, be allocated to both formal and informal socializing. Arrange to meet for dinner the night before. If there are French or Spanish participants, allow two hours for a proper lunch. For some participants this will be the most constructive part of the event.

Preparation

Those toward the systematic end of the organization dimension—Germans, Dutch, Danes—will be well prepared. They will expect briefing papers, which they will study and amend and the implications of which they will have meticulously researched. Those toward the organic end—British, Italians, Spanish, Irish, Greek—will have skimmed through the papers on the plane, and some may still be leafing through them at the meeting. They expect that what is actually said at the meeting has more importance than what is written in the briefing papers.

The chair should ensure that working papers are distributed well in advance with a request for comments on them before the meeting, to check that each participant has received them and, preferably, read them.

Who attends?

The further toward the organic end of the organization dimension participants are—Italians, Greeks—the more unpredictable it is who and how many will turn up, regardless of who has been designated.

If the designated participant cannot attend, those toward the group end of the leadership dimension—British, Dutch, Danes—will send a subordinate, who may be much more junior. Higher up the dimension they will either send an immediate and trusted deputy or no one at all. Unaccustomed to meetings between people of different status, they will ignore the deputies of others.

Punctuality

Everyone will try to be there on time, but only those at the systematic end of the organization dimension can be relied on to succeed. They will expect the meeting to start and end on time even if its aims have not been fully achieved. If the meeting is called half an hour before the formal proceedings start it gives time for the unpunctual to arrive and for the others to socialize over tea and coffee.

Some participants, probably French or Italian, may feel less bound by the discipline of a meeting than others. They may leave to make phone calls or attend to paperwork if the discussion is not immediately relevant to them. One solution is not to serve refreshments during the meeting and to schedule interruptions by breaking every hour for coffee, small talk, telephone calls, and other personal business.

Be overgenerous with time. Add at least half an hour on to the end of the projected schedule for slippage. Punctual people do not mind leaving early.

Agenda

Everyone will expect a prepared agenda, but only toward the systematic end will they expect to keep to it. The moderately organic, like the British, will expect to discuss and amend the agenda at the beginning of the meeting, while the more organic will feel free to introduce unscheduled topics at any time. If possible, agree the agenda with each participant before the meeting and again at the start. Make the individual items as specific as possible, including the desired outcome of the discussion and the time allocated for it.

Those at the individual end of the dimension—French, Italians, Russians—will expect that the agenda is in any case a smokescreen for decisions that have already been taken.

> *Survey*
>
> *"At meetings do they keep to a detailed agenda?"*
>
> Portugal Ireland Czech Belg F Turkey Ukraine
> Cyprus Spain Estonia Hungary N'lands UK Sweden
> Russia Belg W Romania Latvia Japan N.Am Finland
> Bulgaria Poland France Lithuania Norway Austria Switz
> Greece China Italy Slovenia Slovakia Germany Denmark
>
> *no*   *yes*

Chair

Those at the individual end of the leadership spectrum—French, Belgians, Spanish—will expect strong control from the chair over the agenda and the discussion. They will also find it natural to contradict and challenge the chair and vie for the real authority, as distinct from the formal, over the proceedings. Others will expect the chair to be more unobtrusive but for his or her position to be more respected.

At the systematic end participants will expect contributions to be made through the chair when invited. At the organic end they will expect more of a free-for-all and feel less constrained by the formalities of debate.

> *Survey*
>
> *"At meetings do all contribute or does the senior person dominate?"*
>
> Denmark   UK   Poland Spain   Slovenia
> N'lands Ireland Belgium Portugal Germany France Bulgaria
> Sweden Finland N.Am Czech Cyprus Lithuania   China
> Norway   Estonia Austria Italy Hungary Ukraine Romania
> Switz Japan Slovakia Greece Latvia   Russia   Turkey
>
> *all*   *senior*

If possible, it should be agreed before the meeting who will chair it, whether the chair changes according to the topic, and so on. The chair should make clear whether discussion will always be through him or her or not. At first it is as well to make participation as formal as is necessary to ensure both orderly progression through the agenda and the contribution of every participant.

Participation

Participation will be characterized by different styles of contribution depending as much on people's individual personalities as on their nationality. The following discussion is extremely stereotypical and gives examples of different styles that any participant could adopt.

The German style is to be well prepared and to contribute only when they feel well qualified to do so and when they have something useful to say. They will not expect to be interrupted or immediately contradicted and regard their prepared positions as incontrovertible.

French contributions tend to be adversarial, dogmatic, and models of rationality. They expect their own and others' contributions to fit into an overall schema or theory. They expect to be contradicted and to win the argument by logic and assertion.

Italians tend to be innovative, complex, creative, and usually stimulating. Their contributions are embellished with definitions, caveats, analogies, allusions, and asides, and in the opinion of the rigorously pragmatic not always relevant.

British contributions tend to be pragmatic and realistic. They may not always be supported with hard facts, offering opinion and assertion for discussion rather than proposals for adoption or imposition. Their predilection for humor may relieve tense or tedious moments, but it can also be regarded as trivializing. They are the least likely to lose either interest or temper.

The Dutch have a similar approach to the British in terms of seeking a common resolution instead of imposing one, preferring the practical to the theoretical and using humor to defuse conflict and tedium. Their contribution will be brutally frank.

The Spanish tend not to risk embarrassment or discomfort by saying anything that might be criticized, ranging from a poor command of the language spoken to the actual content. This can be mistaken for aloofness. They will participate in emphatic and spirited debate as long as they feel on firm ground.

Consensus

There is a difference between passive consensus, meaning that the participants consent to a course of action, and active consensus, meaning that they are fully committed to it. Those toward the organic end of the organization dimension may give their assent to a decision but may not abide by it. Those toward the systematic end will only assent to what they feel committed to carrying out.

> *Survey*
>
> *"Do meetings end with an action plan?"*
>
> Bulgaria Lithuania Spain Estonia Poland
>   China   Greece Belgium Slovenia Austria Finland N.Am
> Romania Ukraine Cyprus Italy Czech   UK   Norway
> Russia Japan   Latvia Slovakia Ireland Switz Denmark
>   Portugal France Hungary Turkey N'lands Germany Sweden
>
> *no*   *yes*

Those toward the group end of the leadership dimension will look for a genuine consensus based on a synthesis of views. Those toward the individual end will seek consensus based on the adoption of the best idea, preferably their own.

The depth of agreement primarily depends, of course, not on cultural differences but on the underlying business interests that each of the participants represents and how much authority they have to commit them. This may not always be clear.

In any event, it is wise to aim for complete and active consensus. Majority decisions should be avoided and formal voting postponed until the very last minute. Consensus-oriented participants should be prepared for apparently irreconcilable positions to be hotly contested by the others before coming together quickly at the end.

> *Survey*
>
> *"Do they keep commitments without being chased?"*
>
> Bulgaria Turkey Romania Ukraine UK   Switz
>   China   Latvia Greece France Estonia Austria Denmark
> Cyprus Lithuania Spain   Italy Hungary N.Am Finland
>   Czech Slovenia Russia Belg W Belg F Norway Sweden
> Poland Portugal Slovakia Ireland N'lands Germany Japan
>
> *no*   *yes*

Followup

Those toward the systematic end will expect the meeting to have a definable result and a commitment to concrete actions, steps to which everyone is committed and for which responsibilities have been allocated. The more organic will regard the less tangible results of the meeting—mutual understanding, a reaffirmation of the will to cooperate, a sense of where the venture is going—as more important than specific steps. As far as possible the form of the desired outcome should be agreed beforehand. However, it should not be assumed that it will be adhered to by everyone without its being chased up afterwards.

LACK OF SKI POTENTIAL

Which country has the lowest highest point?

    Malta
    Netherlands
    Denmark

Negotiation

Meetings may take place in the context of a negotiation. Specific details of how to conduct a negotiation and construct a deal are outside the scope of this book. However, there are certain values and expectations about negotiation that differ between cultures. Once again, we are dealing with a continuous dimension in which people are unlikely to be at one extreme or the other but the balance between them will be different.

Win/win? Or win/lose?

Some literature on negotiation recommends a win/win approach. Each party not only tries to get the best deal for themselves but also puts themselves in the other's position and makes sure that the deal is mutually beneficial. Parties are seen to be partners striving toward the same shared goal. This is a common strategy in northern Europe and North America.

Others have not read the same book and see negotiation as a zero-sum game in which parties are opponents, not partners. Their goal is to get the best possible deal for themselves and they expect the others to defend their own position. The danger for the win/win negotiators is that they are exploited. The danger for the win/lose negotiators is that they alienate the others.

Survey

"Do they look for win/win or win/lose?"

Turkey	Lithuania	Hungary	Estonia	N.Am		
China	Latvia	Italy	Poland	UK	Japan	Finland
Cyprus	Portugal	Ukraine	Spain	Ireland	Slovakia	Denmark
Bulgaria	Greece	Romania	Germany	Austria	Belgium	Norway
Russia	Czech	France	Slovenia	N'lands	Switz	Sweden

_no_   _yes_

Poker or chess?

For many win/win proponents negotiation is an open game. They believe that a deal will be best and soonest achieved if both sides have all the information, share objectives, and respect each other's integrity. Others believe that the end justifies whatever means are at their disposal to get the best deal.

The dividing line between tactics and tricks is a fine one. A legitimate tactic may be seen as a lack of good faith by someone else. Bluffing, unreasonable demands, time pressure, spurious

deadlines, artificial stalemates, and other ploys may be conventional weapons in the negotiator's armory in one culture but unethical in others.

Beginning and end

It is usually obvious when a negotiation begins. The concept of when it ends is less clear between cultures. At the systematic end of the organization dimension shaking hands and signing a contract are usually seen as bringing negotiation to an end in preparation for implementation. The written contract is the template for implementation, often referred to and meticulously followed. Trying to change it because, for example, market conditions have changed or one partner discovers that there are unforeseen costs is seen as bad faith. In these cultures negotiations are detailed and the resulting documents comprehensive and closely vetted by lawyers.

Toward the organic end of the dimension negotiation is seen as a continuing part of implementation. Practiced negotiators will be on the alert for the "slip-in," a concession demanded after everything has apparently been agreed or after the contact has been signed. The contract is seen more as a guide than a template, if it is referred to at all, and it is acceptable to ask for changes in its terms if conditions change.

Who is in charge?

In cultures toward the individual end of the leadership dimension on the Mole Map, the expectation is that a negotiation will be conducted and a deal structured in which one side or the other is a senior

Survey

    "Do they expect equal partners or one to dominate?"

Cyprus Greece Romania Italy Austria
  Latvia Portugal Slovakia Japan Estonia Belgium Sweden
Bulgaria Czech Ukraine Slovenia N.Am Hungary N'lands
  Lithuania France Russia Germany Poland Finland Norway
Turkey China Spain UK Switz Denmark Ireland

dominate   *equal*

partner. They are uncomfortable with business relationships based on equal partnerships. They do not have the aptitude and skills necessary for shared decision making and accountability. The worst scenario occurs at the implementation stage if both sides believe that they are the dominant partner.

Summary: The negotiator's Mole Map

At the top of the map people are characteristically win/lose negotiators. Their aim is to come out on top of the negotiation, create a deal predominantly in their favor, and remain in a controlling position in any situation resulting from the deal.

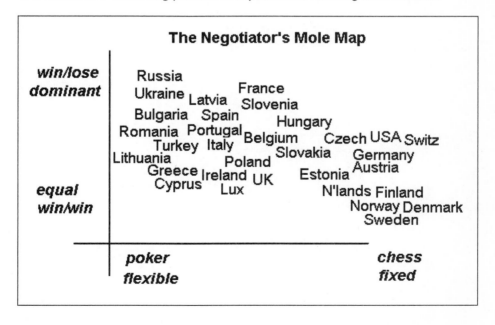

The Negotiator's Mole Map

win/lose
dominant

Russia
Ukraine Latvia France
     Slovenia
Bulgaria Spain
Romania Portugal Hungary
  Turkey Italy Belgium   Czech USA Switz
Lithuania   Slovakia   Germany
    Greece Ireland Poland Estonia Austria
   Cyprus Lux UK

equal
win/win
        N'lands Finland
         Norway Denmark
          Sweden

poker   *chess*
flexible   *fixed*

Win/win negotiators at the bottom of the map characteristically want to find at least a compromise and ideally synergy in the deal. They empathize with the other party's aims, have a problem-solving attitude to negotiation, and are prepared for reciprocal concessions.

The same person or organization can use different dealing modes depending on the circumstances, the size and importance of the transaction, etc. However, each culture has a prevalent mode. The easiest negotiations are with those of the same type. The hardest are with those of the diagonally opposite type on the Mole Map.

GARBAGE

Which country creates the most municipal waste per capita?

Italy

Switzerland

Turkey

PART TWO

THE COUNTRIES OF EUROPE

What is Europe?

This book is full of generalizations, the biggest of which has got to be "Europe." Most of us know what we mean by the word, but in every respect it is hard to define, beginning with the geographic aspects. It is only a continent because Europeans decided on the continents. If Africans or Chinese had named them according to the dictionary definition of "a continuous expanse of land," there would be only Asia from the Atlantic to the Pacific. Those who define the eastern boundary of Europe as the Urals have never seen them—the highest summits are lower than 2,000m.

Diversity and change

What you understand and mean by Europe depends on your generation and your nationality. It can mean western Europe, the European Union, or the territory represented by the Council of Europe from Iceland to the Caucasus. For two generations it meant that part of Eurasia not controlled by the Soviet Union. In Britain European can simply mean foreign. Intellectuals in the pay of the European Union and the Council of Europe agonize in vain on their behalf to come up with a definition of a uniquely European social, political, and cultural identity that will embrace Cypriots and Czechs, Belgians and Bulgarians.

Paradoxically, many people include diversity and change as defining characteristics of Europe. It may seem nonsensical to be united by diversity, anchored in change—and you could say the same about Asians or Africans—but it is essential to bear both of these aspects continually in mind when looking at the Europe in which we live and work.

Geographic diversity

The steeply pitched slate roofs of northern Europe, the tile roofs of the temperate Mediterranean, and the flat roofs of the southern Mediterranean are physical examples of the influence of climate. There are many ways to carve up Europe according to climate, topography, physical and agricultural resources, and so on. The map opposite is based on the oceans and waterways of Europe. What are often thought of as natural frontiers, barriers to communication, in fact function as highways. Rivers, seas, and mountains are avenues of commerce and cultural interchange. Combined with similar geographic environments, they create transnational cultural regions whose inhabitants have more in common with each other than with fellow citizens in their respective hinterlands. Mountain shepherds in Northern Greece have more in common with Bulgarian and Albanian shepherds than with the plains people of the shores. The traders of Greece have more in common with the traders of Turkey and Italy than with the mountain dwellers in the hinterland. Catalonia and Euskadi (the Autonomous Community of the Basque Country) are on either side of the Pyrenees, Savoy and Piedmont on either side of the Alps.

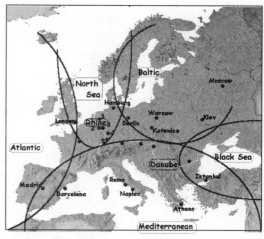

Cultural regions: waterways

cities over 2mm pop •

Political diversity

European political boundaries and political systems are in constant ferment. Most of its states, in terms of frontiers and political institutions, are younger than the United States of America. Many were created at the beginning of the twentieth century, such as Ireland, and some in its last decade, such as Slovakia. The map on political traditions summarizes the position at the beginning of the millennium. It would have looked different ten years before and will doubtless be different ten years in the future. Even if frontiers and institutions do not change they will become less important.

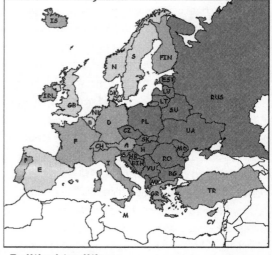

Political traditions

monarchy
republic
ex-socialist

Globalization entails the dilution of national sovereignty in favor of transnational institutions and organizations, including commercial companies.

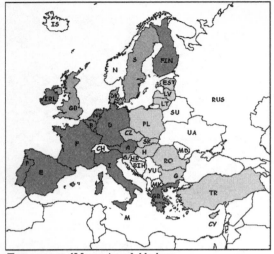

European (Monetary) Union

EU applicants
EU but not EMU
EMU

Nevertheless, politicians and civil servants can relax for the time being. Respondents to the Mole Map Survey listed national government as one of the three biggest influences on their business in all but a handful of countries.

The most powerful agents for political change are European Monetary Union and eastward enlargement of the European Union. The primary objective of European Monetary Union has always been to bring about political union. It is a bold and unique experiment whose true implications for business and the economies of Europe are essentially unpredictable. Half of the respondents to the Mole Map Survey said that the euro was good for business and half were neutral, but as yet it is too early to say. Good or bad, the effect on all European countries, whether inside EMU or not, will be profound in the years to come. If EMU works, national sovereignty over all aspects of fiscal and monetary policy will eventually be surrendered to European institutions.

With the exception of those countries of the former Soviet Union in the Commonwealth of Independent States, the former socialist countries turn west to face their future. Citizens of applicant countries to the European Union could be forgiven for thinking that Fortress Europe is reluctant to lower the drawbridge. While they strive to meet the political and economic conditions of entry, there is mounting frustration at the growing lack of political will and consensus in the EU toward enlargement. The social and cultural adjustments of transition are no less demanding than the economic. Everyone has felt the pain of the transformation that has already occurred—dislocation, alienation, and deep insecurity, both economic and social—but only a few have yet tasted the rewards.

One reason for delay is that the economic cost of enlargement

The Copenhagen accession criteria of 1993 included in the Maastricht/Amsterdam treaty require that "the candidates: (1) have stable governments that guarantee democracy, the rule of law, human rights, and respect for and protection of minorities; (2) have a functioning market economy as well as the ability to cope with competitive pressure and market forces within the Union; and (3) have the ability to take on the obligations of membership, including adherence to the aims of political, economic, and monetary union."

to EU members will be significant. Recipients of EU
budget transfers will find
themselves donors. Coun-
tries such as Norway and
Switzerland, which enjoy
the economic advantages
of the EU through association agreements without
the responsibilities of formal membership, have

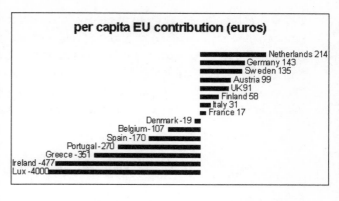

per capita EU contribution (euros)

Netherlands 214
Germany 143
Sweden 135
Austria 99
UK 91
Finland 58
Italy 31
France 17
Denmark -19
Belgium -107
Spain -170
Portugal -270
Greece -351
Ireland -477
Lux -4000

been put on notice that they too will be expected to share the burden.

There will also be a political cost in widening the "democratic deficit," in other words the dilution of democratic control over European institutions. It will be imprac-tical to have all members represented in decision making that affects them. Larger countries accustomed to dominating decision making will have a smaller voice or even, if they are in the minority on a majority vote, no voice at all. Finally, members are voicing the same misgivings about migration and cheap labor as they did before countries such as Spain, Portugal, and Greece were let into the club. In whatever way the issues of enlargement are resolved, the political map will continue to change.

Economic diversity

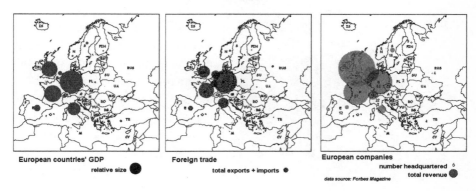

European countries' GDP
relative size ●

Foreign trade
total exports + imports ●

European companies
number headquartered 6
total revenue ●
data source: Forbes Magazine

On a national level half a dozen countries, led by Germany, create the wealth of Europe. They account for 75 percent of the GDP of Europe from the Atlantic to the Urals. Germany, France, and the UK account for over half. These countries are the biggest trading nations in Europe, although Belgium's importance and Spain's lack of it in international trade are noteworthy.

Corporate strength is concentrated in Germany, France, and the UK. The largest

375 companies headquartered in Europe and featured in the *Forbes International 800* generate total revenue of about $5 billion. Over 100 of these companies are based in the UK and account for 25 percent of the $5 billion. Companies based in four countries—UK, Germany, France, and the Netherlands—generate 75 percent. The economic, commercial, and cultural dominance of these few countries, along with that of the US, will probably increase with globalization.

Regional diversity

Gallia est omnis divisa in partes tres. (Julius Caesar)

Commentators have long pointed out the regionalism of Europe. Countries are rarely homogenous. It is a paradox that as the European Union grows in strength, so do the regions. Some of them actively look to Brussels to help them foster their autonomy as national sovereignty diminishes. EU policy makers think in terms of regions rather than countries. They have identified more than 300 separate regions within the EU and its applicant countries. Some regions lie within national boundaries, others lie astride them. There are any numbers of ways to regionalize Europe, depending on what you are looking for and in how much detail. Language and religious traditions are examples of a macro view.

The figure below is an overview of the language families of Europe: Latin, Germanic, Slavic, Greek, plus Finnish and Estonian, Basque, Hungarian, Romanian, and the Baltic languages of Latvian and Lithuanian. These language groupings are of more than linguistic interest, they are maps of ethnicity. Specific ways of thinking and conventions of behavior are associated with each grouping and with their subgroups.

The EU now has 11 official languages. Applicant countries will add another 10. There are about 30 more official or recognized languages and innumerable dialects. Several countries are multilingual. Half of the official national languages are minority languages in other countries. For

Linguistic Europe

Latin   Germanic   Slavic   Celtic   Greek

example, minorities in five countries speak Hungarian. About 50 million of the EU population of 300 million are estimated to be minority language speakers. Spanish is only a second language for a quarter of the population of Spain. Over 90 percent of Italians speak a language or dialect in addition to the Tuscan version known as Italian. Over 50 percent of EU citizens say that they can speak a second European language in addition to their mother tongue—that leaves almost 50 percent who are monolingual. Corporate or personal strategies for Europe must include dealing with the babel.

One solution is English, the *lingua franca* of Europe. Some 35 percent of EU citizens, other than native English speakers, say that it is their first foreign language and that their knowledge of it is good. Top are the Swedes, of whom over 80 percent claim to speak English. Before Anglophones throw away their language books, they should bear in mind that even if initial contacts speak English, they will soon come across some of the 65 percent who do not. French is the first foreign language of 10 percent of EU citizens. While German is not significant in the EU—except of course among the 90 million or so Germans and Austrians—it is a very useful language to know in central and eastern Europe and Turkey.

Native English speakers have the advantage in a global marketplace, for the moment. In countries such as Germany and France, English lessons begin in elementary school. An entire generation of Europeans will be fluent in English. Who will be employed and promoted in the global companies of the future? The polyglots or the monoglots?

Overlapping the linguistic regions but not wholly congruent with them are the historical religions of Europe. In reality, the borders are not as clear-cut as in the map below, which ignores the impact of immigration, resettlement, and war. Each religious tradition has its own sets of social and behavioral values that influence social and individual behavior. Concepts of leadership, authority and hierarchy, individualism and collectivism are among the cultural values promulgated by organized religions in the past and still surviving in secular institutions, including commercial ones.

In some countries it is hard to get people to relocate out of their own region. Even if they are willing to move, account must be taken of local feeling. Posting a Francophone Belgian to

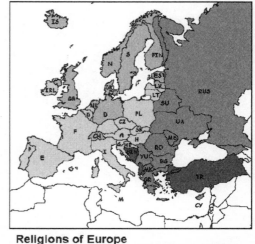

Religions of Europe

Catholic   Protestant   Orthodox   Islamic

Antwerp or a Basque to Seville may make both sides feel uncomfortable. On the level of personal relationships and social contact, it is essential to be aware of regional pride, even if it is only a question of pandering to conceit.

Nevertheless, the significance of the regions should not be overestimated. While there is a difference between, say, Roman Catholic, beer-drinking, extrovert, *Lederhosen*-sporting Bavaria and pietist, sober, modest, thrifty, wine-drinking Swabia, a native of Munich has more in common with a native of Stuttgart than either has with a non-German. And in the context of business attitudes and behavior, the difference in the way that BMW and Mercedes are managed is negligible. Natives of Lille and Marseille come from noticeably different regional cultures, but when they work together in a French multinational they adopt a common business behavior that is clearly French. This is a justification for continuing to structure this book according to countries rather than regions.

LAWYERS
Which country has the most lawyers per 100,000 population?
>   Spain
>   Germany
>   France

Cultural Diversity

The business environment

The grid below summarizes the answers in the Mole Map Survey to the question "What are the most important influences on your business?" Respondents were given a list of possibilities and asked to make their own contributions. In almost all countries government is one of the three most frequent replies. In some decentralized or federal countries local government is more important than national government and in others the weight given to each is equal. However, generally speaking elected representatives and their civil servants have more influence over business than they are sometimes given credit for in an increasingly global marketplace.

In most countries financial markets are one of the top three influences. In the others you have to keep the banks happy instead. That consumers and consumer associations make the list in only four countries reflects either that their influence is overriding or that few companies are genuinely customer driven.

	Govt	Financial markets	EU	Legal system	Banks	Globalization trade information	Consumers	Social elite
Austria			♦		♦	♦		
Belgium	♦	♦	♦					
Bulgaria	♦	♦			♦			
Cyprus	♦	♦	♦		♦			
Czech	♦			♦	♦			
DK	♦					♦	♦	
Estonia	♦			♦	♦			
Finland	♦	♦				♦		
France	♦	♦	♦					
Germany	♦	♦		♦				♦
Greece	♦		♦		♦			
Hungary	♦		♦	♦				
Ireland	♦	♦				♦		
Italy		♦		♦				♦
Latvia	♦			♦		♦		
Lithuania	♦					♦	♦	
N'lands		♦				♦	♦	
Norway	♦	♦				♦		
Poland		♦				♦		
Portugal	♦		♦	♦	♦			
Romania	♦		♦	♦				
Russia	♦	♦		♦				
Slovakia	♦	♦		♦				
Slovenia	♦		♦			♦		
Spain	♦	♦	♦				♦	
Sweden	♦	♦				♦		
Switz.		♦			♦			♦
Turkey	♦			♦		♦		
Ukraine	♦			♦		♦		
UK	♦	♦				♦		

The importance of the legal system in the former socialist countries is interesting. In many of them it has been radically overhauled to meet the requirements of the market economy and is still in the process of refinement and testing through the courts.

Despite prompting, trade unions do not make the list in any country and in most did not come close. Their decline in power and influence in the last decade or so of the twentieth century is notable.

Discrimination

A question in the Mole Map Survey asked: "In order to be successful in a business career… is it a serious disadvantage to be any of these: Asian, black, disabled, female, foreign, immigrant, linguistic minority, national minority?" Respondents in all countries, of all nationalities, and of both sexes were unanimous that being disabled was the most serious disadvantage. The survey did not ask respondents to differentiate between varieties of disability.

```
a serious disadvantage to be…

        disabled

          black

female          foreign
```

There was general agreement among all nationalities in all countries of Europe that being black was the second most serious disadvantage.

The third place among almost all respondents went to immigrants or, in countries like Russia or Romania where there are relatively fewer immigrants, to national and linguistic minorities.

These are serious issues with strong moral as well as political and social implications for globalization. They need to be tackled on both a pan-European and a local level. The business communities in all the European countries have an important part to play in developing proactive policies of inclusion, out of self-interest if not a wider social responsibility.

While they agree about being disabled or black, women respondents in some countries where there were enough female respondents to be statistically significant claim third place for themselves in terms of disadvantage. These countries are Austria, the Netherlands, Germany, Italy, and the UK. Countries where women think they take fourth place, after immigrants, are Belgium, Denmark, Finland, France, Greece, Portugal, Spain, Sweden, and Switzerland.

This was the only question in the Mole Map Survey in which there was a significant difference between men's and women's responses. The main problems specific to women are common to all cultures—combining family and career, maternity leave, provision of childcare facilities, the need to do better than their male equivalents—and far outweigh the problems that women have in different types of business culture.

In terms of organization and leadership, I found little anecdotal evidence of significant differences between men and women. Women behaved in the same way that men did. Those who did well in companies did so for similar reasons to the men. In some countries they owed their first opportunity to family or political connections, in others to professional qualifications, and everywhere their advancement to competence and luck. I could find no evidence that women bring anything particularly female to the job. If they are good bosses, for example, it is in the same way that men are good.

Nevertheless, in order to succeed in business in Europe it is still best to be a fit, white male in your own country.

The generation gap

When I researched the first edition of this book those under 30 insisted that they were different from their older colleagues, more international, better educated, and not imprisoned by national stereotypes. Fifteen years later these people are in their 40s and a new younger generation insist that they are different from their older colleagues, more international, better educated, and not imprisoned by national stereotypes. The marvel is not the generation gap but how soon the young cross it.

The generation gap in business is between those who have professional training and those who do not. A generation of professional managers under 40 years of age, educated mainly in American business techniques and outlook, are challenging the old ways of doing things. The main change in the past decade or so has been that the internationally minded and better-educated people are not confined to a handful of western and mainly northern European countries. The second change is that they acquire their education in Europe. In the past decade business schools and courses have proliferated in western Europe.

Qualifications and training

Educational qualifications are equally prized in all cultures, but for different reasons. In some cultures an organization is made up of experts, professionals, and specialists. From an early age education tends to be vocational and technical. A high priority is placed on technical training at all levels of the organization.

In organic cultures education indicates the sort of person you are, your social position. Experience and common sense, the University of Life, are seen as being of equal or greater value. Training, if there is any, is not prized for itself but as a privilege, an indication of status.

The Mole Map Survey asked what were the most and least important factors in getting ahead in a career. The responses were remarkably similar throughout Europe. Eight factors were mentioned, by far the most important of which was personal contacts followed by education. The work ethic came third. American respondents also put networking and education before hard work, with achievement coming third.

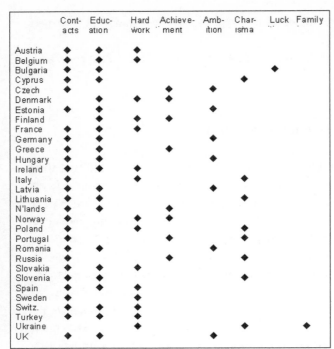

The least important factors of those mentioned by Europeans and Americans were luck and coming from a wealthy family. There is a general conviction that you get ahead through networking and a good degree. This contrasts with Chinese and Japanese responses, where luck joined education and contacts as one of the three most important factors.

Work ethic

It is often said that southern Europeans work to live and northern Europeans live to work. The Protestant work ethic is said to have been one of the vital elements in the development of capitalism. There is a persistent conviction among northern Europeans that southerners are lazy. The different work ethic is said by northerners to be a major cultural hurdle when northern companies head to the sun and the cheap labor of the south.

Recent statistics published by the European Communities' statistical office show how the difference in work ethic translates into reality. The usual length of the working week for full-time employees is longest in the UK with 43 hours and Portugal with 42. The shortest working weeks are in Belgium, Denmark, and Italy with 38 hours each. North and south? Protestant and Catholic?

The argument becomes even more tenuous when one considers paid holidays. Including public holidays, Germans have 39 days' paid holiday a year, more than any other Europeans. Britain has the least with 33, followed by Italy with 34.

The further south you go, the more unreliable the statistics become in evaluating how hard people work. Italy has a "black economy" estimated as the equivalent of 30–40 percent of the main economy. By definition, this does not show up in statistics. In Germany it is around 10 percent and in the UK about 15 percent. In Latin countries there is a much larger proportion of people who have second jobs, made easier by a working day that starts and finishes earlier. Outside the main cities this may include running a smallholding, the labor and fruits of which do not turn up in the statistics.

Observation and anecdotal evidence support the argument that people work as hard in the south as in the north. To claim that one race or culture works harder than another is a subjective value judgment. There are indeed measurable differences between the productive and the less productive economies, yet the underlying cause is not how hard people work but how effectively. The problem is one of management, not motivation.

The former socialist countries

In the former socialist countries the lasting experience of communism remains the biggest influence on the business environment. These countries have made significant progress in transforming institutions and systems, but old expectations and beliefs about business and institutional life remain, even among a younger generation.

There is a deep distrust of corporate or public institutions, a feeling that they are not there to serve the interests of their employees, clients, and customers but the interests of those who have power within them. Instead, people rely on networks of family and close friends for emotional and economic support. With the collapse and transformation of institutions, these networks become even more important.

Feelings of inferiority toward westerners create defensive barriers. A comment often made by people who grew up in these countries is that they were cut off from the rest of the world. They feel that they lack the knowledge, experience, and skills necessary to work on the same footing as other Europeans.

Attitudes such as these influence all levels of interaction, from negotiation to the daily encounters of normal business life. For example, most western employees are used to the management techniques of coaching and evaluation. The basic elements of these techniques—performance measurement, self-appraisal, personal goal setting—can hark back to the self-criticism and public censure of the old days. Those old enough to remember communism have learned to distrust commitment to organizations, to keep themselves to themselves, to be careful not to reveal anything that might be held against them.

Western managers wishing to introduce team-based management methods may also come across resistance from those who remember the teams to which they belonged in the Soviet period. From childhood in the Pioneers and Oktobryaska to work groups in factories and offices, people were organized into teams that competed with each other. However, the organization, goals, and processes of these teams were handed down from above. The idea that a team was autonomous and that individuals within it shared responsibility for goals and performance was discouraged. Far from being empowering, a team was restricting and oppressive.

Appealing to the success of the team is thus not as motivating as it is in some other cultures. Managers who come in from outside with glib talk of teams perhaps should make sure that everyone shares the same understanding of how they should work.

Economic and political restructuring has led to a decline in incomes and living standards and increased social and financial insecurity, especially among public-sector employees. Their condition is in sharp contrast with those who saw the opportunities of privatization, not all of them legitimate, and of the conversion to a cash economy. One symptom of resentment and frustration caused by inequalities and perceived injustices in the new economies is the election of communist parties to power. Another is the prevalence of corruption in the public and private sectors.

Petty corruption, defined as inducements to get people to do what they are supposed to do anyway, is part of the same legacy from "deficit times" as lamentable customer service. In the surplus-based economies of capitalism, the provider tries to induce consumers to buy. In the deficit-based economies of socialism, the consumer tries to induce providers to sell. In the transition economies, despite superficial changes, there are still deficits, and virtual monopolies and old attitudes persist.

Corruption

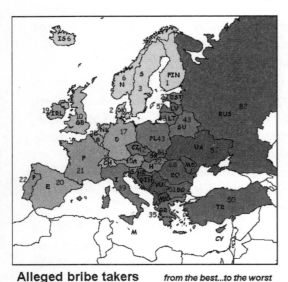

Alleged bribe takers   *from the best...to the worst*

[1] *2000 world rankings*[90]
(blank unranked)

The map of alleged bribe takers is based on the work of Transparency International. TI assembles a number of surveys carried out regularly by other organizations and creates a league table of countries based on the propensity for public officials to take bribes. You can refer to its website (www.transparency.org) for more information and an up-to-date league table of countries.

The TI survey also asks why public officials and politicians take bribes. Low public-sector salaries, immunity of public officials, and secrecy in government were the three main reasons, followed by worsening public procurement practices, the privatization process, and increased foreign investment and trade. This is a strong correlation of these factors with con-

ditions in the former socialist countries. At the same time, western European countries such as Greece and Italy have similar rankings to some of the eastern
Europeans.

The map of alleged bribe payers represents the other side of the
coin, based on a survey by Gallup
International of the propensity of
companies of major exporting
countries to pay bribes (see www.
transparency. org).

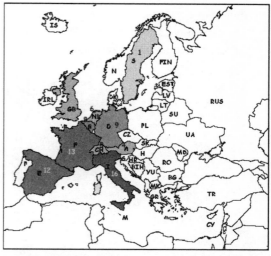

Unethical behavior is not confined to the public sector. The table
below is drawn from responses to
the Mole Map Survey question: "Are
bribes, kickbacks, or other inducements, which are not part of acceptable hospitality, necessary to do
business?" This is not a national corruption index. It reflects the opinions of respondents to the survey
and these may not be typical of the
business sector as a whole.

Alleged bribe payers   *from the best...to the worst*

1 ▢▮▮▮▮▮ 16

2000 world rankings
(blank unranked)

Readers should draw
conclusions from their own
experience about the level of
probity in their own and others' countries. The national
stereotypes to be most wary
of are those propagated by
nations about themselves.

<u>*Survey*</u>
       "Are bribes etc, in excess of traditional hospitality,
             necessary to do business?"

China Lithuania Cyprus Hungary Italy N.Am
  Russia Turkey Japan Portugal France N'lands Finland
    Bulgaria Greece Poland Slovenia F Spain UK Norway
  Romania Czech Estonia Belg Germany Austria Sweden
 Ukraine Slovakia Latvia Belg W Ireland Switz Denmark

always   *often*   *sometimes*   *rarely*   *never*

They express aspiration more often than reality and are rarely held by outsiders.

When I mentioned that I was in the middle of writing this book, the first question that many people asked was which was the most untrustworthy nationality to
do business with. I always named the nationality of the questioner. That wasn't only
a putdown but a statement about the subjectivity and relativity of business ethics.
Those who sincerely believe that they are solely responsible for maintaining standards of fair play and probity in the international community are often shocked to
discover that foreigners think they are crafty and unreliable.

Underlying social values differ from country to country. Attitudes to government, family, local community, employer, and employee also differ. Southern

Europeans castigated by northerners for corruption in public life look with equal disapproval at the collapse of family loyalties in the north. They regard it as a duty to cheat the tax authorities and resent criticism by paragons of civic virtue who put their parents into old people's homes.

The very concept of law—how it is made, observed, and enforced—varies from culture to culture. For example, some people see laws and rules primarily as social contracts that are the responsibility of everyone to maintain and enforce for the common good. Other people see them primarily as manifestations of authority imposed and enforced from above, with or without the consent of those subject to them. Most societies have a mixture of these two concepts, although the differing balances affect not only the rule of law in society but, on a more everyday level, management styles and internal control systems in companies.

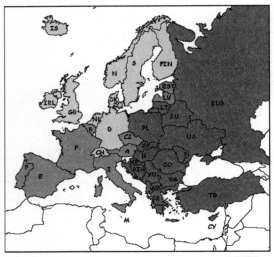

Authority rules?
Or the rule of law?

law
50-50
authority

There are different degrees of belief as to what constitutes actual wrongdoing. What is illegal need not be unethical and vice versa. For example, the status of insider dealing is ambiguous in many countries. Lavish and tax-deductible business entertainment may be considered legitimate in the private sector but as bribery in the public sector. Social security fraud among the poor may be more severely pursued and punished than major commercial fraud.

Values also differ from country to country about personal and civic duty. Would you lie to the police to protect a friend accused of VAT evasion? Would you award a contract to your brother-in-law even if he was not the lowest bidder? Does the likelihood of being found out make a difference? These questions have different answers depending on the social environment. The distinctions between absolute moral codes and the likelihood of being found out, pangs of conscience, and social embarrassment are more blurred in some societies than in others.

In day-to-day dealings conventions of behavior can be misinterpreted. Among many westerners there is a presumption of dishonesty about people from cultures in which it is impolite to look others in the eye. Among Europeans the handshake at the end of a negotiation can be interpreted by one side as a sign that the deal is struck and by the other as a polite leave taking.

Even what is seen as normal practice can still engender mistrust. Delaying payment of invoices until the very last minute is standard among some treasury managers but seen as sharp practice by those from some other countries. Missed delivery dates may be a normal part of doing business in one environment and morally, as well as commercially, reprehensible in others.

Attitudes to agreements differ. Some people look to the spirit of an agreement rather than the letter and are offended when their partner refuses to renegotiate the terms because circumstances have changed. That partner is equally scandalized because he or she believes that the other party is trying to cheat.

Faced with such diversity, the best course is probably to reserve ethical judgment for one's own behavior and suspend it when looking at other people's.

SMOKING
Which country's population smokes the most
(cigarettes per head per day)?
                Greece
                Russia
                Romania

NORDIC COUNTRIES

Denmark

According to Eurobarometer, the majority of Danes are committed Europeans who believe that membership of the EU is a good thing. At the same time, they resist further political integration. With a population of 5.5 million many Danes feel swamped by the other 300 million or so Europeans. Their highly developed but small, specialized, and healthy economy is perceived as having little to gain from the financial and other benefits that some other countries expect from Brussels. They have the highest satisfaction rate in Europe with their domestic institutions and political processes and prefer them to remain uncontaminated by outside influences. In referendums they have voted against the Maastricht Treaty, leading to several key opt-outs, and more recently against joining European Monetary Union.

The Danes' opinion is not uninformed. In public opinion surveys carried out by Eurobarometer, they have the highest percentage of those who declare that they are interested in EU politics. This combination of cooperation and independence characterizes Danish social and business culture.

To the casual observer, social and geographic uniformity may obscure subtle regional differences perceived by Danes themselves. Those from the east of the country, especially Copenhagen, see themselves as lively and open-minded, but they may be viewed as somewhat arrogant in comparison with the quieter, more introverted westerners. Every country has a region whose natives play the role of rustic dimwit and in Denmark's case it is unjustifiably Jylland.

Business environment

Denmark is a model welfare state based on coalition and conformity. Over 800,000 out of a workforce of some 2.5 million are employed in the public sector. At the same time there is a deep commitment to autonomy and independence. The remaining workforce is spread among 6,000 companies and more than half are employed by firms with fewer than 200 employees. Agriculture is based on small farms and smallholdings in a network of cooperatives and the fishing industry is made up of owner-captains rather than commercially run fleets.

All Danish industry and agriculture is in private hands. An entrepreneurial outlook combined with the small size of the industrial base has led to a business strategy based on the exploitation of specialist market niches. Nevertheless, tax rates and benefit provisions make new ventures difficult for entrepreneurs. Marginal income tax is 65 percent, VAT is 25 percent. There are also selective taxes on a number of products. For example, the tax on a car is 200 percent of its import price.

Organization

Public limited companies have a supervisory board, *bestyrelse*, elected by the shareholders. This appoints the management board, *direktion*. Sometimes members of the management board can be elected to the supervisory board as long as they are in a minority. In companies employing more than 35 people the employees are entitled to elect to the supervisory board half the number of members elected by the shareholders. In companies with more than 30 employees they or the employer can opt for a works council to be set up, *samarbejdsudvalg*, consisting of equal numbers of management and employee representatives.

There are many similarities with the business culture of the Danes' North Sea neighbors, the Dutch. Organizations are transparent and the hierarchy purely functional. There is a great deal of sideways communication between areas and a readiness to cut across the hierarchy if necessary. A team-based culture is prevalent and training for it begins at an early age in school.

The boss is considered to be a coach or team leader to the group. Authority is based on professionalism and competence and an authoritarian manner is viewed as rude and unnecessary. Especially among the younger generation, there is an emphasis on open communication and consultation at all levels and sharing of objectives and goals. If something goes wrong the priority is to bring it out into the open and take steps to make sure that it does not happen again.

While accountability lies with individuals, they will rarely take decisions before consultation with everyone affected. Meetings are frequent. They can be for briefing, discussion, or decision making, but it is always made clear what is involved. Meetings always have a stated purpose, an agenda, and they will start and end punctually. If something is not covered properly the participants will reconvene. Preparation for meetings and indeed any discussion is very important. At the same time, lobbying before a meeting may be considered underhand—everybody might not get the same picture.

All participants are encouraged to voice a considered opinion, although consensus is less important than being fully informed. If a vote is taken or the boss makes the decision, everyone will go along with it.

Upward mobility

There is a greater sense of corporate pride in Denmark than in many countries and job hopping is rare. Promotion is on the basis of performance and professionalism.

Among EU countries Denmark has the highest proportion of women in the workforce. There are comprehensive maternity benefits, paternity leave, and child-care provision. Women are commonly found in managerial and professional jobs and there is little discrimination against them.

Etiquette and behavior

These days the polite *De* (you) is only used for formal letters, to the royal family, and on the phone to complete strangers in a business context. Otherwise the informal *du* is common.

Anglo-Saxons who expect foreigners to speak English will not be disappointed in Denmark. They all do, at all levels of society.

Like the Dutch, Danes are plain speaking. Frankness is a sign of honesty and reliability, as is meticulous punctuality in business and social life.

In common with Nordic neighbors, conversations and discussions are serial, that is, everyone waits their turn to speak and listens to the speaker without interrupting.

Social values are egalitarian. Despite a high standard of living, ostentation is frowned on and the outward trappings of success—a more luxurious car than anyone else or a bigger house—meet with strong disapproval. Danes call it *Janteloven*, the law of the Jants, which comes from the name of a fictional town in a 1930s novel by Aksel Sandemose. Nobody should think themselves better or smarter or more important than anyone else. If they do, they are cut down to size. In short, nobody is special, all are equal. This helps to explain punitive progressive taxes, outward conformism, and a mistrust of the flamboyantly successful.

As well as speaking fluent English and probably German, Danes are open and welcoming to foreigners. Most students will have studied abroad for a period. The Danes are dependent on foreign trade and have an international presence greater than the size of their country would indicate. Experience of the outside world reinforces their conviction that the Danish way of doing things is best. It is very difficult to introduce new ideas from outside.

Humor

Danes see themselves as the humorists of the Nordic peoples. (Some might say that they don't have much competition.) Theirs is a wry, understated humor that is not out of place in a business context. It may escape the notice of people used to robust, less subtle humor. It is rarely sarcastic, self-deprecating, or flippant. Irony may be misunderstood by the literal-minded Danes.

Social life

There is often a canteen at work. If not, people bring sandwiches. Lunch breaks are short and it is rare to go out. Lunch is not part of the business day and there is little business entertaining. There is mingling of ranks, but this does not serve a business purpose. People want to turn off for half an hour.

Everyone goes home at five in the evening and there is little social mixing between colleagues outside work. What there is usually takes place at home over an early dinner. Entertaining is informal, except for the Scandinavian custom of synchronized drinking and choruses of *skål* (cheers). The typical atmosphere is a cosy conviviality described by the word *hygge*, the best translation of which is probably "snug."

LANGUAGES

Match up the languages to the countries in which you are most likely to hear them spoken

Sorbian	Greece
Arumanian	Italy
Friulian	Germany

Finland

Finland is Nordic but not Scandinavian. Scandinavia comprises only Iceland, Sweden, Denmark, and Norway.

Finland is the only one of these countries to have joined European Monetary Union. At the same time, according to Eurobarometer, Finns are the least enthusiastic about the euro and the EU in general. Not that enthusiasm is a word to use lightly, or indeed frequently, in a Finnish context. Reserve, rationality, and an acute awareness of self-interest are the dominant characteristics in public affairs.

Statistically the fifth largest country in Europe, a third of Finland lies above the Arctic circle and is mostly uninhabited. Helsinki is the northernmost capital in the European Union. The country's population is 5 million, of whom about a million live in the capital, the only city of any size. The two next biggest towns, Tampere and Turku, have about 200,000 inhabitants apiece.

While it has many social values in common, Finland has several marked points of difference with its Nordic neighbors and partners. For a start, the Finnish language is not Germanic but in a class of its own. Theoretically it belongs in the same language group as Hungarian, although for practical purposes the two are mutually incomprehensible. Finnish is the first language for about 94 percent of the population, Swedish for 6 percent. Both are official languages.

Swedish Finns

Although they comprise only 6 percent of the population, Swedish Finns play a disproportionate role in the commercial and political life of the country. If there is any social division or snobbery in Finland, and compared with most other countries there is very little, the Swedish Finns regard themselves as superior. They are descendants of the old ruling class from the days before 1809 when Finland was a province of the kingdom of Sweden.

Swedish Finns are predominantly merchants and business people and tend to be wealthier, more traditional, and more solidly middle class than their compatriots, owning most of the larger private companies. They are regarded by Finnish Finns as more outgoing, better at languages, and more at ease with foreigners. They attend Swedish-speaking schools and universities. While these schools are state funded on the same basis as any other and would deny any charge of élitism, some Finnish Finns deliberately send their children to them under the impression that they will gain an advantage in life.

There is no easy way to identify a Swedish Finn. People whose last names end in "*-onen*" are invariably Finnish Finns, otherwise names can either be Swedish or Finnish.

The Russian connection

Finland is where Russia borders directly on the European Union, both by land and sea. It is the only western country with the same rail gauge as the former Soviet Union. Finland has a long association with Russia going back to when it was an arch-duchy under the Czars. It has a minority group of Russian speakers and Orthodox Christian is the second official state church, along with the predominant Evangelical Lutheran. Since the October Revolution Finland has maintained its independence from Russia through the most testing of times. It has a great deal of experience to offer the newly independent Baltic states, especially Estonia, whose language is a sister of Finnish.

Finland is well positioned to take advantage of the resurgence of the Baltic as a major regional market in international trade. There is substantial and growing Finnish investment in Russia, and Finland's financial, commercial, and personal links with both Russian and the other Nordic countries give it a strong competitive advantage with all the states bordering on the Baltic.

Industry

The economy depends heavily on forestry and Finland is one of the world's leading manufacturers and exporters of timber, pulp, and paper products. These account for nearly 30 percent of exports. Over the past generation the economy has undergone a rapid transformation from almost total dependency on forest-based products to metal and engineering industries, which are now the largest source of industrial employment and account for almost 50 percent of exports.

A small number of companies in the capital-intensive forest, metal, and engineering industries dominate Finnish business. They have close ties to the banks, which are allowed to control up to 10 percent of equity. Some of the major companies are state owned, although a policy of limited privatization is being spasmodically implemented. About 85 percent of industry is in private hands and the emphasis is on private enterprise, albeit under the watchful eye of the close-knit financial and industrial establishment.

Exports are of major importance, amounting to over 40 percent of GDP. Industrial policy has focused on exploiting international market niches. These include manufacturing control systems, environmental protection, and high-value fashion. For example, the electronics company Nokia is the second biggest supplier of handsets for mobile phones after Motorola and is the biggest supplier to the British market. For a Nordic country Finland has a relatively small public sector, employing a sixth of the workforce. The rest are in the private sector.

Organization

Industrial companies are dominated by engineers. Management has a strong technical orientation. The engineering mentality is reflected in a precise and systematic approach to organization. A respect for systems and procedures goes hand in hand with a distrust of improvisation. Finns become nervous if they feel that things are not totally under control. A high value is put on efficiency and effectiveness. While not on the Swedish level of an obsession, punctuality is important.

Delegation consists primarily of setting targets, benchmarks, and detailed budgets. Within this framework employees are expected to use their initiative and detailed action plans are not forthcoming. Outside Helsinki companies operate in a socially conscious, even paternalistic environment, based on the kind of mutual loyalty that is now only a folk memory in the market-driven economies further south. However, job hopping among Helsinki-based companies is becoming more prevalent.

Leadership

Authority is oligarchic rather than collective, the responsibility being taken by a core team of senior people. If there is an individual driving force at the top it is usually not immediately obvious.

Decision making is slow and deliberate and takes place against a background of deep conservatism. There is a long process of consultation and debate in which anyone with an opinion or an interest is heard. Perseverance, described as stubbornness by some outsiders, is a Finnish characteristic. Innovation and change for its own sake are not highly valued. To put over ideas and win arguments one needs to fight a war of attrition rather than a brilliant pitched battle. As soon as disagreement or confrontation occurs the subject is dropped, only to be brought up again on the next occasion. Tactical victories are usually hollow. Public contradiction is to be avoided and the worst tactic is to force opponents into a corner or make them look foolish. It is unwise to bring up a new idea at a meeting without having first lobbied it privately with all those concerned.

In the presentation of ideas and proposals Finns are deeply suspicious of anything resembling a sales pitch. They prefer to base decisions on a worst-case scenario and consider optimism as frivolous.

Meetings are an important forum for information sharing, problem solving, and debate. A well-managed, efficient, and time-driven meeting may be an aspiration, but it takes second place to hearing everybody out. A thorough agenda is agreed, although the need to elicit everyone's contribution and achieve consensus means that it is rarely completed. Board meetings are the exception. They are not usually a forum for discussion and debate but for the formal ratification of decisions that have been made previously.

While a participatory style of management is becoming more accepted, especially among newer companies and younger managers, and is certainly more highly developed than in most other European countries, Finland should not be lumped together with the thorough-going industrial democracies of Sweden and Denmark. Among older managers and traditional industries participation is still regarded as populist and inefficient.

Serial conversation

Finnish conventions of communication can be offputting to outsiders. Serial conversation is the rule, that is, each person takes it in turns to speak while the others listen intently without interruption or even signs of attention and encouragement. When the speaker has finished, the other party may meditate on what has been said before responding. The Anglo-Saxon style of interrupting, finishing sentences, and leaping in with an instant reaction and comment of one's own is considered disrespectful, while the Mediterranean style of simultaneous conversation in which everyone speaks at once is incomprehensible. Such conversationalists are apt to think, mistakenly, that Finns do not understand what is being said, or if they do that it is penetrating very slowly.

As foreigners are unlikely to attempt Finnish, the language of choice is likely to be English or, if it is a common language, Swedish. However, Finnish linguistic conventions still apply. A strong value is placed on speaking plainly and openly, without exaggeration or understatement, and if possible with statements expressed in facts and figures. At the same time, the presentation is low key and laconic to the point of being cryptic. It is not done to be expressive, assertive, or emotional, nor to say things more than once. The Finns' natural reserve is compounded by a reluctance to speak foreign languages if there is a risk of making mistakes.

Attitudes and behavior

There is no taboo on humor in a business environment as there is in other some other cultures, but by English or Irish standards it simply does not occur very often. Good humor rather than humor characterizes business relationships. Finns are the first to acknowledge that they are not good at small talk. Conversation for its own sake is regarded as a waste of breath. Their natural shyness derives largely from a strong concept of personal privacy, even insularity, from which strangers are excluded.

A lack of ostentation is reflected in self-presentation. Despite their fashion industry, Finns do not regard themselves as smart dressers and this is not disputed by outside observers. For men, sober jackets and ties are conventional at most levels, perhaps a gray or a brown suit, but there are many companies in which casual wear is acceptable. Dark suits are for very serious occasions.

Status differences are minimal and the younger generation of managers at any level pride themselves on being approachable. There is slightly more formality about the use of last names and titles than in, say, Sweden or Denmark, although usually one rapidly gets on to first-name terms with people at any level of seniority and regardless of gender. In conservative circles, which usually means Swedish Finns, this takes longer and the more traditional and upper class will wait for an invitation to do so from the senior person.

Women

There are no gender distinctions in the Finnish language, no "he" and "she," "his" and "her." This is why Finns with less than fluent English often mix these up. Perhaps it also has an influence on the war of the sexes. Finland was the first European country to give women the vote, in 1906. About 40 percent of members of parliament are women.

In business there is a significant and increasing number of women in senior management and directorial positions. This is made possible by practical measures, such as the provision of comprehensive nursery care, and by social attitudes. It is perfectly acceptable for both men and women to leave work or even break off a meeting with the explanation that it is their turn to collect the children from school or to take it in turns to stay at home if children are sick.

Saunas

For such a fitness- and health-loving culture, the Nordic predisposition to consume prodigious amounts of vodka is a consolation to otherwise less clean-living Europeans further south. However, it should be put in perspective. Finns' annual per capita consumption of alcohol is half that of the French and Spanish and two-thirds that of the British. The difference is that they try to drink their ration all at once rather than a little every day. The habit is waning, however, among a more health- and fashion-conscious younger generation, who prefer a glass of wine. Finns have the distinction—and this may be connected—of drinking more coffee per capita than any other European nation. (On the other hand, they spend the least on clothing and furniture.)

They pay for their vigorous consumption of stimulants with the rigors of the sauna. The Lutheran approach to the sauna is in sharp contrast with the unreformed orthodoxy of the Russians over the border. In Russia the sauna is an excuse for indulgence; in Finland it is expiation. A "sauna beer," a grilled sausage, and a rustic speciality or two are the most that one can expect during the ordeal.

The sauna has a special role in domestic life but it is not a regular feature of business-related social life. For Finns themselves the sauna is to be shared with family and close friends. First-time visitors may be treated to one, which they should accept even if they do not regard it as a treat. An important business meeting may be followed by a sauna in which the conversation is continued on a more informal basis and things can be said that are harder to articulate with clothes on.

In general, business life and personal life are kept separate. Socializing does not go much beyond an occasional beer after work with colleagues or a modest lunch with visitors. An invitation to dinner at home is a major step in a personal relationship. It is not that a personal relationship arises out of a business relationship, but that it is irrelevant. Finns are wary of new relationships and slow to open up. Newcomers should be reconciled to a lengthy period of establishing credentials and building up trust and credibility.

LITERATURE

Authors of which country have won the Nobel prize for literature most often?

    France

    Italy

    UK

Norway

Norway belonged to the Kingdom of Denmark for 400 years and was taken over by Sweden at the end of the Napoleonic wars. It gained independence from Sweden, peacefully, in 1905. Since the 1930s it has been governed by coalition, led usually by the Labour Party and sometimes by the Conservatives.

Politically and socially Norway is similar to other Scandinavian countries. Egalitarianism underlies a democratic and consensus-based sense of community combined with a self-image of individualism and independence.

Independence is reflected in the referendums of 1972 and 1994 in which Norwegians voted against membership of the European Union. They like to have it both ways: They belong to the European Economic Area and the Schengen Agreement, which removes border controls between member states. This means that they have all the economic rights and advantages of the European Union, including free movement for their citizens, without the duties and disadvantages of membership. They may not avoid the costs or membership for long, however. By virtue of its EEA membership the European Union wants Norway to pay its share of the expense of EU enlargement.

These rugged individualists, like their Scandinavian neighbors, are happy to pay a marginal tax rate of 50 percent for the state to look after them from the cradle to the grave.

Languages

There are two official written languages. Bokmål ("book language," otherwise known as Riksmål, "state language") has many similarities with Danish. It was the language of the urban, ruling class. In the middle of the nineteenth century Nynorsk ("new language") was concocted by nationalists from local dialects. Norway is *Norge* in Bokmål and *Noreg* in Nynorsk, both of which you will see on the stamps. Schoolchildren learn to write in both. Norwegians also speak one or more of several dialects.

The two written languages reflect a cultural divide: Nynorsk representing a Norse culture, traditionalist, rural, puritan, and Europhobic; Bokmål a Germanic culture, urban, innovative, modernizing, and internationalist. Not only is the country split between these two, as reflected in the EU membership referendum, but so are individuals.

A Norwegian respondent said, "If you want people to work 8–4 in factories go to Sweden. If you want people to work in storms with ice in their beards without a break for three months go to Norway—if you don't mind them being drunk for the next three months." This is certainly true of the 5 percent of the workforce employed in fishing and on oil rigs. Meanwhile, the 40 percent employed by the state and the 20 percent in the retail and catering trade opt for a quieter life.

Traveling around rural Norway, it is striking that there are few villages and market towns compared with, for example, Mediterranean countries where people congregate in villages and isolated houses are rare. Norwegians prefer to keep themselves to themselves. Small, independent communities are replicated even in the cities; not that the cities would count as more than market towns in bigger countries. Oslo has a population of half a million and Bergen, the second city, less than a quarter of a million.

Norwegian national pride is distinctly rural and egalitarian. It glorifies the scenery and the simple life rather than extolling military power, political pomp, and urban grandeur, like the former colonial powers of Europe. The national anthem proclaims a country of *"Hytter og hus, men ingen borge"* (cottages and houses, but no castles). Like their Nordic neighbors, most Norwegians prefer to spend their vacations in primitive, isolated cottages, skiing or fishing. In common with Finland and Sweden the *Allemansret/Allemansrätt* ("Everyman's Right" of public access to the wilderness) gives everyone free access to forests, lakes, and uncultivated land.

The Laws of Jante

Norwegians have a strong antipathy toward social hierarchies, social climbers, and any kind of exhibition of wealth, status, or success. The negative aspects of egalitarianism are satirically expressed in the famous (in Scandinavia) Laws of Jante, the *Janteloven*, which they share with the Danes. Nobody should think themselves better or smarter or more important than anyone else. If they do, they are cut down to size.

Despite the highest standard of living in the world, Norwegians cultivate frugality and simplicity. There are heavy taxes on "luxury goods," and wine and liquor can still only be purchased in state monopoly stores at exorbitant prices. Designer clothes, luxury cars, and the good life are considered definitely un-Norwegian. On SAS (Scandinavian Airlines) flights you can tell the Scandinavian businessmen apart: The Danes wear tweed jackets, the Swedes natty Italian suits, and the Norwegians dress like English solicitors.

Business sector

The traditional industry in Norway is fishing. The country exports 90 percent of the catch, making it the world's largest exporter of fish. It is also the world's largest exporter of farmed salmon. Along with Japan, Norwegians hunt whales in the face of an international ban. This is an unprofitable activity, subsidized by the state, in order to keep small fishing communities alive by giving them something to do in the summer, the low season for fishing. Half of the catch is exported to Japan and the rest eaten locally or used for pet food.

The second traditional activity is shipping. Norwegians account for 7 percent of the world's fleet, the fourth largest. Other commodities include aluminum, forest products, and above all oil and gas. It is oil that gives Norwegians one of the highest per capita incomes in the world. Norway is the seventh largest oil-producing country in the world and the second largest exporter, energy group Norsk Hydro being its largest company. The government is preparing for the time when the oil runs out by pouring its vast revenues into a fund invested in foreign equities.

Led by engineering and construction company Kvaerner, the dominant industries are engineering and energy-intensive industries such as metal production, industrial chemicals, and pulp and paper. Shipbuilding and the construction of oil platforms are important segments of the engineering industry. Manufacturing accounts for about 15 percent of total employment.

Business attitudes and behavior

Norwegians are pleasant and informal, but difficult to get to know. It is not only foreigners who find them reserved and distant—they are like it with each other. Close colleagues of many years will not have any social life together. An invitation to a private home is unusual. Personal relationships are unimportant in a business context. Indeed, Norwegians are uncomfortable with personal relationships that contain any element of obligation or indebtedness.

Entertaining is not an essential part of doing business as it is in more southern countries. One returns a favor or a gift almost immediately, and measures the return with careful precision. Even if people know each other well and will have ample opportunity to reciprocate, they pay their own way. They do not seek to create relationships and networks based on mutual obligation.

At the same time, Norwegians work consistently well in teams. While acknowledging the need for strong leadership, the leader is part of the group. The responsibility for decision making and implementation is seen as belonging to the team rather than its leader. Like their Nordic neighbors they are strongly consensus-oriented. They prefer a poor compromise to disagreement and are reluctant to act unless everyone is in positive agreement.

Communication

Norwegians express themselves plainly and sincerely. Understatement, exaggeration, irony, and flippancy are rare. Being quiet and soft spoken is the accepted norm and those who are loud of speech or manner are disapproved of. Interrupting others when they are speaking, completing their sentences, or openly contradicting what they have said is considered ill mannered. Children are taught to think twice before speaking and to utter only their most firm beliefs, and then only when there is a considered intention. Small talk is seen as "dead talk."

PENGUINS
Where is the biggest penguin colony in Europe?
  Crete
  Edinburgh
  Tallinn

Sweden

The "Swedish model" is still the bane of liberals, free marketeers, and tax cutters. It is a paradigm of high taxation, a dominant public sector, and enforced egalitarianism. Nevertheless, the Swedes must be doing something right. Sweden's economic and industrial power is out of proportion to its size; its population of nine million is smaller than that of Greece, Portugal, or Belgium. Yet it has the seventh biggest economy in Europe and is fourth in the world in terms of GDP per head.

As regards ethnicity, religion, and language, Sweden was until recently a relatively homogenous society. There are a minority of Finnish speakers and a few thousand Lapps in the far north. The dominant religion is Lutheran. Only recently was it made possible to opt out of paying church tax and very few avail themselves of the concession, although only a small minority go to church.

Recent immigration from southern and eastern Europe during a period of rising unemployment sparked an anti-immigrant backlash in some sectors of the Swedish population. It is a measure of public sensitivity that to be classified as an immigrant one needs only one parent to have been born abroad. By this definition 10 percent of the population is immigrant. However, generally Sweden has an exemplary record of human rights and social tolerance. Immigrants and refugees benefit from a wide range of social benefits, including compulsory but free Swedish lessons.

The population is the oldest in the world, defined by the proportion of it who are over 65. The young have to work to support their elders. The country leads the world in the percentage of the population in the labor force, at 70 percent. It is not and has never been true that social and climatic stress leads to an unusually high suicide rate: Hungary ranks highest and Sweden only 17th in the world. Instead, Sweden has Europe's highest murder rate.

Egalitarianism

Although the addition of Sweden brings the number of monarchies in the European Union to six, the dominant Swedish social value is egalitarianism. This does not connote bland uniformity. The bedrock of the political system is a network of grassroots organizations called popular movements that unite different and often conflicting interest groups.

Consensus and compromise are deeply ingrained into every aspect of Swedish social and business life. In the legal sphere the adversarial system of litigation is alien. An extensive range of arbitration procedures and tribunals takes the place of court proceedings. This is coupled with exemplary openness of government. Since 1766 any person, Swedish or foreigner, has had the right to inspect any government record or document kept in central or local government files.

A universally high standard of living and a relatively small differential between the highest and the lowest paid, both enabled through the tax regime, foster a society in which visible differences in status are suppressed. Although the spread between highest and lowest incomes is growing, it is still the smallest in Europe.

It would be a mistake to think of the country as one vast commune, however. The sense of community is on a social rather than a personal level—on the latter Swedes are deeply private, competitive, and individualistic.

In common with the other Scandinavian countries the status and role of women are enviable to those in other countries. The number of women with paid jobs equals that of men. They are not in low-paid part-time jobs but spread through the workforce. It has been calculated, although with what precision is not clear, that 20 percent of all those in management positions are women. Most preschool childcare is publicly funded and there is generous maternity and paternity leave.

Urban and green

Environmental issues are at the top of the political agenda and represent a strong social value. There is no law of trespass. The right of common access, the *Allemansrätten*, allows people to walk where they like in forests or across open land, to pick mushrooms or tie up their boats anywhere they want so long as they do not do any damage or actively intrude on the privacy of the owner of the land. Many people have country cottages where they live the simple life for a few weeks a year.

Swedes have a town dweller's love of the countryside. They have experienced one of Europe's fastest rates of urbanization, which has left much of the countryside depopulated: 85 percent of people live in small towns. The largest urban area, Stockholm, has about 700,000 inhabitants. The southernmost third of Sweden is the most densely populated region, with more than 80 percent of the total population. The north, for sound climatic reasons, is very sparsely populated.

Industrial concentration

While Sweden is totally committed to a welfare state, its industrial policy is only indirectly interventionist. A mere 5 percent of industrial assets is state owned, one of the lowest state holdings in Europe.

The fortunes of Sweden were based on forests and iron ore. Timber pulp and paper still represent a major export sector. Rather than steel making, advanced engineering and capital goods now dominate the industrial sector. Swedish industry is concentrated in a small number of high-quality engineering companies producing mainly capital goods and vehicles. The 20 largest companies account for more than 40 percent of exports and employ four times as many people abroad as they do in Sweden. Many of these companies are household names: Volvo, Electrolux, Ericsson, Saab-Scania, Nobel, SKF, Atlas Copco.

In such a small country this situation has been made possible by a domestic industrial policy favoring merger and cooperation. Companies have been allowed to profit from domestic monopolies in order to compete more effectively in world markets. In recent years there has been an upsurge of new IT and telecommunications ventures created by a young and now wealthy entrepreneurial class.

These companies have thrived alongside the world's strongest trade union movement and the largest public sector relative to the country's GDP. The tax burden is 55 percent of GDP, one of the highest in the world. An aging population, resulting from increased longevity and a declining birth rate, aggravates the burden. The public sector absorbs a third of the workforce, most of which are engaged in administering the welfare system. Only basic industries such as energy, forests, and the domestic telephone network are state owned.

There is one respect in which Sweden is a small country: 15 families own 35 percent of industrial assets. While nepotism and old-boy networks are severely frowned on, it nevertheless helps if you belong to one of them. The crown jewels of Swedish industry are shared out among three groups of owners who, while taking care to protect their own interests, prefer to compete abroad rather than with each other. The greatest of these groups is the Wallenberg family, who have dominated Swedish industry for more than a century. The core of the family interests is a diversified industrial holding company with minority stakes in international companies such as Electrolux, SKF, Atlas, Ericsson, and the pharmaceutical company Astra. They share Asea Brown Boveri with a Swiss dynasty.

The Volvo/Skanska group does not have a controlling owner. Rather, it protects itself from outside depredation by a complicated system of cross-ownership. Volvo manufactures vehicles while Skanska is involved in construction. This group and the Wallenberg companies are closely associated with the largest Swedish commercial bank, SE-Banken. Swedish banks may not own industrial shares, but through their investment funds and main board directors they are predisposed to associate themselves closely with the fortunes of their corporate customers.

The third group is centered around the Industrivarden investment company. Its holdings are mainly in domestically oriented companies, with the exception of

Ericsson, which it shares with Wallenberg. It is associated with Sweden's second bank, Handelsbanken.

Practically all wage earners belong to unions affiliated with the Swedish Confederation of Trade Unions (LO). If a company has more than 25 employees, they may appoint a representative to the board of directors. Those with more than 100 appoint a blue-collar and a white-collar representative.

Softly softly management

Managers see themselves as coaches—in the English not the American sense of planners and coordinators and trainers—rarely giving what would pass for orders in more directive cultures. Both managers and managed are embarrassed by what in other cultures would be regarded as clarity and decisiveness in giving instructions. Managers wait for employees to show initiative while employees expect only suggestions. The assumption is that the person doing a job knows more about it than anyone else, including the boss, and is willing to do it well. Conversely, bosses are not expected to have the answers to problems that their employees encounter.

Anything less than unanimity and active consensus is seen as unsatisfactory. There is little sympathy with the idea that any decision is a good decision as long as it is made. Decisiveness for its own sake is not especially prized and the word "compromise" does not have any negative overtones. This makes decision making very slow, infuriatingly so to people from more action-oriented cultures, but is compensated for by more efficient implementation.

If this creates the impression that Swedish corporate life is cosy and conformist, this would be mistaken. The belief that each person has a positive contribution to make does not imply that everyone is in agreement. This is a collegiate but not collectivist society. Swedish managers are obliged to dedicate a greater amount of time to listening and persuasion and reconciling contradictory positions than, for example, French or Anglo-Saxon colleagues would be prepared to tolerate. Disagreement and rivalry can be rife, but at the same time subjected to the stronger value of ultimate reconciliation. Negotiating skills based on a combination of personal conviction and self-restraint become second nature. Collegiality is symbolized by the ease with which Swedes move rapidly to a first-name basis with one another regardless of job title, gender, status, or age.

Systematic but flexible

There is a deeply systematic approach to organizational life in Sweden. Structures and procedures are designed to minimize the need for uncertainty and improvisation. This is most evident in a concern for punctuality and time keeping that makes the Swiss seem sloppy. If a meeting is scheduled to end at a certain time it will end, even if it is incomplete. Not to be punctual is more than inefficiency and rudeness, it is a character defect.

A systematic approach to organization does not imply rigidity in chains of command or channels of communication. Organizations are typically shallow, with a great deal of informal interaction between all levels. Matrix management, whether formal or informal, works better in a Swedish environment than in those where well-defined chains of command and clear reporting lines are seen as desirable. Organizational management is based largely on target setting and budgetary control.

Etiquette

In some cultures a business relationship precedes a personal relationship; in others vice versa. In Sweden they tend to be kept permanently separate. A heightened sense of personal privacy maintains corporate life on a strictly business level.

It is not necessary to mug up on art and politics before going to a business dinner with Swedes: The fortunes of the national football team will be culture enough. This is certainly not because they are philistines, but because such topics do not belong. Personal issues should not interfere with or cloud business judgment. However genial their company, more southerly Europeans rarely feel that they get to know their Swedish associates.

Open communication

Swedes are among the world's best English speakers—and that includes native Anglophones. They do not have the allusive, understated style of the British, but possess a directness and openness that can be sometimes disarming and occasionally alarming when it is interpreted as abruptness. Swedes would, however, be surprised if they were ever accused of being abrupt. There is a strong measure of conflict avoidance that can be frustrating to those who prefer to "have things out."

Swedes share with other Nordic peoples a serial conversational style: Each person takes it in turns to speak, while the others listen intently without interrupting or even showing signs of attention and encouragement. Silence is not abhorred as it

---

PHONES

Which country has the biggest telecoms company in Europe?

> Germany
>
> France
>
> UK

---

is in more garrulous cultures and there is no social pressure to keep the conversation going. An aptitude for small talk—or "dead talk" as it is usually called in Sweden as well as Norway—is regarded as a social liability rather than an asset.

BALTIC COUNTRIES

It is misleading and undiplomatic to consider the Baltic States of Estonia, Latvia, and Lithuania as identical. They are substantially differentiated by language, ethnicity, and religion as well as the size and character of their economies. However, there are many similarities in their past and present, which are summarized here in order to avoid repetition.

The most obvious difference between the three states is language. Lithuanian and Latvian are the two surviving languages of the Baltic group. This is very different from the neighboring Germanic and Slavic groups although, like them, it is directly descended from the original Indo-European. As the more endangered language Lithuanian has been deliberately reconstructed and preserved and keeps many of its ancient forms. Latvian has developed under German and Russian influence. Estonian is in the totally different Finno-Ugric group of languages and is closely related to Finnish.

Since the Middle Ages the Baltic States have exploited their geographic position astride important trade routes east–west between northern Russia and northern Europe and north–south through Belarus and Ukraine to the Black Sea. Fish, timber, furs, and minerals were the traditional commodities. Industrial products and oil are now equally important.

The Russian influence

From when Peter the Great built St. Petersburg, the Baltic Sea has been of vital strategic and economic interest to Russia. St. Petersburg itself is closed by ice in the winter. Kaliningrad, the Russian enclave within Poland, and the ports of Lithuania are the only ones that remain naturally ice free in the winter. The pipeline from the northern Russian oil fields ends in Latvia.

It is remarkable that such small nations should have retained a distinct identity over centuries during which their countries have been independent for fewer than 50 years. For most of the past 500 years the Baltic States have been more or less unwilling parts of the empires of their larger neighbors, Sweden, Denmark, Germany, Poland, and Russia. By the beginning of the twentieth century they had become part of the Russian Empire. The Russian Revolution of 1918 gave them the opportunity to seize independence. This lasted just over 20 years until 1940 when they were annexed by the Soviet Union as part of the Molotov–Ribbentrop Pact, by which Stalin and Hitler divided up central and eastern Europe. Political institutions were dismantled and large numbers of the middle classes and intelligentsia were deported to Siberia.

In 1941 Germany broke the Molotov–Ribbentrop Pact, invaded the USSR, and occupied the Baltic States. The Germans were treated as liberators until conscription, labor camps, and the Holocaust changed that opinion. In 1944 the Red Army recaptured the Baltic States and Stalin's unfinished business was continued. Stalinist policy was to wipe out any lingering attachment to the West and to integrate economic and political systems into the Union. Like all Soviet peoples, those in the Baltic States were the victims of Stalinist terror and oppression, including more mass deportation to Siberian work camps. Partisans in the forests continued to fight a guerrilla war until the mid-1950s. Memories of these times still color relations with Russia and the Russian minorities within the three countries.

At the same time, the new republics were industrialized. Traditionally their economies had been based on trading, fishing, and agriculture. Heavy engineering, chemicals, and electronics were among the sectors created from scratch. As the states had very little industrial expertise, raw materials, energy, or labor, these were imported from Russia. Production was exported back to Russia. Russian immigrants provided most of the workers and bureaucrats for the factories. At a time of great material hardship, they were given preferential treatment in housing and employment. In time they became the economic masters, a colonial class.

Independence

With the collapse of the Soviet Union in 1990 the republics seized the chance of independence. After confrontation and sometimes violence, they all achieved it by 1991. The last Russian troops did not leave until 1994, however, and a large number of Russian immigrants and their descendants still remain. As they are mainly resident in the cities, they account for up to 50 percent of the urban population. What have now become their host governments impose stringent residence and language requirements before they can acquire local citizenship. They remain classified as resident aliens, although they can apply for passports.

On independence, the respective governments would have liked to see the immigrants follow the troops back to Russia. But where would they go? They are not Russian citizens, most have no other home, and Russia does not have the resources to absorb them. Many do not wish to apply for citizenship either, as they would then need visas to visit family and do business in Russia. Others prefer to be under the notional protection of Russia and to have a safety net in case anti-Russian discrimination worsens. A few die-hard irredentists see the independence of their states from Russia as temporary. Against all this is balanced the attractiveness of eventual EU citizenship.

In science fiction, the term "parallel universes" describes two separate realities existing in the same space–time continuum. That also describes the Russian and Baltic communities. While they live in the same places, they have virtually no contact with each other. They do not mix socially or commercially. They know the streets by different names and patronize different shops and restaurants. While there are Russian television channels, Russians prefer to tune in to programs from Moscow, although the quality of local television is hardly an incentive to do otherwise. The business sectors operate separately. Russian-owned companies employ Russian staff and deal with Russian companies. The way of doing business is different. Baltic people regard Russians as more extrovert, dramatic, and spontaneous. They are more entrepreneurial but less meticulous in execution. Personal relationships are more important to them in business.

Many suspect that Russians control a greater part of the private sector than native citizens and more of them are rich, but they do not publicize their business activities. Wealthy entrepreneurs try to remain anonymous to avoid the attentions of politicians, the public, and Russian-dominated organized crime. As time goes on they are growing even more apart, as a young generation of Baltic language speakers prefer to learn English rather than Russian. The existence of such large minorities within small countries creates a potentially explosive situation, which will at some time have to be resolved.

Conversely, the Baltic nations have a substantial diaspora in North America, Australia, and western Europe, who have preserved traditional cultures that have evolved or dissolved in the home country. They have also acquired education, technical skills, and a familiarity with a wider world that are much in demand in the new states. Whether they come back to practice them is another matter. Since independence between 5 and 10 percent of the respective populations, predominantly younger and better-educated people, have chosen to study and work abroad and there is little sign as yet of them returning.

Post-independence politics have been a tussle between members of the independence movements and former communist party politicians. With greater or lesser speed the Baltic countries are reorienting to the West. They are progressing toward membership of the EU and NATO and have joined institutions like the IMF and the European Bank for Reconstruction and Development. They formed their own free-trade area in 1994. At the same time, they must retain constructive relationships with Russia, to which geography and economics still bind them.

Transition to a market economy

The transformation from a centrally planned to a market economy has followed similar stages in each country. Currencies were pegged to the Deutschmark—now the euro—and backed by foreign exchange reserves. Monetary and fiscal policies were introduced and developed. Budget deficits were reduced by shrinking the public sector through privatization and cutting welfare payments.

Transition has not been without hardship. Many people found themselves worse off than before and without the safety net of social provision. Nor does privatization necessarily create a free market. Transferring ownership into the private hands of former managers and officials or to foreign companies does not necessarily mean more efficiency and competition. In basic sectors such as utilities and raw materials, organizations continue to operate as monopolies under government protection.

Financial and banking systems have been re-established on commercial lines. Stock exchanges have been opened. Steps have been taken to reform the legal system, including commercial law, tax, land ownership, and intellectual property. Foreign trade legislation has been liberalized and investment laws created to facilitate foreign investment.

The institutional reform process is not yet complete, however. Property rights are often disputed, financial statements are not always what they seem, and an essential requirement for any business, however small, is an experienced bookkeeper who can navigate the complexities of bureaucracy. Land acquisition is complicated by the policy of reparation for property expropriated by the USSR. Certifying that there are no prior claims is not straightforward.

All of this has created severe demands on a limited pool of expertise. In the early days it was striking how young the policy makers and technocrats were. Unless they were returning emigrants, people over 30 did not have the necessary education or background. It also created social stress. The privatization process was not transparent and was often corrupt, as managers and politicians manipulated the process to their advantage. It is ill mannered to ask owners how they acquired their business or otherwise refer to the murky period of spontaneous privatization. Social benefits were considerably reduced, unemployment rose steeply, and the standard of living of most of the population fell sharply.

In contrast, the minority who saw the opportunities of the free market to set up new businesses or who were sufficiently well qualified to be employed by foreign companies did well. Enthusiasm for the free market encouraged many new ventures and the expansion of privatized companies. In some cases naïveté and well-intentioned but incompetent management led the new companies into failure.

The widening gaps in income and expectation, the novelty of a money-based economy, and the constant change and fluidity in institutions and systems created an environment that encouraged a "shadow market" estimated at around the equivalent of 25 percent of the official economy in Lithuania and 20 percent in Estonia and Latvia. It also encouraged organized crime and routine corruption.

Hard information is a scarce and valuable commodity to be hoarded and traded. Gossip, rumor, and conspiracy theories flourish. There is often the suspicion that other people hold things back, are not telling the whole story, and that even the most open and clear proposal conceals an ulterior purpose.

The defense mechanisms that have preserved the identity and pride of peoples subject for centuries to occupation and oppression cannot be expected to disappear overnight when meeting foreigners, even those with good intentions. While they have an acute sense of 50 misspent years, they deeply resent being patronized by westerners. There is an assumption that greater powers are out for what they can get, whether they are Russian, German, or American. A culture of resilient self-belief, with accompanying skepticism and obstructionism, served the Baltic peoples well in the past. Sooner or later foreigners encounter the "it will never work here, we are different" attitude against which patience and perseverance are the best devices.

It is remarkable that these countries have survived at all, let alone recreated themselves as modern, viable states. Against a difficult and unpredictable background reform has unleashed a dynamism and an optimism in a new generation, and among some older people too, that have transformed the region. There is a sense of exhilaration at again being open to the world and an enthusiasm to work with foreigners in order to be incorporated once more into Europe.

> **GOLF**
> Where is the biggest golf course in Europe?
> Corfu
> Malta
> Jersey

Estonia

Estonia is the smallest of the Baltic States, with a total population of 1.4 million. About 70 percent are Estonians whose first language is Estonian and whose religious denomination is Lutheran. There is a substantial leavening of people who have returned from abroad. Indeed, there are several notable political and military figures who have dual nationality, still holding on to their American or Canadian passports. About 30 percent of the population is of Russian origin. Although they may vote in local elections and are represented by their own party, they have no national voting rights or other privileges of citizenship and are described as aliens. The divide is particularly marked in the capital, Tallinn, whose population of 400,000 is almost equally split into two separate communities.

After independence Estonia single-mindedly embarked on the economic and legal reforms necessary to a free-market economy without the backtracking and excessive corruption that have bedeviled other countries in similar circumstances. Agricultural and industrial products are now of sufficient quality that in a few years after independence the majority of exports were switched from Russia to the West. Finland and Sweden are its main trading and investment partners.

Communication

Many Estonians speak fluent Russian, Finnish, and English and some also have good German and Swedish. They like to be considered as Scandinavian and do not appreciate being compared with Russia or reminded of their Soviet past. With Finns there are reciprocated feelings of superiority.

When meeting for the first time, the polite greeting is a stony stare. The polite plural and last names are used. After the initial formal encounters people get on to first-name terms. Since independence the traditional formalities have been eroded and colleagues, including those at different levels of seniority, are usually on first-name terms and use the second person singular. However, informality does not go so far as familiarity. There is a distinct line between personal and professional relationships.

The secret of good Estonian pronunciation is to move the lips as little as possible. Estonian communication style is similar to Finnish. There is not very much small talk, idle chat, or conversation for its own sake. Silence is perfectly acceptable if there is nothing meaningful to say or if what has just been said deserves serious consideration. It is ill bred to interrupt others or finish their ideas for them, or to say anything unless you are sure that the other person has finished. People speak plainly, without exaggeration or understatement, and if possible with statements expressed in facts and figures. Humor is not frowned on but is rarely evident in a business context.

Assertiveness and self-promotion are not virtues. A natural reserve and sense of personal privacy can be mistaken by outsiders for coldness or introversion. The relaxed side of the Estonian character is more often to be seen privately in the sauna or over a bottle of vodka than in the office.

The spoken word is not taken lightly and is usually preferred over the written word to communicate or request important information. However, written minutes, instructions, and detailed plans, with appropriate signatures, are the basis for action. With such instructions and authorization, execution is usually impeccable.

Like their Finnish cousins, Estonians are keen on mobile phones and the internet. Estonia is the leading country for internet connections per capita among EU associate members, and ahead of EU member states such as Belgium and France. Retail and commercial banking, including payments, are highly automated.

Business etiquette

The Estonian business community is small. Close personal contacts and relationships are inevitable, but they are not a necessary precondition of a business relationship. Foreigners are not expected to network and many find it difficult to break in to a small and tight community. Hospitality and socializing are not an integral part of business life and it is unusual and a privilege to be invited to a private home. Social life outside the office is also confined to small groups of close friends. Business entertaining is discouraged by the taxation system, which treats expenses as income rather than a deduction.

During the week some business people use the sauna, and the food and drink afterwards, for relationship building. Nevertheless, for most people the sauna is a weekend pastime, usually associated with their little house in the country.

A Scandinavian concern for punctuality is indicative of an ordered approach to organization and a mistrust of spontaneity. At the same time, the centralization of authority is markedly un-Scandinavian. A tactless observer would find more parallels with a Russian management style.

In traditional companies the senior manager takes decisions of any importance. The concept of a team is that of a platoon of disciplined people waiting for orders and expecting blame if they make mistakes. There is a reluctance to take initiatives or responsibility without clear authorization. Meetings are rarely used as management tools for discussion and problem solving; when they do occur there is little concern for sharing contributions. In contrast, some newer companies and foreign multinationals try to develop a more participative and empowering style.

Another un-Scandinavian characteristic is the role of women in society and in business. As a younger generation brings back attitudes from abroad, an older, patriarchal generation will eventually have to make uncomfortable adjustments.

CHRISTIANS

Which was the last European country to be converted to Christianity?

> Lithuania
> Russia
> Malta

Latvia

With neighborly disdain, Estonians call Latvians "neither fish nor meat." They are referring to the strong German, then Swedish, then Russian influence on their history. This is reflected in the way the Latvian language has developed and in the richness and complexity of Latvian culture.

The population of Latvia is around 2.5 million, of whom 25 percent are non-citizens of Russian extraction. Those who profess a religion are likely to be Lutheran or Catholic, with those of Russian origin being mainly Orthodox. Most Latvians speak Russian, albeit reluctantly, with English or German as a third language. Those in the rising generation do not learn Russian and prefer English as their first foreign language. Many Latvian-Americans have returned to Latvia to assume leading roles in government and business.

Until Soviet occupation Latvia was primarily an agricultural country, with fishing and forestry also important. Timber, wood products, and fish are still significant exports. After 1945 heavy industrialization concentrated on vehicle, rolling stock, and machinery production, but this is now being replaced by light engineering and electronics.

With a population of 800,000, Riga is the region's largest city. Its size, industrial hinterland, and trading traditions have long made it the most important commercial and financial center of the region. It was the Soviet Union's second biggest port and remains the main pipeline outlet for Russian oil into the Baltic and an important entrepôt for other Russian exports. Much of this business is handled by the Russian community, the largest in the Baltic States.

The transition from a centrally planned to a market economy has been spasmodic as the political balance has swung between reformers and traditionalists. Despite extensive privatization and the emergence of new private-sector companies, some foreign owned, central government has retained more power than in the other Baltic States. There is still a core of bureaucrats and managers whose outlook and way of working were formed in the Soviet period. This includes institutionalized practices such as favors and kickbacks. As in other countries that have emerged from the Soviet Union, government bureaucracy, corruption, and organized crime are significant features of the new economy.

Communication

After the first formal introductions people get quickly on to first-name terms and, if they are speaking a language that permits this, to the second person singular. Titles,

Kundze for a woman and *Kungs* for a man, follow the last name. Instinctively, "s" is added to a man's first and last names and "a" to a woman's, including those of foreigners.

While polite, Latvians are generally circumspect about what they say, especially on first meetings. Openness and directness of speech are reserved for people they know well and in informal surroundings. Circumlocution is especially evident when a refusal or a negative is called for or a problem needs to be aired. Neither should a "yes" be taken at face value.

Humor is rarely used in a business context, being reserved for those who know each other well. It is a wry, ironic sense of humor, like that of the Danes, and relies on anecdotes and stories. Word play, sarcasm, and other forms of verbal humor will not be readily understood.

Business etiquette

Latvia has a small business community in which everyone knows each other. While networks of people united by school, university, or military service are as important in Latvia as in any former socialist country, personal contacts are helpful to outsiders but are not essential in a business context. It is not necessary to build a personal relationship before getting down to business

The Latvian equivalent of playing golf is hunting. Business lunches and cocktail parties are also common. While business life is generally taken seriously, office celebrations as a means of reinforcing team commitment are becoming more widespread. They begin formally with toasts and speeches, but are soon overtaken by a more anarchic party spirit.

While Latvians are naturally cooperative and work well in teams, leadership in most organizations is centralized with senior management. Bosses keep a distance from the people they manage. While clear direction is necessary, consensus is not. Team-based participative management learned in business schools and foreign multinationals is fashionable, although not widespread. Managers are well advised to follow up on implementation to ensure that commitments and deadlines are met.

A German and Swedish past has left its mark on Latvian attitudes to organization. Methodical and structured processes are preferred, which sometimes contrast with the improvisatory approach favored by their Russian counterparts. Meetings are structured and orderly and result in action plans that are respected as long as they are minuted and approved by an appropriate authority.

In general, written instructions are respected without reminders, whereas oral agreements are more questionable. People work best with a concrete and written course of action. They are less effective when creative solutions or initiatives are required.

POLICE

Who has the smallest police force in relation to population?

  Ireland
  Malta
  Finland

Lithuania

The National Poet of Poland is Adam Mickiewicz. Poles will tell you that to understand the Polish soul you should read his epic "Pan Tadeusz," or at least see the movie. To Lithuanians he is known as Mickevièius, National Poet of Lithuania. After all, the poem begins "Lithuania! My Fatherland." He was born in what is now Belarus, studied in Vilnius, lived most of his life in exile, and is buried in Krakow. He was a Russian subject and wrote only in Polish. Not only did he write and fight for his Fatherland, but he also embodies its historical and cultural complexity.

Lithuanians were late to convert to Christianity when they formed a joint monarchy with Poland at the very end of the fourteenth century. They were Christianized by Poles who told them that God did not understand Lithuanian so they must pray in Polish. The ruling and merchant classes spoke Polish and looked down on Lithuanian as the language of pagans and peasants. This view persisted after Russia annexed Lithuania in 1795. Only on independence in 1920 did Lithuanian become an official language and was its decline arrested.

During this first period of independence the capital was Kaunus, now the second city. Poland had annexed the third of Lithuanian territory that was Polish speaking, including the current capital Vilnius. Vilnius was also home to the most important Jewish center of scholarship in Europe until it was destroyed in the Holocaust. In 1940 when the Soviets occupied Lithuania, part of the country was ceded to Belarus and Vilnius was returned to Lithuania. When the Russians reoccupied Vilnius in 1945 they made Russian the official language. Lithuanian language and identity struggled against Russification until the second independence in 1992.

Lithuania is the largest of the Baltic States with a population of 3.6 million. Over 80 percent are Lithuanian and mostly Roman Catholic, with 8 percent Russians and 7 percent Poles. Excluding the 50,000 Russian troops and their families returned to Russia, about 150,000 Lithuanians have emigrated since independence.

While Estonia and Latvia are essentially city states, Lithuania's regions are more independent and there are five relatively large cities with their own cultural and business life. Vilnius itself still has the feel of a university town rather than a commercial center.

Since independence there have been several changes of government veering between reformed communism and social democracy. In small countries where politicians and leading business people have known each other since schooldays, politics is more a tussle between competing personalities and interest groups than ideology. As a result structural reform, especially in banking, has been slower than in the other states and obstructed by vested interests. Nevertheless, the budget deficit has been reduced, non-inflationary growth has been achieving around 3 percent, and official reserves cover the money base. Telecommunications, banking, and shipping have been largely privatized.

Lithuanian exports are predominantly furniture, textiles, and light industrial products. While the country has attracted substantial foreign direct investment, it has lagged behind its neighbors. Leading investors are Sweden and Denmark, followed by the US, Germany, and Finland. The barriers to foreign investment are labor inflexibility, land ownership, and stifling bureaucracy.

The legal framework, for example the audit law or labor law, is still in need of further modernization. Intellectual property laws are harmonized with EU directives, but practice does not fully conform to what is on the statute books. Respect for contractual arrangements has been improving over the past few years. Agreements and contracts should be written, clear, and comprehensive. If they are written in parallel languages, having the translation independently verified may be a worthwhile investment.

Communication

The last-name formality of first meetings, with the titles *Ponas* or *Pona*, soon develops into first-name informality. During the first stages of acquaintanceship, politeness and courtesy get in the way of frank discussion. Saying "no" is especially troublesome. When relationships develop to greater familiarity people speak more directly and often bluntly, especially to other Lithuanians.

Among the Baltic nations Lithuanians are reputedly the most extrovert. Nevertheless, they are less naturally communicative than westerners, to whom they may appear sullen or diffident. A common expression of enthusiastic approval is *Na bulgay*, not bad. Faced with what seems like a veil of indifference, outsiders should persevere until they are absolutely convinced that it is genuine. Humor is used sparingly in business situations, when personal relationships are sufficiently relaxed.

Business etiquette

Members of the business community all know each other. Networks based on family, school, and military service were vital under socialism and so they remain. Personal relationships outside networks of friends are cordial but functional, and hospitality and socializing are not essential to developing a business relationship.

Lithuanians prefer to demonstrate individuality and to compete rather than collaborate. It is not a naturally egalitarian society. People are less than happy to talk seriously with those of lower status. The art of delegation is still being learned, with varying degrees of enthusiasm. Lithuanians find equal partnerships more difficult to manage than those in which one party is in undisputed control.

If teams are to work well they should have a strong leader who takes responsibility for decision making and implementation. Experienced leaders do not wait for spontaneous contributions to the team effort, but take pains to elicit them. It is helpful to establish unambiguous responsibilities and precise performance expectations and then to follow them up to make sure they are being fulfilled.

Punctuality is usually respected and schedules normally adhered to. In a volatile and changing environment, a higher premium is placed on flexibility than on planning and preparation. There is a strong sense of urgency. Action is valued more highly than deliberation, which means that things get done, although of necessity several times over.

There is a strong belief in education, but also that one can only do things for which one has received appropriate training. An International School of Management has been opened with Norwegian sponsorship and more business courses are available. These are stronger in technical subjects such as accounting than subjects such as marketing and business policy. In general, Lithuanians prefer to go abroad to study and work if they can.

In business and outside Lithuania is a male-dominated society. Women are as well educated as men, but concur with their inferior status in the workplace.

DIVORCE

Which country has the highest and which the lowest divorce rate?

  Finland

  Greece

  Hungary

BRITISH ISLES

Ireland

Ireland and Spain are the countries that have changed the most since the first edition of this book. The original description is unrecognizable to a new generation of young Irish professionals. Secular and materialist Ireland has joined modern Europe.

Eire is only used in Gaelic. In English the country's official name is the Republic of Ireland.

Gaelic is an official language in Ireland and Brussels. According to Eurobarometer, it is designated as a "foreign" language by 38 percent of Irish people. While fewer than 100,000 people, living mostly in the rural areas of the west of Ireland, speak it as a first language, it has sentimental and nationalist importance. It is taught in schools, and government servants, including teachers, must pass an examination in Gaelic as a condition of employment. It is not used in business.

In 1922 the island was partitioned between the six counties of Ulster, which remained part of the United Kingdom, and the other 26, which formed the Irish Free State, a Dominion in the British Commonwealth. It became a fully independent Republic in 1949.

Partition and its consequences distort the image that Ireland presents to the world. The Northern Ireland question is a political responsibility and unification is an ultimate ideal that few would consider feasible—or desirable—in their lifetime. It is not a domestic political issue. Sinn Fein—the political branch of the IRA (Irish Republican Army), dedicated to the political and economic independence of a united Ireland—has few seats in parliament and the events over the border are as remote for most Irish citizens as for British subjects over the water. If they consider it at all they look down on Northern Ireland as backward and puritanical, an interesting reversal from a generation ago.

The population of Ireland is just under 4 million, of whom over 1 million live in Dublin, the only major city. It is the youngest population in Europe, with over 40 percent under the age of 25. Economic growth has had a significant impact on previous demographic patterns. In the past Ireland's most consistent export was enterprising and energetic people. While many people travel, study, and work abroad, they are no longer under an economic obligation to do so. Ireland is now a net immigration country and a destination for economic migration from eastern Europe and Asia, a development with which some citizens are struggling to come to terms.

The main regional difference is between the dispersed rural areas and the urban middle classes of Dublin. Republican hopes and aspirations for an egalitarian society after the departure of the British have been unfulfilled. One of the several legacies is an elaborate class system based on education, wealth, and professional status.

Perhaps the greatest social change at the end of the twentieth century was the collapse of allegiance to and influence of the Roman Catholic church, to which over 90 percent of the population nominally belongs. The cultural influence nevertheless remains in social and political behavior, which is more akin to southern than northern Europe.

Economy

Until recently the Irish economy was inextricably linked with that of the United Kingdom through geographic proximity and centuries of colonial dependence. With little industrial heritage or natural resources, Ireland's role was to provide foodstuffs to the UK in return for manufactured goods. For many years the twin prongs of Irish economic policy were to diversify trade into the rest of the EU and the US and to build a manufacturing and services sector largely through the encouragement of foreign direct investment.

The UK still accounts for 26 percent of total foreign trade, but this is well down on the 40 percent of a decade ago. The investment strategy has also been extremely successful, bringing in companies in clean and advanced technology industries such as electronics and pharmaceuticals. Foreign penetration of business is the highest in Europe. The largest percentage of companies are American, followed by British and then German. Ireland receives 50 percent of US foreign direct investment into the EU. This is partly as a base for export into the EU and partly as a low-cost source of product for export back to the US.

The economy has traditionally been state led with direct government ownership, employment schemes, subsidies, and tax breaks. State involvement is mainly through semi-state companies in utilities and transport, and the development agencies promoting inward investment and supporting indigenous companies.

The cosy relationship between business and government resulted in cronyism and corruption, examples of which were brought to justice during the 1990s and are still being pursued. The government is implementing anti-corruption legislation to bring Ireland into line with the Organisation for Economic Cooperation and Development (OECD) Convention on Combating Bribery.

Celtic tiger...

After a period of stagnation and inflation in the late 1980s, the Irish government radically overhauled its economic policy. Public expenditure and the government deficit were slashed and corporate tax rates were cut to attract foreign investment. As a result, Ireland's economic performance in the 1990s was spectacular. The average annual rate of increase in GDP was 9 percent over the seven-year period 1993–99.

Over 15 percent of GDP is represented by combined exports and imports. The small size of the home market obliges successful Irish companies to expand abroad. Six of the largest Irish companies have overseas investments accounting for over 80 percent of annual turnover.

...or Celtic fat cat?

An ingredient of Irish prosperity has been EU subsidies. In 2000 Ireland's net receipts amounted to €1.8 billion, which per capita was more than twice that of other net recipients such as Greece, Portugal, and Spain. EU transfers amounted annually to about 5 percent of GDP. The prospect of losing the subsidy and perhaps of becoming net donors to Brussels was an important factor in a 2001 referendum rejecting ratification of the Treaty of Nice, which provides for EU enlargement.

In general the Irish have used their subsidies wisely, investing considerably in education, for example. While educational standards according to the OECD are below the European average and per capita expenditure is still one of the lowest in Europe, progress has been remarkable. Irish respondents to the Mole Map Survey were unusual in not listing personal contacts as the main success factor in an individual's career. Instead, pride of place went to a good education. This does not mean that Irish business people do not depend on networking and personal contacts as much as those of any other country, but it does reflect the importance of education in Irish values and its resulting quality.

Organization

Company structure is similar to that in the UK. There is no significant difference between the structures of public and private limited companies. The board can elect one of its members as managing director or appoint a general manager. Supervisory boards are not recognized in law or practice and employees have no representation rights on the board. Many companies have works councils with rights of negotiation with, and representation to, management.

Irish people have a more flexible approach to organization than do the British. This is reflected in the importance given to personal relationships, a talent for improvisation, and a dislike of rigid systems and bureaucracy. The old image of quaint inefficiency is a thing of the past, if it was ever true. The workforce is by over-all European standards young, well educated, computer literate, and professional.

In common with their British neighbors, the Irish have a highly pragmatic and unintellectual approach to problems. They are more traders and dealers than long-term investors, and short-termism characterizes their approach to planning and strategy.

Among the younger generation the aversion to women in business is losing ground, although general attitudes regarding women in the workplace remain tra-ditional and conservative. The Irish and the Belgians share the greatest antipathy in the EU toward working women.

Irish are essentially cooperative and work well in teams. Teams do not neces-sarily need a strong leader, but if they have one they should make sure that they are part of the team and not stand apart. Teams will commonly accept collective responsibility for decisions and implementation. Active consensus in decisions is usually desirable.

In management meetings everyone is expected to make a contribution and it is rare for the senior person to dominate. They will not feel restricted by an agenda, if there is one, but at the end an action plan is usual. People can normally be relied on to carry out the commitments it lays on them without being chased.

There is an outward deference to authority combined with strong reservations about accepting it. The Irish respect authority more if it derives from competence rather than being based solely on status. Success is admired but begrudged. The role of the boss and the way in which he or she is regarded by subordinates are more Gallic than Anglo-Saxon. Bosses expect to have to impose their will. However, the younger generation and those in American-owned companies look to Ameri-cans rather than Europeans as managerial role models.

Communication

When communicating or asking for something important, more weight will be given to the spoken than the written word. Among their neighbors Irish people have a reputation for ease and elegance of speech and a readiness to put it into practice. Fluency does not always imply openness, nevertheless. Rhetoric can be used to conceal as well as communicate.

Etiquette and modes of address are similar to those in the UK, but Irish manners are less reserved and they are considerably more amiable, relaxed, and gregarious. Important discussions and decisions often take place in an informal environment outside the office. There is a pervasive informality and an antipathy toward pretense and pretension. This can be misleading, however. In the practicalities of negotiation the Irish are anything but easy-going. Amiable frankness is combined with astuteness and often stubbornness.

Among those I talked to, the Irish were the only ones to complain about the British lacking a sense of humor at work. Great store is set by crack, whose meaning should not be confused with that in American English. (To avoid this confusion it is often given the Gaelic spelling, *craic*.) It means fun in the sense of good humor, and can range from crude anecdotes to subtle wit before which nothing, even the sacred, is sacred.

WORK

Where do people have the highest and the lowest average working hours?

Turkey

France

Germany

United Kingdom

Those who refer to the citizens of the United Kingdom as the English rather than the British risk irritating citizens of Scotland, Wales, and Northern Ireland. Scotland has its own parliament and legal and educational systems, and Edinburgh is a financial center second to London, albeit somewhat smaller. Wales has a parliament and finds its identity in language. In some rural areas Welsh is the first language, and it is taught in schools and used on radio and television. Although British society and culture are essentially homogenous, outsiders who work with people from these regions are advised to acknowledge the pride taken in what may appear to be superficial differences between them.

Northern Ireland is characterized by an inability to govern itself through sectarian discrimination and violence. Unless they are directly involved in business there, it is unnecessary for outsiders to become any better informed about the political situation than are those on the mainland.

Outside Northern Ireland religion plays little part in everyday life. In Britain 35 percent of the population claims to have no religion, the second highest proportion in Europe after the Netherlands. Disinterest creates an atmosphere of religious freedom and tolerance.

The British population has long been characterized by internal and external migration. There is a constant drift to the more prosperous south. Out of a total population of about 60 million, 50 million live in England. The emigration rate is almost exactly balanced by the number of immigrants, mainly from the Caribbean and the Indian subcontinent.

Political and economic decision making and administration are highly centralized in London. The countries surrounding the capital are known as the Home Counties, as if the others were extraneous. The area within a couple of hours' drive from London is known as "the South." The rest of the country is known as "the North." The South is perceived by those who live there as superior in wealth, sophistication, and social status. It owes its image to the preponderance of service, high-tech and other growth industries, while the north is associated, anachronistically, with heavy industry, engineering, mining, and unemployment.

The UK is an urban society. A fifth of the population of mainland Britain lives in eight cities, the largest being London with seven million inhabitants. There is a wide spread of living standards, from some of the worst slums in Europe to the affluent estates of the south. In London only the very rich or the very poor live in the center. The majority of the rest live in the suburbs or in dormitory towns and villages up to 100km away.

Historically the UK has been a divided society, adversarial in the relationship between classes and institutions. The dismantling of redistributive socialism, the decline of public services, and the widening gap between rich and poor begun under the Thatcherite Conservative government have been seamlessly continued by New Labour. The postwar period of political consensus and cooperation, deriving from the shared experience of war and the ideals that created the welfare state, has now reverted to a more traditional spirit of independence and competition. The British manner of politeness, reserve, and restraint that kept these in check is also giving way to a thrusting individual assertiveness more in keeping with the British bulldog.

Image

Much rhetoric has been devoted to the breaking down of old cartels and interest groups and what is described as "the establishment." This was once defined as the whole matrix of official and social relations within which power is exercised. It consisted of people from a number of recognizable pillars of society such as the Civil Service (the administrative arm of government), the legal profession, the Church of England, Oxford and Cambridge Universities, business figures, and a pool of acceptable individuals known as "the great and the good." It has proved resilient under attack, not least because it is such a fluid and almost intangible group of related interests. Some of them, such as business, have grown in importance at the expense of others, such as Oxford.

The UK is one of the few EU countries not to have proportional representation at elections. This favors the two main parties and a government that has a freer hand than most others in the EU. The effective collapse of the Conservative (Tory) Party has given New Labour even greater scope to propound social democratic reforms.

Political and legal systems are based on precedent, compromise, and negotiation. There is no written constitution, bill of rights, or legal code. The introduction in 2000 of the European Convention on Human Rights, with its codified system of law, was a significant innovation. The role of the monarch is symbolic and ceremonial rather than constitutional.

The political system epitomizes the British aversion to working within a rational and systematic framework. They take pride in "muddling through," in "getting there in the end." This should not necessarily be construed by outsiders as intellectual idleness. British thinking is interpretive rather than speculative. It prefers tradition and precedent and "common sense," in other words the interpretation of experience untrammeled by theory or speculation. This usually involves finding the expedient rather than the innovative solution.There is a deep skepticism about great schemes and constructs on a macro- or microeconomic level.

This finds expression in attitudes to the European Union. There is deep mistrust and misunderstanding of the grand design for Europe, and British policy is to thwart attempts to implement it in regulatory structures.This is not regarded by the British as negativism but as pragmatism.

Business and government

There is no national agenda for economic development in the UK. The government's policy is to create a competitive environment for private business with a minimum of state intervention. Privatization of state-owned manufacturing industries was followed by that of infrastructural and monopoly services such as water, gas, and, disastrously, railways. Nevertheless, about one in three employees remains in public-sector occupations, compared with 30 percent in Germany and 20 percent in Italy.

There has been a significant shift from manufacturing to services. Other than for defense contractors, there is no protection against foreign takeover. Major sectors such as the car industry and merchant banking are in foreign hands and further inward investment is actively encouraged. The UK has become the gateway for many non-EU companies into the EU.

Labor

British industry is labor intensive, with manual workers making up 45 percent of the workforce, reflecting the dominance of services and the low level of capital investment. The British prefer to work for others rather than themselves; only 13 percent are self-employed. About 40 percent of employees are trade union members; 75 percent in the public sector compared with 30 percent in the private sector. Employment legislation has concentrated on curbing union power and making industrial action more difficult.

Wage negotiation has been decentralized and employee protection reduced in the interest of creating a flexible labor market.The British labor market is the least restricted by labor legislation: Companies have a greater freedom to hire and fire than in other EU countries, and worker participation at board or any other level is strenuously resisted by government and business alike.

The City

The business community is dominated by the banks, insurance companies, and other financial institutions collectively known as the City. Large financial conglomerates, mostly foreign owned, operate within a loose legislative framework, optimistically relying on self-regulation by the institutions' own trade associations and professional bodies. Dealing institutions are regulated by the Securities and Investments Board (SIB), whose job is to protect the interests of investors.

The UK stock market is the largest and most active in Europe and the principal source of capital for companies. There are about 4,000 public limited companies (plc) with shares traded on the Stock Exchange or the Unlisted Securities Market. For smaller companies and new ventures there are various forms of private placement available.

Privatization has not significantly increased the number of active private shareholders. Institutional shareholders are far more significant in size and power, and they exert considerable influence over company managements, either through informal pressure or through action in the market.

Business organization and structure

The board of directors is the principal decision-making unit of a company and the source of power within the organization. A plc must have a board of at least two directors appointed by the shareholders. One is the chairman, who may also be the chief executive. If not, the chief executive will usually be called the managing director. Besides the chairman there will be a company secretary, in charge of legal compliance and administration. All other board members are discretionary. There is usually a finance director and other directors representing the main operating units of the company.

A holding company with a structure based on subsidiaries will have tiers of boards, usually with the same chairman. These may be called local boards, consisting of local directors.

A private limited company (Ltd) need only have one director appointed by the owners. Otherwise its structure and the legal framework under which it operates are very similar to those of the plc.

Large companies may have nonexecutive directors whose theoretical role is to keep an objective eye on matters, although their responsibilities are rarely well defined. Their real function is to provide contacts with government and the establishment. Aristocrats, politicians, and retired civil servants are typical appointees. The board will then appoint an executive committee consisting of executive directors and a managing director to manage the company. This is the closest that British companies get to the continental twin-board system. It is resisted by executive directors, for whom it represents a curtailment of their traditional role.

Beneath board level the nature of the organization is less clear cut. The traditionally British concept of organization is a many-layered and vertically oriented pyramid based on a vertical chain of command. Its primary purpose is seen as transmitting orders down the line from the top. Where top-down, structured hierarchies have been abandoned, there is an antipathy to what is pejoratively described as "bureaucracy," procedures that have lost sight of their ultimate objective. In some cases this includes all systematic decision-making processes, clear lines of authority, and channels of communication.

Organization charts are less a map of the business than a depiction of the social hierarchy. There is a legal requirement for written job specifications, but outside senior levels of management this is rarely translated into a meaningful description of specific responsibilities and goals.

Planning

When asked about planning, most British managers immediately think of financial forecasting and budgeting. The annual budget is the backbone of the organization and is the major exception to the otherwise inconsistent approach to systems. Most companies have a sophisticated process of annual budgeting, in some cases extended to a three- or five-year forecast. Typically, line managers make first drafts that are consolidated, processed, amended by senior management, and fed back down to the line managers for implementation or further amendment. The forecast is monitored on a regular basis, usually monthly, and divergences explained. Bonuses and incentives may be based on meeting or outperforming forecast. The process is closely allied with the accounting function.

It is only in the largest and most sophisticated companies that this process is influenced by considering changes in the external environment. Planning in the sense of forecasting long-term changes in the overall environment, analyzing the impact on specific markets, and identifying market opportunities is rudimentary. There is a practical reason for this in addition to the British preference for pragmatism over theory, opportunism over planning. The short-term goals of City investors do not match the long-term needs of manufacturing investment and research. Managers are called to account primarily for quarterly earnings per share and annual dividend. In the past 10 years dividend distribution in real terms has increased fourfold while investment has fallen.

The pressure on management is increased by the freedom given to predatory financial engineers. While they have indubitably accelerated the restructuring of British industry and improved its profitability, they encourage management to concentrate on immediate results at the expense of the longer term.

Leadership

Managers aspire to be effective, decisive, and tough under the motto "managers have a right to manage." But these and similar macho traits were never mentioned by any of the British I talked to when asked what qualities they looked for in their own boss. Those most often described were the abilities to conduct meetings efficiently and to establish good relationships with subordinates. Outsiders should be careful to distinguish between the image and the need.

It is a convention that instructions should be disguised as polite requests. People expect their boss to give them instructions and then let them get on with the job without interference. Combined with British reserve and an inbred awkwardness in personal contact, this creates an arm's-length relationship in which both sides are on their guard. Using the boss as a sounding board for personal or professional worries is difficult for both sides. Fairness in relationships is more important than closeness. The concept of the boss as a coach, creating an atmosphere of support and encouragement and providing constant feedback on performance, is making ground but is by no means universal.

Ambiguity and debate about the role of the boss have been heightened by the breakdown of hierarchical systems of control and a transition to systematic, market-oriented structures. There is a wide divergence of views between and also within companies about the relationship between superiors and subordinates. Some attribute this to the fact that the UK is the only large EU country not to have military conscription. While the military model may not be the most appropriate in a modern business environment, and while it only concerns the male half of the workforce, it means that there is no national consensus among managers under the age of 45 about the nature of authority systems.

Teams

The British joke about their love of committees. The most important committee in a company is the board of directors. Even detailed decisions within the competence of a director may have to wait for formal approval by the board. Beneath the board is a complicated network of other committees, formal and informal.

The British prefer to work in the security of a group within an established order with which they can identify. They are motivated by work that is seen as valuable not only to themselves but to others and that contributes to a common goal. Opinions are encouraged and listened to, although the extent to which they are taken into account depends on seniority. It is not usual for everyone to be well prepared. Even when papers are distributed in advance, they will not always be read. Lack of preparation does not inhibit the passing of opinion and judgment.

Passive consensus is important. A concern to avoid disharmony among the group and disloyalty to the boss will smooth over all but the most fundamental disagreement.

The process at a decision-making meeting may be adversarial. A designated individual will present a proposal to the group and defend it. If it is approved, he or she is mandated to implement it. It is not usual to lobby individual members beforehand, since they will not make a commitment to an idea before they have learned what the others think. Even if they have contributed to the formulation of a proposal, they play an objective role at the meeting.

Communication

Formal and articulated systems for sharing information throughout the organization are not common. Information systems are designed primarily to channel hard information to senior management and directions from them to the rest of the organization. Unless people are in an open office and visible to each other, they will tend to use the phone in preference to a personal visit. Since the number of meetings in the working day means that people are often away from their desks, the use of internal memos or emails is widespread.

Upward mobility

British companies spend on average a sixth of what German and French companies do on training. There is a particular deficit in training at lower levels of the organization. Four out of five manual workers and three out of five nonmanual workers have received no training after leaving school. At higher levels training is regarded as a reward for promotion rather than a preparation for it.

Many science and engineering graduates are creamed off into financial services, consultancy, or accounting. This is partly because of better pay and conditions, partly because education at the highest level, even in applied subjects, is not seen as vocational. There are a small number of business schools and most universities offer undergraduate and postgraduate business-related courses. However, the most valued and widespread qualification is accountancy, for which a university degree is not required. Chartered accountants proliferate not only in their field but in general management.

The prime requisite for success is performance. Nepotism and personal influence are less important. People may be selected because they are the right class or type, but if they attempt to capitalize on this by "pulling strings" they risk being rejected.

Company loyalty is less common now than before the radical corporate restructuring of the past few decades. This brought to management levels the enforced job mobility that had previously been confined to workers. Younger professionals incorporate a regular change of companies into their career planning.

Women

Women make up 45 percent of the workforce, a larger percentage than in other countries despite the UK having the lowest maternity benefits and negligible child-care facilities. Economic necessity and greater opportunity outweigh the difficulties. Female workers are cheaper than male, and since half are part-time, they may be less protected by employment legislation.

Women are more often found in managerial positions than in most EU countries, especially in service industries and the public sector. There are fewer women in manufacturing industry, although this is only partly because of discrimination. For social and educational reasons outside the workplace, fewer women than men qualify in technical subjects.

Etiquette

Foreigners believe that the British are more formal than they really are. First names are used immediately among colleagues of all ranks and both sexes, and are increasingly common among all business contacts, even on the phone when there has been no personal introduction. Those who have been knighted are addressed as Sir with the first name only. Doctor is only applied with medical doctors and other academic titles are not used.

Men should not refer to themselves as Mr. So-and-So, they should use their last name only or the first and last name. Women may use whichever title they prefer to be known by—Mrs, Miss, or Ms—and last name. There is no equivalent in a business context of the title used on its own. Superiors are sometimes called "Sir" by male subordinates who wish to ingratiate themselves and by those in a servant role: chauffeurs, doormen, receptionists, and so on. "Madam" is rarely used.

Handshaking is for first meetings and reunions. People who meet regularly do not shake hands. The greeting "How do you do?" is not an inquiry but expects the reply "How do you do?" and nothing more. The sensible American habit of introducing oneself, rather than waiting for an introduction to be made by a third party, is becoming widespread. Nevertheless, increasing informality has not broken down the barriers of reserve. Understatement may give the impression of coolness and indifference. At the same time, overt standoffishness is avoided. Male colleagues close in the hierarchy cultivate a matey, old-boy atmosphere.

The British are uneasy in situations where everyone has similar status. The complexity and subtlety of British class consciousness, with its meticulous distinctions, snobberies, and snubs, are mirrored in corporate life. The principal divide is between managers and other ranks. Within these divisions there is a fine gradation marked by a host of minor privileges.

The most important symbol of rank is the car. A company car is a widespread method of tax avoidance and three-quarters of new cars are bought by companies. Even if the company fleet is of the same make, the market demands a large number of superficially different models to satisfy the status requirements of its customers. The mark of superior rank is to have a car that is a different make from the company fleet, and a chauffeur is a sign of absolute seniority.

On a social level it is important to be a "nice person," meaning courteous, unassuming, and unabrasive. Some older men still cultivate a "gentleman amateur" image. False humility and self-deprecation are more typical than self-assertion, especially in senior people with their juniors. This is changing among a younger generation who have no inhibitions about treating business seriously and energetically. "Intellectual" is a term of disparagement. Those with a theoretical bent are advised to conceal this under a veil of pragmatism.

Politeness and reserve are reflected in conversation, which is typically imprecise and vague, full of hints and subtleties, especially in the south. Facts and figures and definitive statements are avoided, as are direct confrontation and argument. For outsiders used to clarity, decisiveness, and demonstrative professionalism this can be misleading. It is less true of northerners who have a reputation for plain speaking.

The British quickly lose their reserve when their basic assumptions about themselves are challenged. While they have grown reconciled to losing economic and military superiority over other nations, they become flustered and aggressive if their moral superiority is questioned. One should not make fun of even the more outlandish traditions and customs, especially if they involve royalty. In everyday conversation it is best not to question the assumption that British television is the best in the world and British weather the most interesting.

Dress

The British are experts at classifying each other by tiny details of speech, manners, and dress. Men's clothing is more an expression of affiliation than taste and the popularity of chainstore off-the-peg clothing has made good tailoring optional. Ties are an important signal. Men will wear old-school, army, university, or club ties and, if they do not qualify, something that mimics the real thing. Since these are intended to be recognized it is not good manners to ask what they mean. It is also a social error—a *faux pas*—to wear a tie to which you are not entitled.

Women have less of a problem. The more senior and authoritative a woman wishes to appear, the more her clothes should resemble men's, except that a skirt should be worn rather than trousers.

Formal evening occasions, the annual dinner of a trade association for example, may be dignified by dinner suits, which are obligatory if the invitation says "black tie." This need not represent a major investment, since it is acceptable to hire a suit. At formal lunches and dinners smoking may not be permitted until after the meal. The signal for this is the "loyal toast," when everyone stands up and toasts the sovereign.

Punctuality

In a social context the British have formalized unpunctuality so that it is impolite to be on time. For social occasions this means arriving between 10 and 20 minutes after the stated time. Sometimes invitations acknowledge this by specifying, for example, 7.30 for 8, which means arriving no later than 7.50. This is extended to the business sphere. People are 10 minutes late for work, for meetings, for lunch. In many companies there have been recent moves to improve the efficiency and punctuality of daily life as part of the quality movement.

Humor

There is an aversion to seriousness. Humor is expected at all levels, between all levels, and on all occasions. It is important to be entertaining on every possible occasion, public or private. There are many public figures who are not entertaining but this is regarded as a deficiency. The only public figure exempt from this expectation is the sovereign. Outsiders need not attempt to join in, but should not be surprised at levity in what they might regard as inappropriate circumstances.

In a culture where the direct display of feelings is suppressed, humor is a cover for embarrassment and aggression. It can be self-deprecating, ribbing, sarcastic, sexist, jocular, racist. Women participate in humor, including sexual innuendo, with the exception of sarcasm and the needling remarks that men use to score off each other.

Socializing

Colleagues usually lunch together at work. How much mingling there is between ranks depends on circumstances. In many companies there are still segregated canteens. The directors' dining room also remains common. Within a single-status restaurant, although different grades may stick together, it is acceptable to take the opportunity to mix with subordinates.

Business dinners are less common than lunches. For many a business lunch is the main meal of the day. There are no conversational rules; it depends on whether you are eating with a "gentleman amateur" or a dedicated professional. Actual negotiation is not usual; this takes place afterwards at the office. An invitation will be more for business than friendship, but should nevertheless be treated as if it were a personal favor.

Mostly entertaining consists of meals, but there may be invitations to socially acceptable sporting and cultural events. Partners will often be included. While entertaining may be lavish and expensive, there is no taint of corruption as long as it is in a corporate context and the recipient is deemed to be a corporate representative.

Socializing at the pub immediately after work is frequent among peers and their immediate bosses. There may be some socializing among peers at weekends if they live in the same area, but regular social events including partners are not common. The preponderance of meetings and the general inefficiency of working life mean that managers at all levels frequently work late hours and take work home with them. After hours is accepted as time for private work and only for the most urgent and informal meetings. Phone calls at home are permissible. Working at weekends is not unknown, although it is less common than in the US. There is a growing tendency for senior people to demonstrate indispensability by not taking their full holiday entitlement.

At least once a year there will be a social occasion for all employees, often including partners. This can be as elaborate as a dinner dance in a hotel or a simple office party. Senior people are expected to make an appearance and to mingle with all employees. Intoxication and other indiscretions at the end of the evening are part of office party folklore and are not held against the miscreants afterwards. There may also be a social club for excursions, events, or a children's Christmas party. Large companies may have their own playing fields and facilities. While ranks will readily mix, more senior managers are not likely to attend.

VOTES FOR WOMEN
Match up the dates that women got the vote to their respective countries.

1906	Switzerland
1945	Finland
1971	Italy

LOW COUNTRIES

Belgium

Belgium was created in 1830 from the Catholic provinces of the Low Countries. United in religion, it remains deeply divided culturally, politically, and economically into two communities identified by language. About 5.5 million of the total population of 10 million live in the northern part of the country, Flanders, and speak Flemish, a close relative of Dutch. Wallonia, the southern part, is populated by about 3.5 million French-speaking Walloons. Except for a small German-speaking minority along the German border, the remaining million or so live in Brussels, a predominantly French-speaking enclave in Flanders.

Most Walloons cannot speak Flemish and some hard-line Flemings, although fluent in French, still refuse to speak it even to foreigners. Individuals think of themselves as Walloons or Flemings first, Europeans second, and Belgians third. There is a much weaker sense of national identity than in more homogenous and nationalistic countries and a correspondingly greater enthusiasm for European federation. The monarchy and the church, both deeply conservative, are the only two national institutions of real significance, and their influence is in constant decline.

The antipathy between the two communities goes much deeper than language. Until the 1970s Wallonia was the dominant partner, its wealth based on mining and heavy industry. Flanders was mainly agricultural, poorer, and less sophisticated, except for the port city of Antwerp. The standard of living, education, and public services was much higher in Wallonia. Flemish was considered the language of the lower classes, French that of the upper class and bankers.

The tables were turned with the collapse of the mining and steel industries in Wallonia. At the same time, the EC was bringing prosperity to the farmers and development to Antwerp, which competes with Rotterdam as northern Europe's entrepôt. Flanders was faster to adapt to the new economy of Europe. It attracted investment from its Dutch and German neighbors and other countries looking for a gateway into the rest of Europe. Its greenfield sites and less unionized labor force drew in new high-tech industries. It is now economically the more powerful part of the country.

For Walloons there is a growing realization, especially among the young, that they are no longer automatically superior to the Flemings and even—unthinkable to an older generation—that they ought to learn Flemish if they wish to make a career inside Belgium.

Meanwhile Brussels, burgeoning home to Eurocrats, Natocrats, and regional headquarters of multinational corporations, has been able to remain neutral. As its role as a national capital becomes less commanding, the city is making a concerted effort to become the capital of Europe. Geographically part of Flanders, it is 85 percent French speaking and English is increasingly acceptable in international business as well as public places. Over 30 percent of its residents are non-Belgian. While the city as a whole is becoming increasingly cosmopolitan, the Flemish minority is more and more fearful of being swamped and their sensitivities should be recognized in everyday dealings.

In 1989 political disintegration culminated in the creation of three virtually autonomous regions, including Brussels, and three language communities, Flemish, French, and German. Domestic functions have been handed over but many of the national institutions remain intact. For example, most ministries are duplicated on a national and regional level—there are now about 65 ministers in all—and their respective responsibilities are not always clearly defined. Meanwhile the three main political parties, Socialist, Christian Democrat, and Liberal, have divided along linguistic lines with varying degrees of acrimony; the two halves of the Socialist Party fight but the Liberals work together. The transition to what many Belgians believe will be a fully fledged federal state is clearly not yet over.

Business environment

Belgium is heavily dependent on international trade. Like the Netherlands, about 60 percent of its GNP is accounted for by exports. Antwerp, the third largest port in the world, is the rival to Rotterdam as a gateway to the rest of Europe. It is also a target for foreign, mainly French investment. There are direct investment incentives for private companies designed to reduce unemployment and foster high-tech projects, and tax breaks for foreign multinationals setting up regional headquarters. Among the intangible assets are a strong work ethic and language skills.

Three labor organizations correspond with the main political parties. They negotiate on a regional level with the employers' organization, VBO–FEB (*Verbond der Belgische Ondernemingen–Fédération des Entreprises Belges*) or on an industry basis. The relationship is generally regarded as reasonable and cooperative and is characterized by compromise rather than confrontation.

All companies of more than 100 employees are obliged to set up a works council with equal numbers of management and employee representatives. Every company with more than 50 employees must set up a safety committee as well.

It is usually obvious whether a company is Walloon or Flemish from the initials after its name. Flemish companies are either NV if public or BVBA if private (*Naamloze Vennootschap* or *Besloten Vennootschap met Beperkte Aansprakelijkheid*). Walloon companies are SA or SPRL (*Société Anonyme* or *Société Privée à Responsabilité Limitée*). The shareholders of an SA/NV elect a minimum of three directors and a statutory auditor. The owners of an SPRL/BVBA appoint one or more directors.

Organization and leadership

Walloons and Flemings have less in common with their French and Dutch neighbors than many outsiders assume. They also have more in common with each other than either would like to admit. There is a recognizably Belgian approach to many social and business issues.

The Belgian solution is based on compromise. Adaptability, flexibility, intellectual humility, and an avoidance of dogmatism set Belgians apart from their immediate neighbors. A preference for the middle way came out in all my conversations with foreigners and Belgians alike. It is hard to pin down a definitive style, an elusiveness that some outsiders characterize as blandness. There is a greater concern to find a solution than to win the argument. The process is gradualist, pragmatic, and to more effervescent outsiders agonizingly deliberate. Despite this, the end result can be surprising and creative. A classic example from the political sphere occurred in April 1990 when the king felt that his conscience would not allow him to give his assent to abortion legislation passed by parliament—so he abdicated for a day.

Flanders

In dealing with Flemings in any circumstance it is vital to acknowledge their sensitivity about the French language. They resent the assumption by most foreigners that French is the dominant language in Belgium. Even if French is the language that you have most easily in common, it is advisable to struggle through a few words of Dutch or English or German, after which you will be invited to use French.

Walloons tend not to speak Flemish and Flemings tend to be bilingual, which is why most government staff positions requiring fluency in both languages are held by Flemings. When French-speaking Stella and Flemish-speaking Jupiter merged to form Interbrew, English was chosen as the corporate language.

Although Flemings often refer to their language as Dutch, it is more mannered and ornate than the version of their more plain-spoken neighbors. There is a similar distinction in tastes and manners. Flemings enjoy good food and living well and other un-Calvinist indulgences. They are also more outwardly formal. Progressing from *Meneer* and *Mevrouw* with last name to first-name terms takes longer than with the Dutch, if it happens at all, and the polite plural is more common than the informal singular. Nevertheless, relationships are relaxed and low key. Assertiveness in manner and speech is likely to be interpreted as arrogance.

Unless the targets are Walloons or Dutch, humor tends to be mild and self-deprecating rather than ebullient, good humored rather than funny. In a business context it is acceptable in informal circumstances, but making jokes or bantering at the beginning of a meeting or during a presentation is regarded by all Belgians as an Anglo-Saxon eccentricity.

Organizational structures are flat and procedures unsophisticated. Offices tend to be simple and functional. Titles, type of office, perks, and other status symbols are far less important than take-home pay.

The Flemish approach is characterized more by conscientiousness than imagination. French managers may be better at designing systems—and then ignoring them—but Flemings are more disciplined in applying them. In more traditional companies hierarchical lines and formal channels of communication are adhered to, although tempered with active and informal networking, *ad hoc* meetings, and so on.

Flemings prefer participative authority and leadership. The boss is expected to be approachable, to "walk the job," and to base their authority on competence rather than hierarchical position. They expect participative decision making, active consensus, and delegation of responsibility.

Wallonia

Walloons resent being regarded as quaint French people. Like the Irish in Britain, their achievements tend to be subsumed into their more powerful neighbor while their eccentricities—and their accent—are made fun of. There is a risk in describing their attitudes to organization as a watered-down version of the French.

While they regard themselves as more punctual, harder working, and more practical than the French, there are similarities in their preference for a structured, formal organization with a clear hierarchical system and a directive style of leadership. Rules and procedures are important and in the main adhered to. Distinctions of rank are important, with attention paid to job title, size of office, quality of furniture, parking space, and so on.

Subordinates will feel free to contribute information and suggestions to the boss, but the clear expectation is that the decision is the latter's alone. Once taken and promulgated in writing, it will not be questioned. Whether it will be carried out may depend on the boss's competence in following it up. Traditional relationships between managers and subordinates are distant and formal, although a younger generation of managers is slowly introducing a more egalitarian style.

Meetings are more for exchanging information and discussing alternative proposals than for decision making, which is not regarded as the function of a group. Indeed, little importance is given to groups in any context and working relationships are primarily vertically oriented.

All of this is subject to the Belgian talent for compromise and negotiation. Because Belgians avoid extremes and season everything they do with common sense, there is less perceptible difference between what is supposed to happen and what actually does. For other northern Europeans this more transparent and less dogmatically assertive environment is more comfortable. The most noticeable difference to France is in problem solving and decision making. While the French take a deductive, dogmatic approach, Belgians are inductive and pragmatic.

Etiquette is more traditional than in France. The transition from *Monsieur* or *Madame* with last names and the polite plural to first names and the informal singular takes longer, and is for close colleagues in informal circumstances. The Walloon sense of humor exhibits a Gallic preference for wit and irony, usually at someone else's expense. The main difference is that Belgians can laugh at themselves. Just as the Irish have the best Irish jokes and Jews the best Jewish jokes, Belgians have the best Belgian jokes.

AIDS
Which country has the highest and which the lowest incidence of AIDS?
         Belgium
         Finland
         Portugal

Luxembourg

The most significant feature of this chapter is that it exists at all. Luxembourgers celebrated the 160th anniversary of their independence in 1999 with pointed enthusiasm and they find every opportunity to remind visitors of it—albeit, being
Luxembourgers, in a most polite and unassuming way.

Luxembourg is usually lumped in with Belgium, with which it joined in a monetary and tariff union in 1922. In 1944 the Netherlands joined them to form Benelux,
the prototype of the EU. While Benelux provides a political and economic orientation, Luxembourg's primary business orientation is toward Germany.

Luxembourgers' sense of identity is based on their language, Luxembourgisch.
This is spoken mainly at home and on social occasions. It causes great resentment that
foreigners who have lived and worked in the country for many years do not take the
trouble to learn even a few words. Not that there is much incentive: Luxembourgers
at all levels learn and speak French and German as fluently as their own language and
in most companies the *lingua franca* is French, both spoken and written. Nearly half of
the population speaks at least two foreign languages and 45 percent three or more.

Business environment

There are not many Luxembourg companies and the chances of readers working
with one are statistically small. People who do work in Luxembourg are more likely
to be employed by one of the 100 or so international banks or the multinationals
that use it as a European distribution center. In many ways Luxembourg provides an
interesting example of what results when the different business cultures of northern Europe meet.

The population of Luxembourg is about 410,000 and the workforce is around
160,000. Despite the rationalization of the steel industry, Luxembourg's traditional
indigenous industry, there is little unemployment. A third of the workforce comprises *frontaliers*, frontier commuters from Belgium, France, and Germany, and
longer-term immigrant workers, mainly from the EU. Luxembourg has learned to
manage this cosmopolitan workforce, drawn from all over Europe, without a major
strike after 1922. Folklore has it that since the last war there has been one strike lasting one day starting on Friday afternoon. Absenteeism is low; government sources
put it at less than 5 percent.

Unemployment can be controlled and troublemakers weeded out with the
closely monitored work permit system. Nevertheless, Luxembourg embodies in

miniature a collaborative and institutionalized approach to industrial relations. While employers find this irksome and employees often have to be urged by their representatives to take an interest, it is often associated with productivity rates much higher than those of countries with a confrontational approach. The basis is a complex legal and administrative framework for negotiation and conciliation at factory and national level.

Business structure

Every company with over 15 employees must have an elected staff representative committee. If there are over 100 employees there will be several committees representing white-collar, manual, and, if there are enough, an under-21s committee. In companies employing more than 1,000 a third of the board of directors is elected by the staff committee. All employees in the country elect their representatives at the same time every four years.

In addition, any company employing more than 150 has to have a joint works council consisting of an equal number of management representatives, appointed by the chief executive, and employees, elected in a secret ballot with proportional representation. The council must be consulted on financial results, investment plans, changes in production methods, and so on, in addition to terms and conditions of employment.

Organization

For many years the Luxembourg economy was based on the steel industry. Around it were gathered numerous family-owned businesses, mainly in steel fabrication and tools, united in a cosy relationship with each other, the banks, the government, and the unions. The traditional Luxembourg business culture, still in evidence in older-established companies, follows a French/Belgian pattern of a strict hierarchy under an autocratic patron. Major decision making is a private affair between family members. Formal meetings are for briefing and formalizing decisions made by the boss with input from relevant experts.

More recently founded and entrepreneurial companies, managed by young executives educated abroad, are developing a new style of management based on participation and informality in decision making and communication.

There is no university in Luxembourg, so professionals, whether Luxembourger or foreign, are recruited from universities and business schools all over Europe. This results in a mix of backgrounds and cultures that can be very productive, and can also produce interesting comparisons of national characters. One chief executive who deliberately recruits a mix of nationalities described French and Italians as expert at projecting and selling themselves, Germans as clinically honest and accurate about their strengths and weaknesses, and Luxembourgers as overmodest.

Etiquette

Luxembourgers tend to be reserved in both business and private life, which they keep clearly separate. The working atmosphere will generally be collaborative and consensus oriented, so it is not wise to assert a position unless you are very sure of your ground—and even then in a modest way. Assertiveness, strong criticism, and especially personal remarks, even if meant lightheartedly or humorously, are seen as aggressive and rude. Outside working hours, foreigners often have to take the initiative to establish social relationships, so a few words of Luxembourgisch go a long way.

If the modest and bourgeois social values of Luxembourg seem claustrophobic to more extrovert outsiders, it is perhaps part of the price that a small community has to pay for autonomy, social harmony, and one of the highest standards of living in Europe.

FURNITURE
In which country do people spend the biggest proportion of their domestic budget on furniture and which the smallest?
Czechia
Luxembourg
Finland

Netherlands

Holland is a region and not a synonym for the Netherlands. While the Dutch accept the confusion among tourists, the country should be referred to by its correct name.

Despite the size of the country and its density of inhabitants, they draw clear distinctions between different regions, *gezellig* (affable) Brabant, for example, or cheese-eating Friesland, which has its own language. To an outsider the most noticeable difference is between the Randstad and the rest. The Randstad, or "city on the edge," is the flat and sprawling conurbation between Amsterdam and Rotterdam, The Hague and Utrecht. This is the home of the entrepreneurial, hard-headed, maritime Dutch, of industry and ports and intensive agribusiness. The rest of the country, including the rolling and wooded hinterland, is more rural and traditional, less obviously dedicated to the relentless pursuit of wealth. However attached the Dutch are to their home region, they are united in a fierce nationalism centered on the monarchy. Folklore has it that the orange carrot was developed from its natural purple variety by Dutch breeders out of patriotism to the royal House of Orange.

The principal divisions in the country are not by geography but by religion. The original provinces of the Low Countries that achieved independence from Spain in the seventeenth century parted company because of conflict between Catholics and Calvinists. The Catholic part broke away in 1830 to form what is now Belgium, although the Protestant Netherlands under the House of Orange retained a large proportion of Catholics in the south. The two persuasions have arrived at an exemplary accommodation, assisted by the particular style of Dutch Catholicism that, to an outside observer, appears to genuflect as much to Geneva as to Rome. A third group, the Liberals, is nondenominational.

Thus there have been three versions of many political and social institutions—Catholic, Protestant, and Liberal—from political parties to labor unions and social clubs. In recent years the groups have reformed on a political level into Christian, Liberal, and Socialist, but social clubs, education, and so on still tend to be organized along traditional lines.

Until the beginning of the twenty-first century sectarianism and discrimination were not serious issues. Tolerance and openness are active social and civic virtues in the Netherlands. The relationship between the elements of society is characterized by dialog and a search for accommodation based on what the Dutch call "columnization." This does not mean consensus. Society is thought of as consisting of various columns or pillars, each maintaining their own identity and values and supremely confident of their superiority over the others. Coexistence and not integration is the glue holding society together. In the political and social arena the cosy compromise cultivated by the ruling parties is showing signs of unpopularity, however. In business a partnership with a Dutch company will tend to work better as a marriage of convenience between independent entities than as a total merger.

"God created the earth but the Dutch made the Netherlands," goes the saying. Some 20 percent of the country has been reclaimed from the sea and the process continues. The entire landscape, urban and rural, is an artefact designed to accommodate the most congested population in Europe. It is the most obvious manifestation of the Dutch belief that everything, whether land, society, or business, can be molded by human aspiration and reason and effort. At the same time, there is an admission that dykes, societies, and wealth are subject to external forces that have to be respected. You cannot afford to take chances with nature, physical or human.

There are several aspects to the Dutch. One is a willingness to innovate and experiment, sometimes on a massive scale: Witness the sheer nerve of blocking off what was the Zuider Zee, now known as the IJsselmeer. There is a sense that the world is its oyster, not only because theirs is a small country bursting at the seams, but because it is there for the taking with intelligence and courage. This is the Netherlands of enormous multinationals, technology-based agriculture, enlightened experiments in control of illegal drugs, and penal reform.

Another strain, at first sight contradictory, is deep conservatism. You must innovate and be bold to survive, but at the same time minimize risk. Change for its own sake or change that has not been thought through is to be avoided. The boy with his finger in the dyke is a symbol of failure as well as heroism—what happened to the safety margin? This is the bourgeois Netherlands of straight streets and clean windows, order and conformism.

The values of the Dutch are predominantly egalitarian rather than aristocratic, rural rather than urban. Independence and self-reliance are associated with an outward-looking and entrepreneurial maritime tradition. At the same time, physical proximity and the need for total cooperation in the management of limited resources have created a social system based on negotiated interdependence.

Internationalism

The Dutch, along with the Belgians, have one of the most open economies in Europe. Imports and exports each account for 60 percent of GNP. Half of Europe's truck fleet is owned by the Dutch. It is a maritime, colonial, and trading nation forced to make a living from a tiny base with no natural resources, at least until natural gas was discovered.

The Netherlands is an economy of traders and middlemen, adding value to imported raw materials and re-exporting them. A good example of this is the thriving and entrepreneurial agricultural sector, which accounts for 20 percent of exports. How does a small, urban, crowded country find the land and the resources to be the world's largest exporter of poultry and dairy products? To be the largest exporter of house plants and flowers? By importing feed, manufacturing fertilizer, and forcing produce with cheap energy from natural gas. In Dutch agriculture "organic" refers to the chemistry, not the food.

Therefore the probability of being in partnership with a Dutch person is as great as that with business people from much larger countries. Dutch investment in the US is the third largest after the UK and Germany.

Foreign investment in the Netherlands is encouraged with considerable subsidy and incentives, but these are by no means its only advantages. Other than those in tiny Luxembourg, the Dutch are the most multilingual people in the EU and have an international outlook to match. A frequent strategy for companies wishing to exploit the single market is to acquire a Dutch company and let its staff get on with the job.

Business environment

To the rest of the world Dutch business is typified by the great multinationals, Philips, Unilever, Royal Dutch/Shell, and, for the connoisseurs, Akzo. However, these are typical only of each other and of other major multinationals, not of the rest of industry consisting largely of small and medium-sized privately owned enterprises.

Frugal to the point of parsimony in their private and business affairs, the Dutch have been profligate in public spending. Natural gas proved to be a mixed blessing in fostering consumption and, as a proportion of GNP, financing the highest welfare expenditure in Europe. People from countries where the fiscal relationship between the state and individuals or corporations is adversarial should be aware that in the Netherlands it is generally above board. Tax avoidance is highly developed and there is a growing gray market, especially in the private building industry, but outright evasion is considered reprehensible and extremely risky.

The pillars of the business establishment are the banks. They have a universal role, acting as investment, commercial, and merchant banks. They are directly represented on the stock exchange where they have a predominant influence on the German model. While competing strongly among themselves, they tend to close ranks against foreign predators.

Industrial relations

There are two main union groups, the Protestant CNV and the Catholic and non-denominational FNV. These represent about 40 percent of the workforce on an industry basis. They negotiate with the two employers' associations, the predominant, nondenominational VNO and the joint Protestant–Catholic NCW. The policy of nonconfrontational industrial relations based on negotiation and debate is called the *polder* model (*polder* is land reclaimed from the sea).

At the individual company level, those employing more than 35 people must set up a works council, *ondernemingsraad*. This is entitled to receive financial information, plans, and forecasts, and to be consulted on major changes such as investment and mergers and all aspects of personnel policy. Otherwise the employees have to be given the opportunity to question the management board at least twice a year.

Business organization

The two most common sorts of company are NV, *Naamloze Vennootschap*, a public limited company, and BV, *Besloten Vennootschap*, a private limited company. Both have to have a management board and a managing director. In addition, a "large" company—defined by its capital and whether it has 100 or more employees in the Netherlands—must have a supervisory board of at least three people. Shareholders, works councils, and the management board can nominate candidates and the first two have a right of veto. The supervisory board members, *commissarissen*, cannot be employed by the company. Their job is to approve the strategic direction, appoint the management board, finalize the annual accounts, and ratify major management decisions.

The supervisory boards have many powers that in countries like the US or the UK are vested in the shareholders. There is strong protection for managers against shareholder interference. Decisions on mergers and acquisitions lie with the board rather than the shareholders. Dutch managers of an independent company feel much more secure than their counterparts in other takeover-happy countries.

The Dutch countryside was described by an English writer, Aldous Huxley, as a rationalist's paradise, "like a tour through the first books of Euclid." There is a rationalist's aversion to the nonessential, an approach that permeates all aspects of social and organizational life. A Dutch organization aspires to a rigorous system that, more importantly, is respected and adhered to by all its members. They are not obsessive legislators. There are right and wrong ways of doing things, but only the essentials have to be codified into procedures. These are taken very seriously.

The Dutch are frugal, careful with money as individuals and companies, if not as governments. Organizations are lean and practical. There is a strong belief that the main function of business is to make profits. The bottom line is paramount. At the same time they are not obsessed with numbers. A strategy has to be qualitatively and conceptually right and not quantified in detail, unlike the operating plan and profit reports.

The strategic orientation is made clear down to relatively low levels in the organization. While there is a belief in hedging the unexpected by careful planning and study, the plan is not characteristically a highly developed and numbers-based document. The Dutch avoid the grandiose in favour of cautious, pragmatic, and step-by-step development. If reality does not conform to their projections, they are prepared to improvise.

The flexibility of personal pension schemes makes job hopping increasingly common, although there is not much incentive to move for pay. Pay agreements are highly standardized and collectivized and individual performance-related pay would be against the collective ethos. Dutch people's motivation comes more from job satisfaction and the congeniality of the team with whom they work.

Progress through a Dutch company is slow and methodical. The scope for promotion is largely determined by educational background. There are not many shopfloor-to-boardroom stories. Most of the senior people will have received a vocational education at the universities of Delft, specializing in engineering, Rotterdam, for economics, or Leiden for law and the humanities. These are the basis of a powerful old-boy network. There is also an aristocracy, which forms a clubbish group mainly within the banks and the diplomatic service. For the less exalted the apprenticeship system, along German lines, is still important.

Business behavior

The Dutch are so adept at dealing with foreigners that you will usually find you are using your own etiquette. Among themselves they tend to combine a frank, no-nonsense informality of manner with strict observance of basic etiquette. Unless there is a large generation or seniority gap, colleagues at all levels will rapidly come to first-name terms instead of *Mijnheer* or *Mevrouw* and use the informal singular form *je*, rather than the polite *U*. Titles like Doctor or Professor are sometimes used. If it is not apparent from the first introduction that the other person prefers you to use a title, it is not necessary to do so, even if it is on their business card.

Dress is informal, the degree depending on the conventions of the industry. In some companies this may mean open-necked shirts and sweaters and unpolished brown shoes, with a suit reserved for outside meetings and special occasions. In the bourse and banks dark suits are worn. In any event, taking off your jacket means getting down to work. In some companies informality of dress, as far as jeans and T-shirts, may be a privilege of seniority.

Whatever style is current, it is more important to avoid pretension than a breach of formal manners. This includes self-deprecation or diffidence. To be businesslike and straightforward to the point of bluntness is a greater mark of respect than is ostentatious graciousness.

In accordance with the basic value of frugality, flamboyance is to be avoided in all circumstances. While accumulating money is a virtue, spending it is a vice. Offices are simple, clothes are subdued, cars are modest, even the notepaper and letter-head are basic and unadorned. Those who put on style are considered not merely wasteful but suspect. Frequent mention of frugality and modesty perhaps gives a false impression that the Dutch are meek and dour. In most circumstances they are assertive, forceful, and stubborn, as well as tough negotiators.

Communication

Most Dutch you will meet in a business context are virtually bilingual in English, although they are very un-English in their use of language. They are the first to acknowledge that their openness and straightforwardness can be disturbing to foreigners, especially those used to hedging and hinting, understatement and politeness. In discussion there is a sense that ideas are objective and independent of the people uttering them. The directness of comment might seem offensive to those from cultures where the quality of an idea is more closely identified with the identity of its originator.

One of the few exceptions to bluntness is sometimes a reluctance among business partners to give a straight "yes" or "no" to a proposal. A concern to avoid conflict and a reluctance to postpone the definitive decision lead to phrases like "Let's take it a bit further," meaning "yes," or "This could produce problems," meaning "no."

Speeches and formal presentations are frequently tinged with humor, but informal business discussions tend to remain serious. Humor is jocular and earthy rather than witty, while irony and sarcasm invariably backfire with people who prize plain speaking. This literal approach to language favours humor based on logical absurdity and paradox.

Leadership

A very high value is placed on working in teams. Hierarchical systems are generally shallow and boundaries flexible. People will cut across reporting lines if necessary. The egalitarianism and openness evident in society are reflected in the workplace. The Dutch are easily shocked by the hierarchical discrimination practiced in many other cultures. Seniority is a necessary convenience and power is camouflaged rather than flouted. The boss is a *primus inter pares*, "one of us." He or she is therefore seen as the most important collaborator. The Dutch resent managers who take action or make decisions without consulting them.

Relationships between all levels are generally natural and highly tolerant. Communication is open and transparent. There is a preference for *buurten*, which means "visiting" in the American sense, over written communication. The Dutch are not good at keeping secrets and are uncomfortable with deviousness, their own as much as other people's. Everyone is expected to make suggestions and contributions and assumes that their upward communications will be listened to with respect. At the same time, people are conservative and resistant to change. While brainstorming and kicking ideas around in a group are perfectly feasible and nothing will be dismissed outright, ideas have to be well researched and thought out before they are taken seriously. There is a mistrust of intuition and a requirement for clarity.

Regular and frequent meetings form part of the team-based consensus culture. They are primarily for decision making after thorough discussion. While this is exhaustive, it is usually concise and to the point. It is essential to come well prepared and not to utter ill-informed opinions, however scintillating. All members are expected to contribute, whatever their seniority. The role of the senior person present is to steer the discussion and facilitate participation rather than impose direction. Despite an informality of manner, the Dutch stick to the basic protocols of keeping to an agenda, speaking through the chair, and so on.

Individuals are held accountable for decisions, but only after active consensus has been established. Every interested person has to be fully committed. Obedience is not an overriding virtue and people will not assent to a position unless they are convinced that it is right. Vote taking or any other formula that leaves a dissenting minority would be regarded as high-handed. It treads on individuals' rights to make themselves heard and to hold a different opinion. At the same time, considerable pressure is put on dissenters to conform to a majority view and this will persist until they have done so. The process is therefore slow and ponderous and, for some outsiders, frustrating. However, once a decision is made, implementation is fast and efficient because it has been thoroughly thought through and everyone knows what their role is.

Organization

The Dutch look for solid business relationships based on interdependence and reliability, mutual respect and mutual profit. It is important to honor commitments, however trifling. There is much more importance attached to the spirit than the letter of agreements, which, if they are written at all, are cursory. Schedules, routines, and diaries are carefully structured and adhered to.

Lateness, missed appointments, postponements, and late delivery are not merely inconvenient—to a Dutch person they mean untrustworthiness and will quickly sour a relationship. While a high value is placed on punctuality, a compulsion to make productive use of every minute sometimes puts a strain on the timetable.

There is no tangible dividing line between formal and informal contacts, no sense of occasion about a monthly meeting or a conversation with the boss. There is not a rigid barrier between home and office. People will take work home and can be telephoned there on important matters.

Job descriptions tend to be oriented less toward tasks and targets than toward how an individual interrelates with colleagues. Cooperation and trust are valued more highly than individual performance and all forms of one-upmanship are frowned on. It is important to attribute success to the team and not to oneself or another individual. Conversely, there will be little blame or recrimination if things go wrong. It is important to avoid embarrassing other individuals. Overt cooperation does not, however, preclude covert rivalry and as much behind-the-scenes politicking as in more openly competitive societies.

It would be misleading if this gave the impression that the Dutch are obsessively collaborative and conciliatory in manner. They dislike being answerable to other individuals and, to those from a more directive culture, may appear unyielding and opinionated. They regard interference in what they view as their sphere of responsibility as an infringement of trust.

Socializing

Socializing takes place over coffee rather than meals. Food is not an important part of the social culture and Dutch cuisine is not a source of pride. Meals are plain and private. Their place is within the family and not for social entertaining. Lunch is a necessity not an event, and a sandwich at the desk is the norm. The works canteen, if there is one, is for workers. The business lunch is often perfunctory, although there is a growing trend of eating in restaurants. Business entertaining is regarded as a personal occasion and not corporate entertainment.

Social occasions at work include staff parties at St. Nicholas on December 5 and other times during the year. Birthdays are celebrated with cakes and coffee. Colleagues may mix socially at weekends or evenings if they are neighbors, but not immediately after work. People go home promptly and eat dinner early with their family.

Entertaining colleagues or business partners at home is not common and it is more usual to be invited after dinner rather than for dinner. This should not be taken as a sign of a lack of hospitality and it is advisable not to eat much beforehand. Guests are plied with plentiful snacks and sandwiches along with drinks and the inevitable coffee, but the indulgence and slight embarrassment of a formal meal are avoided.

MEDICAL CARE
Which country spends most and least on health per person?
>
> Switzerland
>
> Estonia
>
> Romania

GERMAN-SPEAKING COUNTRIES

Austria

Austria is a landlocked, mostly mountainous country whose restricted size and role in world affairs today are in stark contrast to its recent history. Vienna was the capital of two great empires. The Austro-Hungarian empire, embracing much of what is now called central and eastern Europe, was dismantled in 1918. The vibrant intellectual and artistic realm of Mitteleuropa, embracing the German-speaking intelligentsia of central and eastern Europe, was crushed by the Nazis, not least because of the central role therein of Jewish thought and culture. Modern Austria, a small, neutral country of 8 million people, was created in 1955. Nevertheless, Vienna remains an international commercial and political center on a different scale to its hinterland.

Austria is predominantly Roman Catholic and Germanic, with a few minorities reminiscent of the old empire—Croats, Slovenes, and small groups of Hungarians, Czechs, Slovaks, and Italians. About 1.5 million live in Vienna, whose urban sophistication contrasts with the simpler and more provincial values of the rest of the country. The second city, Graz, has only 240,000 inhabitants. About 45 percent of the population is classified as rural, although urban areas continue to grow as the farm population leaves the upland valleys and as the tourist industry increasingly develops in the Alpine areas.

Vienna's empires were founded on Austria's command of east–west and north–south trade routes. The Danube links western and eastern Europe, while north–south Alpine passes connect the country with the Mediterranean and the Balkans. It is a road, rail, barge, and airline transport hub for the region. International trade accounts for just over a third of GDP, 40 percent of which is with Germany and 15 percent with eastern neighbors. While careful to maintain their own identity and culture, many Austrian business people are adept at dealing with those of others, especially their German, Italian, and central European neighbors.

The country accounts for 10 percent of western investment in former eastern Europe and 25 percent in the Slovak Republic. During the Cold War, through its historical and personal connections with its former empires and its meticulous neutrality, Austria nurtured its role as the primary commercial link with the eastern bloc. As a consequence, there were sophisticated commercial and financial structures already in place to take advantage of the burgeoning markets of the former socialist countries. With the demise of the Soviet Union and the rise of the new Europe, Vienna has moved from the fringe to the center of Europe. It has attracted foreign residents at all levels of society, from bankers and business people to immigrants from the former Yugoslavia and Turkey.

In spite, or perhaps because of, its many international borders and the impor-tance of foreign trade and tourism, Austria has remained in many ways a closed and introverted society. The undercurrent of wariness about foreigners occasionally erupts into chauvinism and the maltreatment of minorities. Austrians' desire to pro-tect their own identity extends to their German neighbors. It is no less irritating for them to be lumped together with Germans than it is for Canadians to be regarded as Americans or Irish as British.

Industrial structure

At the heart of Austrian business life is the concept known as *Sozialpartnerschaft*, social partnership. This is based on a comprehensive system of chambers and asso-ciations that conduct labor relations on behalf of their members. Industries, trades, and professions have their own chambers and associations under public law. Mem-bership is compulsory. Chambers of labor protect the interests of employed per-sons. The Federation of Austrian Industrialists (VÖI) is a voluntary association of industrial entrepreneurs. About two-thirds of all employed persons belong to the Austrian Trade Union Federation, which has no political affiliation. There are several well-honed mechanisms and forums for chambers and associations to negotiate and disputes and strikes are very rare.

In a country of small towns and ethnic and religious homogeneity, there is a deep sense of community. This embraces the sense of belonging and mutual responsibility between companies and their employees that is only now beginning to succumb to international market forces. While redundancy is increasingly com-mon, in most companies it is accompanied not only by a lump sum but by retrain-ing and outplacement provided by the ex-employer.

Until recently the sense of community was reflected in companies' annual reports, which invariably began with a tribute to workers past and present and the picture of a country chapel or some similar commemorative icon. Unfortunately, in today's global markets, all European annual reports now look as though they have been produced by the same PR agency.

Loyalty and conservatism are also reflected in outside business relationships. It is difficult to break into existing supplier arrangements and then only if the type and standard of service are radically different. Buying the business is not usually effective.

Historical experience and economic necessity have taught Austrians about accommodating to change. When asked to describe their national characteristics, Austrians are likely to mention flexibility. Traders and negotiators, they are friendly but circumspect in initial contacts and take care not to show their hand too soon.

While not afraid to assert a strong position, they are always prepared to change it in order to reach an accommodation.

Organization

Outside Vienna Austrians are early risers. Most are at work at 8am and finish around 5pm. In Vienna the timetable slips an hour. Excessive hours are considered a mark of inefficiency rather than industry. However important the proceedings, people will stop for lunch. Outside Vienna where commuting distances are very small, it is not uncommon to go home for lunch. It is usually not worth the trouble of trying to get hold of someone after noon on a Friday, especially in the skiing season.

A Germanic sense of punctuality is part of a disciplined approach to working life, which those from more improvisatory environments will find irksome. Some companies work by the academic quarter of an hour, but this is also a fixed convention.

There is some flexibility and compromise within a well-structured framework of systems, controls, and procedures, but it is usually as well to stay within guidelines. Improvisation and creativity are regarded as symptoms of inadequacy rather than desirable competencies. Minutes, action plans, and other records of past decisions and instructions are not consigned to oblivion in the bottom drawer of the desk.

Roles and responsibilities are well delineated in an organization chart that on the whole reflects how the organization actually works. Nevertheless, delegation tends to be target driven rather than process based, at least in the middle and upper reaches of management. Policy and targets are set by senior managers and handed down for implementation.

Leadership

Managers are not overly troubled about ensuring consensus and agreement among their staff. They are prepared to claim personal responsibility for decisions that in more participative cultures would be ascribed to a team. If they feel that the situation demands it, they can be directive to the point of autocracy.

In informal situations, and especially among the many family-owned companies, bosses will demonstrate their paternalistic benevolence to employees at any level. Nevertheless, this should not be confused with egalitarianism. There is a respect for status and a deferential sense of hierarchy that distance bosses from their employees.

Meetings at which a senior person is present will be controlled by that person. The agenda will be respected. It is important to come well prepared for meetings. Flicking through the papers for the first time as you sit down is not well regarded. However, in an individualistic leadership culture meetings have a less important function than in team-based cultures. Among peers and in the absence of a senior person, meetings may well turn into a less structured discussion without time pressure and are likely to disintegrate.

Communication

Many Austrians speak good English, although they often stick to German wherever possible, even in a multinational context. They have a factual, numerate, and direct approach to communication that is intolerant of euphemism and allusion. While frankness may be sweetened by charm, it is perfectly acceptable among peers. There is an adversarial approach to discussion and problem solving. Confrontation is not avoided and discussions can become heated. To senior people, however, dissenting opinion is neither offered nor solicited.

Austria shares with other German-speaking countries a preference for last names and titles. These may be job descriptions—*Herr Kommerzialrat*, for example—as well as *Magister* or *Doktor* to denote university degrees. Educational qualifications feature largely on cards, letterheads, and luggage tags, as well they might: Austrians take up to ten years to acquire them.

It is not unknown for the sons in family businesses to address their fathers by their title during working hours. A transition to first names is a mark of intimacy and is at the discretion of the older or more senior person. Celebrating it by a formal *Brüderschaft* ceremony is still common. The pair drink to their new relationship with their colleagues as witnesses. Among younger people and in newer industries this convention has become less rigid, although they tend to revert to the formal *Sie* and last names when senior management is around.

Attitudes and behavior

One way in which Austrians have resisted outside influence is in the preservation of traditional central European politeness. Those from cultures where to be businesslike is to be assertive and brusque may find this cloying. Others may find it refreshing. Courtesy goes deeper than mere politeness. There is an engaging cordiality and genuine hospitality about Austrian manners. The word that crops up most often in discussing this topic with outsiders is "charm." Provincial Austrians are likely to use the word *schmalzig*—unctuous—about their Viennese compatriots, who are often thought to overdo the charm.

Vienna is certainly more formal. There is still a tradition of reserve and formality among some Viennese in contrast to the relaxed and informal style characteristic of provincial Austria. In Vienna, men's suits are conventional and they dress up to socialize in the evening. In the towns, suits and ties of sober cut and hue are more common and they dress down to go out. On formal occasions the equivalent of the dinner jacket or tuxedo is a splendid gray flannel jacket with embroidered lapels. In these and other material aspects, Austrians have a preference for quality and the most superior brand names.

Women who visit Austria may be charmed by old-fashioned courtesy. This goes hand in kissed hand with traditional discrimination against them in business. It is rare to find a woman in a senior management position.

Formality is worn lightly and counterbalanced by a more easy-going approach to life than is prevalent among German and Swiss neighbors. The quality that Austrians value most in their social life and their personal relations at work is *Gemütlichkeit*, best described as comfortable geniality. They like to feel that they are easy going and enjoy life with a touch of laziness. It is conventional to exchange the friendly *grüss Gott* with everyone, including strangers in lifts and corridors, as well as a ritual handshake with all colleagues at the beginning and end of the day.

Humor is acceptable in informal circumstances but never at a formal meeting, most easily defined as whenever senior people are present. Jokes tend to be earthy rather than subtle. A custom that surprises many foreigners in some provincial areas is a mid-morning beer break instead of coffee. This does not mean sneaking round to the *Gaststube* next door; it is served in the works canteen.

Friendliness and hospitality among business colleagues have their limits. There is a clear demarcation between business and personal life, especially if foreigners might be involved. Regular socializing after hours or at weekends is uncommon. While hospitality is readily offered to outsiders, it is usually in restaurants and rarely at home. Home telephone numbers are not distributed and it has to be a real emergency to make a business call at the weekend. While a business relationship may develop into a personal relationship over time, the latter is not a necessary constituent.

POLLUTION
Which country emits the most greenhouse gases per capita (CO, CO_2, SO_x, NO_x and VOCs)?
Norway
Slovakia
Russia

Germany

Germany dominates Europe. With 83 million people it has the largest population. It accounts for 25 percent of the EU's GDP and is the world's third largest economy.

The two great changes that have taken place in Germany in recent years have been reunification and the demise of the Deutschmark. They mark the end of a 50-year renaissance and have profoundly affected the sense of German national identity, purpose, and place in the world.

Reunification is a misleading term. It implies the joining together of two halves of a previously single country, but the two states that now form Germany were as unlike their common predecessor as they were each other. In many respects, above all political and economic, it was the unification of two new countries. Indeed, unification of whatever kind is a euphemism. It was the wholesale takeover of one country by another with no process of convergence or compromise. Overnight, 15 million people found themselves in another country.

For West Germans, *Wessis*, the immediate impact of reunification was an increase in taxes to pay for it, about which there were frequent and vociferous complaints. For *Ossis*, every aspect of their daily life was touched, every process, every procedure, down to the *Pfennigs* in their pockets. The struggle to cope was not compensated for by the promised benefits of capitalism, affluence and employment. In the new Germany it was *Ossis* who had to change their social values from community and egalitarianism to individual achievement and success. A senior executive of the Treuhand—the government organization that took over ownership of East German companies for reorganization and privatization—was asked how it dealt with the East German participative management style exemplified by the use of *Du* at all levels of hierachy. He said that it was one of the first things the West German managers knocked out of them.

On the surface, the former East Germany has been transformed in the past ten years. The transport and communications infrastructure is new, its residential and commercial buildings have been renewed, and its industrial structure completely changed from heavy industry, mining, and chemicals to a modern service-oriented economy. Productivity, skills, and training have been radically overhauled. This has not been without pain, especially to older and older-thinking citizens. It has bred feelings of inferiority and resentment to match the condescension and resentment of the *Wessis*. It is only the youngest generations of former East Germans who feel that they properly belong in the new Germany.

The *Wessis* are more affected by the euro. For many, the Deutschmark was the symbol of stability and security and the achievements of the past 50 years. To have it now submerged in the euro is demoralizing and disturbing. German conservatism and dislike of the unpredictable are challenged by the uncertainty of the euro's future.

Regionalism

The *Länder* making up the Federal Republic have real economic and political independence. It is difficult to identify a simple geographic pattern. There is a traditional north–south divide, with northerners following the custom of dismissing southerners as lazy and soft while the southerners reciprocate with taunts of dour and dull. A less tangible divide contrasts the solid Saxons in the east with the cosmopolitan Rhinelanders. However, Germany is better thought of as a patchwork, with enclaves and cities reflecting the tribalism and eccentricities of the old dukedoms and principalities.

Germany has several capitals, depending on your interest. Berlin is the political capital. Frankfurt is for banking and finance, Hamburg for trade, Munich for sunrise industries, society, and the arts, Düsseldorf–Dortmund–Essen for heavy industry. If you want to know about the largest automobile industry in Europe you have to go to Munich (BMW), Stuttgart (DaimlerBenz, Porsche, Mercedes), Wolfsburg (Volkswagen), Cologne (Ford), or Rüsselsheim (General Motors, Opel). If you are interested in publishing you have to go to Munich, Frankfurt, Stuttgart, Hamburg, and, for the biggest publishing group in Europe, the small town of Gütersloh, the headquarters of Bertelsmann. There is no dominating metropolis. This is why communications are so good and why road and rail networks are in a convenient matrix rather than a centralized spider's web. And why Germany has more and bigger trade fairs than other countries.

National identity

In the past 100 years Germans have gone through the menu of political systems, including monarchy, empire, republic, dictatorship, federal democracy, and democratic republic. If there is any consistency, it is the determination to exploit whatever is on hand to the limit of its potential. In a *British Social Attitudes Special International Report*, British and Germans were asked to rank various reasons for being proud of their respective nationalities. In similar proportions the British gave the monarchy as their first choice, with 37 percent, and the Germans the *Grundgesetz* or "basic law," with 30 percent. Second place in Germany, with 17 percent, went to economic achievement, while in Britain this ranked bottom with 2 percent. Germans take business very seriously indeed, which those coming from countries with less regard for it would do well to bear in mind. They are justifiably proud of German abilities and achievements—some self-critical German commentators have said too proud, if not to the point of arrogance then certainly to the point of complacency. A newcomer will soon come across the firm conviction that German products, German management, and the German way of doing things are best.

Government intervention

Whatever the reasons for German economic success, a free-market economy without government intervention or control is not one of them. The German "social market" economy is based largely on free-market principles, but with labor, wage, and regulatory issues being largely decided by a broad consensus of government, business, and unions. Its past success does not make it immune to the need for reforms to reduce budget deficits, tax rates, and the inflexibility of labor markets.

Apart from state monopolies in most public services, the federal government has major shareholdings in hundreds of German companies. In addition, the *Länder* have proactive and interventionist policies often amounting to direct shareholdings. Regional and industrial subsidies are extensive and financed by one of the highest rates of corporate taxation in Europe.

The attitude to government participation in industry is not based on ideology but on a sense of partnership with the business community and wider social obligations. Unlike, say, Anglo-Saxon orthodoxy, enhancing shareholder value is not the overriding performance goal. It is this sense of community of interest that has undermined successive privatization attempts. It extends to the local level, where local authorities, unions, schools, banks, and businesses combine on a town, district, and *Land* level to establish policies of mutual benefit.

Government intervention in business is most noticeable to the outsider in the panoply of regulations. Germany may not be the most regulated business environment in Europe, but it is certainly the one in which regulations are most adhered to. In addition to regulations there are a host of guidelines and principles covering every aspect of running a business. In the unlikely event that a loophole is discovered, it is customary not to exploit it but to refer to the appropriate authority for a ruling.

Some sections of the business community look enviously at other countries' moves toward deregulation and the increased competition that ensues. The counter-argument is that a genuinely competitive market can only exist if it is regulated. The Law Against Restraints on Competition is particularly strong and energetically enforced by the Federal Cartel Office. Its principal brief is to guard against the abuse of market dominance, which it does by preventing companies from achieving a dominant position in the first place. Mergers and acquisitions of whatever size come under close scrutiny and the onus is on the companies to disprove the immediate assumption that their association will be detrimental to the marketplace. Unless the particular market is highly fragmented, horizontal mergers are unlikely to succeed.

The banks

Banks dominate business. The big three—Deutsche, Dresdner, and Commerzbank—combine the roles played in other countries by commercial bank, investment bank, merchant bank, savings bank, stockbroker, and institutional investor. They are aptly described as "universal banks." Their strength derives from the immediate postwar years when the shortage of investment capital meant that bank finance was the only source of equity as well as working capital. They are based in northern Germany. In the south the Vereinsbank and Hypobank have a similar but more regional role. In addition to the big five, there are many other banks no less influential on a *Land* level.

The banks' role of principal provider of funds, while it may serve well at times of economic crisis, exacerbates the difficulty in good times of finding capital for new ventures. Their natural conservatism and the lack of an active and independent stock market tend to stifle entrepreneurial growth and innovation. The benefits of collaboration between government, banks, and business are seen to outweigh the dangers of a conflict of interest. Business people from countries where banks and government are kept at arm's length or played off against each other need to modify their customary attitudes. A closely woven network of connections and loyalties and an innate distaste for stepping out of line mean that those who break ranks quickly find themselves isolated.

Family companies

Antitrust laws, the tight grip of banks over the stock market, and strong regionalism have preserved the position of family-owned small and medium-sized companies, defined as those employing fewer than 500 people. They account for 50 percent of total corporate turnover and 60 percent of all employees. Foreigners working with these companies may find more of a paternalistic environment than they are used to at home. They may discover a sense of social responsibility and concern for long-term employee welfare that are alien to their experience. They may also feel excluded from policy making among family interests outside the forum of professional management. A constant challenge for German companies is to bridge the gap between the family firm and multidisciplinary professional management.

Long-termism

The dominating position of government, banks, and closely held family companies means that Germany provides few pickings for stock-market operators. Hostile takeover bids are almost unknown and it is extremely difficult to enter the German market by acquisition. While this will be deplored by those who believe that predators maintain the health of the herd and the financial health of shareholders, it does mean that managers can devote their time and energy to managing the business instead of fighting off bids, planning management buyouts, or worrying if they will have a job next year. They can afford to take a longer-term view than can those preoccupied with tomorrow's share price and the quarterly results. They will adopt a strategic view of the development of their market without the pressure for immediate returns. They have to concentrate on achieving long-term growth internally rather than through acquisition or manipulation of assets. This is one reason, coupled with high labor costs, why continuous capital investment is an article of faith in Germany.

Industrial relations

Although unions are no more welcomed by management than in other countries, they are acknowledged as an inevitable and necessary member of a partnership. While both sides are imbued with a sense of social responsibility and the admission that what is good for one side is similarly good for the other, they are also circumscribed by a comprehensive legal framework.

Full-scale strikes during negotiations are rare and a last resort following prescribed and detailed arbitration and balloting procedures. More frequent, although still uncommon, are short work stoppages during negotiations with individual companies. They rarely last for more than a few hours and are designed to underline a point rather than disrupt production. A favorite period for a work stoppage is 48 hours beginning four o'clock on a Friday afternoon.

Restrictions on union activity are balanced by stringent employee protection and welfare laws. Dismissals and layoffs are complicated and expensive to carry out. However, the area that management finds most tiresome is the system of worker participation, *Mitbestimmung*. This provides for elected employee representation on the *Aufsichtsrat*, or supervisory board of outside directors.

Any company employing more than five people must set up a *Betriebsrat* or works council if the employees request it. This is composed solely of employees elected by secret ballot. It must be consulted by management every three months on all changes affecting working conditions, including production methods and new investment, as well as personnel questions such as working hours, holiday schedules, incentive payments, and so on. It must also be consulted about hiring, firing, and transferring employees. By law, management again has the last word, but in practice is best advised to maintain a constructive relationship. There is a saying that managers get the *Betriebsrat* chairman they deserve. Sooner or later in their careers managers will be judged on their ability to work with the *Betriebsrat* while keeping it in line.

Business organization and structure

Business organizations in Germany are oligarchic. Power is concentrated in a small number of people at the top. Public corporations (AG) and limited companies (GmbH) with over 500 employees have a supervisory board (*Aufsichtsrat*) which consists of up to 21 members. It appoints the management board (*Vorstand*), which has the last word on management policy matters. Since the directors (*Vorstandsmitglieder*) are reappointed every four years, they tend not to exercise this prerogative too freely. In smaller private companies that do not have to have an *Aufsichtsrat* the directors are appointed directly by the shareholders and are known as *Geschäftsführer*.

All decisions of any importance are taken by the *Vorstandsmitglieder* or *Geschäftsführer*. (These are not to be confused with *Direktoren*, who are the top level of middle management.) While each of them may have a particular expertise or functional role, they share responsibility jointly for the management of the company. Because the *Vorstand* is legally collective, the chairman (*Sprecher* or *Vorsitzende*) is less powerful than the equivalent in other countries.

The participative element of German organizational culture stops here. Below the *Vorstand* or *Geschäftsführung* there is a strict vertical hierarchy. The organization and the individual's role within it are logical, methodical, and compartmentalized. Functions and the relationship between them are thoroughly defined and documented. Procedures, routines, and doing things by the book are important. Cutting corners, taking initiatives, and skimping on the formalities are frowned on. Newcomers are well advised to stick closely to the rules until they are absolutely sure of the acceptable way in which these can be tempered by pragmatism.

What would lead to a bureaucratic nightmare in other cultures works in Germany because of a respect for perfectionism extending to all areas of business and private life. However, when the unexpected does happen, even in the best-run organizations they are less well equipped to handle it. They look for a mechanism that has already been worked out and if it does not exist they tend to be at a loss. This also means that German organizations are not good at maintaining a process of constant and regular change. They are better suited to a manufacturing environment where major decisions have a long life span.

Planning

Germans are uneasy with uncertainty, ambiguity, and unquantifiable risk. Experience and temperament have fostered a strong fear of insecurity. Faced with the choice, they will take the most conservative option. Opportunism is viewed less as a talent than a failure to organize.

Planning is seen as the responsibility of senior management and not of those lower down in the organization. If there are several people involved it requires constant discussion and complete consensus. Anyone with expertise and knowledge will be asked to give a considered opinion and will be seriously listened to. While studies and analysis are important, these are tempered by intuition and common sense. It will be a cautious decision, loaded with fallback positions, contingency plans, and alternatives, and subject to empirical testing. The approach is best described as "systematically pragmatic."

Once the decision is collectively made it is translated into rigorous, comprehensive action steps that are carried out to the letter without question. Alternative solutions are not encouraged to permeate upwards or sideways from people not recognized as qualified to contribute to them.

Leadership

Germans look for strong, decisive leadership from people who know what they are talking about. There is a universal deference to people in authority and subordinates will rarely contradict or criticize their boss. Superiors expect to be obeyed and in return are expected to provide unequivocal direction.

It would be wrong to regard this as subservience. Orders are obeyed out of respect for the boss's functional role and competence. Some may take advantage of this to indulge a dictatorial manner. Although it is certainly not done to answer back, such behavior is no more acceptable to Germans than it is to others. Greater store is set by managers who rely on technical competence rather than force of personality. People from countries where outbursts of temper are a privilege of seniority and a sign of getting tough should know that in Germany they are regarded as uncouth and evidence of weakness.

Doing the minimum to get by is abhorred at all levels of the organization, especially senior management. It is important that bosses be seen to be working hard, getting their hands dirty. Although the upwardly mobile expect to be rewarded, the chance to take it easy while others get on with the job is not associated with promotion.

Employees readily obey instructions, but they prefer to be left to carry them out without interference. Delegation is clear, precise, and preferably written. Relationships between bosses and subordinates tend to be distant and awkward. While bosses may deliberately keep an open door, most people are too intimidated to walk through it. Younger employees often want their bosses to be more accessible. They expect more participation and feedback and have fewer inhibitions about asking for it, with which older-style bosses have difficulty in coping.

The kind of appraisal system in which performance and progress are frankly discussed is not common in traditional companies. Employees do not expect to share in setting objectives. They are censorious about even minor failings, especially if a procedure has been broken or ignored. Feedback has to be precise and objective, since criticism is neither given nor received easily.

Teams

The concept of a team is a group of individuals each with a given expertise, under a strong leader, with a specific objective and a recognized place in the overall organization. *Ad hoc* groups across hierarchical lines do not obtain whole-hearted commitment. They have to be properly constituted, have a place in the timetable and the organization chart, and not add to the members' workload. Those used to more fluid ways of working should not misinterpret reluctance to cooperate as a lack of goodwill and certainly not idleness. It derives from a strong sense that everything should be part of a methodical pattern.

Germans feel most comfortable with a thorough integral analysis of a given problem, in which all the team members contribute their expertise. When everyone knows what is expected of them they work independently until the next and probably final meeting to coordinate their results.

Meetings

Germans are much more relaxed in individual discussions than at large meetings. Unless there is a dire emergency, meetings of any sort will be scheduled weeks in advance. They are formal with an agenda and minutes. There is possibly a polite period of small talk first while a secretary serves tea or coffee, but thereafter meetings are strictly functional.

Meetings between boss and subordinates are usually for coordination, briefing, or formal ratification of decisions. The decision-making process—identification of the problem, consideration of alternative solutions, and so on—will have been largely carried out beforehand by the relevant experts. The meeting will be dominated by the senior person. It is less likely to be a forum for upward communication or alternative opinion than a mechanism for giving orders. Divergent opinions are rarely welcome; differences should have been resolved in advance or saved until later.

Compliance rather than consensus is expected. It is assumed that everyone will work to implement decisions regardless of how they feel about them. When giving instructions it is not important to explain and persuade, but it is very important to be clear and decisive.

Meetings between peers or at a senior level, when major decisions or policy issues are being discussed, tend to have a different character. There is much more discussion, even debate. Nevertheless, it is important to come very well prepared and not to comment on things about which you are not qualified to speak. Proffering uninformed opinions, dogmatic statements, and premature conclusions, however inspired or elegant, is to be avoided. It is unwise to spring something new on a formal meeting. It is more acceptable to remain silent if you have nothing to say than to make a contribution for the sake of it.

Communication

Communication is primarily top down and on a need-to-know basis. Information is required to flow upwards only when asked for. Due to a pervading deference to authority, people accept that superiors should be better informed than they are. While there is a hunger for information and no shortage of politicking, Germans do not suspect great secrets and conspiracies. The main concern is to get on with the job.

Many German companies thrive on a massive amount of written communication, elaborating and confirming what has been discussed and agreed face to face. Germans have not mastered a telephone manner, unlike their Latin neighbors who can be as loquacious and intimate over the phone as around the table. Germans are more inhibited, especially on conference calls. They miss the cues and feedback and the setting.

Upward mobility

There is no dominant élite in Germany, no equivalent of the *Grandes Ecoles* and prestigious universities. Those with a technical background have the best chance of rising to the top.

An engineer has greater status than a marketing or financial specialist. Higher education, both in the well developed apprenticeship system and at the universities, is mainly vocational. Some 70 percent of the workforce is occupationally qualified. Training, predominantly technological, continues throughout an employee's career. Management education as a separate discipline is not viewed with great enthusiasm. Companies prefer to instill their own methods.

In most companies a fast-track career is rare. Positions are permanent and there is a recognizable prospect of planned, steady progression. Getting ahead is not merely a question of what you know. The *British Social Attitudes Special International Report* stated that when asked to rank the factors influencing getting ahead in life, Germans put education first, ambition second, knowing the right people third, hard work a surprising fourth, and ability fifth. This is a glimpse of a not wholly technocratic society, one where competitiveness and who you know are important.

Most people prefer to stay in their home town or region, which limits the scope for taking jobs elsewhere. In some industries it is seen as a major professional weakness and even job rotation is viewed with skepticism. Job hopping used to be more frequent between foreign-owned companies than family-owned ones or the large conglomerates. It was common for people to rise through the ranks from humble beginnings to the *Vorstand*. A survey by Youssef Cassis (*Big Business*, OUP, 1997) showed that 43 percent of chief executives came into their present firms at senior management level and 45 percent in junior management. Only 12 percent started with the company. As in most other European and North American countries, it pays to move around.

The rewards of success are not noticeably financial. The spread of earnings between the highest and the lowest paid is the smallest in the EU. Performance-related pay, at any level, is not a significant feature of salary structures. People are expected to do the best job they can and to be rewarded by eventual promotion.

Attitudes and behavior

Germans are competitive and ambitious. They are very critical of themselves and others. They do not identify or sympathize with failure. It is shameful to be out of work and bankruptcy is a social and professional stigma. They place a great deal of importance on individual success and its outward trappings. The car you drive, the size of your office, and where you take holidays are all important.

There is a clear demarcation between private and business life. Germans leave work as punctually as they arrive and rarely take papers home. They do not like being called at home on business unless there is a very good reason. People at all levels take their full holiday entitlement and they do not keep in touch with the office when they are away, nor do they expect to be called.

There is not the same alliance building across boundaries as in many other companies. Informal contacts are more within functions than across boundaries, although they are frequent and important. On a personal basis colleagues like to know a great deal about each other. They are very liberal and uncensorious about private life, but they like to know who they are dealing with.

There is a high value placed on *Kollegialität*, coupled with a strong distaste for nonconformism. At the outset newcomers will be treated with a certain degree of mistrust until they establish their credentials, their ability, and whether they pose a threat. Once they are established they will be treated much less defensively than in less structured organizations.

Women

The people who are least likely to make it to the top are women. Among Europeans, Germans hold the most traditional views of the role of women in society. There are some structural reasons for them finding it harder, of which the bias against girls taking technical subjects at school, the time it takes to get a university degree, and the lack of sex discrimination laws are some. However, the fundamental reason is that German males are chauvinist.

Etiquette

Some newcomers find the stiffness and formality of social and business contacts inhibiting. Germans have a strong sense of privacy and their protective shell extends much further into public life than in many other countries.

There is a notable feeling of community and social conscience, which to some may appear to be based more on social tidiness than genuine neighborliness. There is a great antipathy toward stepping out of line, out of your prescribed role. Eccentricity of the mildest sort will attract open criticism. While there is an instinctive dislike of personal confrontation, there is no hesitation in pointing out to someone that they do not meet acceptable standards of behavior. This may be for something as trivial in your eyes as taking off a jacket at a meeting or parking in the wrong place. Policing each other's behavior is not seen as offensive but as a social duty.

Unlike some countries where men wear jackets as a sign to fellow commuters that they have a job, and then leave them hanging on the back of the door until it is time to go home, in most German offices you keep your jacket on and buttoned up unless you are alone. Shirt sleeves are a sign of relaxation, not getting down to work.

Public behavior is in sharp contrast with the informality and warmth of private life and genuine friendships. Intimacy is not freely given, but is much more durable than the instant variety peddled by more informal societies. There is a strong desire for belonging, for *Brüderschaft*. Sometimes this spills over into sentimentality, although for the most part it is kept on a tight rein.

This demarcation between public and private is illustrated by the way people interact. The general rule is for everyone to address each other by *Herr* or *Frau* followed either by their last name or, if they have one, their title and then the last name. *Frau* is almost always used instead of *Fraülein* for single women. The title is either a professional qualification or a position in the company. It is a lapse of etiquette not to use a person's title, if they have one, or to get it wrong. If in doubt, look on their business card.

If you are speaking German, the polite plural, the *Sie* form, is almost always employed. Close colleagues of a younger generation tend to use first names among themselves. At a meeting, in front of strangers, or in front of the boss, they will revert to last names or titles. The informal singular, *du*, is only used by agreement among close friends and the transition is a significant event. It marks the entry into each other's jealously guarded "private space" and should never be taken lightly. It is a sign that familiarity at work has expanded into a lasting personal friendship. It is usually initiated by the senior person, in rank or age, and is marked by a ritual—a drink or a meal and a formal agreement. It is usually the result of something shared: a project, a business trip, or a specific piece of collaboration. The friendship is expected to continue even if careers take you different ways.

If you are American or British, do not be surprised that your German colleagues have read their etiquette guides too, probably more thoroughly than you. They will be prepared to adopt an easy Anglo-Saxon familiarity, but only while they are speaking English. If you switch to German you should revert to the formal style. If you are both using English as a second language then you should probably remain formal.

There are exceptions in some areas and some industries and among some younger people, notably computer specialists. There is something about working with computers, perhaps because it is a young profession, that induces informality in dress and manners the world over.

However informal the relationship, politeness and good manners are essential. Colleagues expect each other to be reserved but friendly. They are careful to greet each other properly in the morning and evening and also with *Mahlzeit* ("meal time") when they go to lunch.

Punctuality

It is very important to be punctual, which means on the dot. Only in academic circles is the professor's ten-minute delay acceptable. It is also permissible to leave work on time. There is a strong sense that the relationship between the company and the employee is contractual: You are paid for so many hours and you work as hard as you can, but that is the end of it. There is no particular kudos in working over unless you are paid for it or there is a deadline to meet; even then, it may be regarded as inefficiency rather than diligence.

Humor

The old *canard* about humorless Germans is not borne out by acquaintance, whether of wry Hamburgers, witty Rheinlanders, or jocular Bavarians. Nevertheless, levity does not belong in the workplace. Like so many aspects of German life, humor is strictly compartmentalized. The more formal the occasion, the less humor is acceptable. Far from putting Germans at their ease, joking among strangers or new acquaintances often makes them feel uncomfortable. At meetings or presentations, while Americans or British might feel obliged to sprinkle speeches or presentations with jokes, or Italians or French would indulge in occasional witticisms, Germans remain consistently serious.

In some countries people feel that they can relax more as they become more senior. In Germany the opposite happens. Seniority is a mantle of responsibility that the holder must be seen to deserve and take seriously.

Among close colleagues in private there is banter and joking. It is usually sharp and biting and directed toward incompetence, mistakes, and nonconformity. It is rarely facetious, especially about money or business, and never self-deprecating. To admit inadequacy even in jest is incomprehensible.

Socializing

When colleagues get together after hours, great store is set by *Gemütlichkeit*, a combination of camaraderie and having a good time. The ease with which it is indulged in varies between less inhibited southerners and more low-key northerners.

At the workplace colleagues will often lunch together, especially if there is a staff canteen. This is not usually an opportunity for networking or talking shop. Although staff restaurants are often single status, people will tend to keep the same company at the same table every day. A drink after work is common but not a regular end to the working day and rarely across ranks. Many large companies have a *Kasino*, or club, for senior managers.

Office parties are frequent but remain on a restrained, formal level. Birthdays are often celebrated with coffee and cakes or drinks in the office after hours. There is a constant chink of collection envelopes for birthday presents, which are formally presented and must always be greeted with surprise. The annual Christmas party is not an opportunity to show the real you underneath the business suit. People are on their best behavior. If someone were to get drunk or flirt outrageously it would not be forgotten. If things get lively at all it is at the very end of the evening when the bosses have left.

While Germans can be very hospitable toward business partners from abroad, and expect reciprocity, there is little mingling among colleagues out of hours and even less between ranks. Lunching with the boss usually takes place in the context of a business trip, fair, or similar occasion when the stiffness of formal invitations and the danger of favoritism can be avoided.

If German working life seems dull and over-regulated to people used to informality and confusion, there is circumstantial evidence that Germans share this opinion. They may apply themselves when they do work, but statistically they put in fewer hours than fellow Europeans. They are not fond of unpaid overtime, clock watch at the end of the day, and rush off home without lingering with colleagues. It is frequently difficult to contact colleagues on a Friday afternoon, especially in the south.

Carnival, *Fastnacht* or *Fasching*, gives an interesting glimpse of another side of the German character. It is associated mainly with Catholic areas and cities like Cologne and Mainz, but is celebrated to some degree in most areas of Germany, including Frankfurt. The jollity is not confined to leisure hours. People come to the office in funny costumes, poke fun at their bosses, and crack rude jokes. On women's day, the Thursday before Shrove Tuesday, men are advised to come to work with old ties as women will cut them off in symbolic revenge for the discrimination they suffer throughout the rest of the year. Colleagues eat and drink together and generally indulge in disorder, insubordination, and *Gemütlichkeit* until it is over and they go back to sobriety and formality for the rest of the year.

AID

Who gives most aid to developing countries per capita?

> Austria
> Luxembourg
> Denmark

Switzerland

What chance does a landlocked country have, much of it uninhabitable, with few natural resources, a population the size of London's, half Catholic and half Protestant, four languages, weak central government, and 26 virtually autonomous local governments? Answers on a postcard please from the most prosperous and socially cohesive country in Europe. Switzerland has the highest productivity, lowest unemployment, lowest inflation, most generous welfare benefits, highest per capita income, smallest gap between high and low earners, and least child poverty of any western country.

The population of Switzerland is about seven million, 65 percent of whom speak German, 20 percent French, and 10 percent Italian. They like to live in small communities. Only 380,000 people live in Zurich, 180,000 in Basel, and 170,000 in Geneva. Bern, the capital, is almost a village by the standards of neighboring countries, with 140,000 people. Around 20 percent of the population is non-Swiss. In some cantons such as Geneva, foreigners make up 30 percent of the population. In addition, many workers commute from nearby countries.

Unlike their neighbors, the Swiss do not feel the need for charismatic leadership. The government is headed by a Federal Council of seven ministers of equal status, except that the ceremonial presidency rotates among them annually. The real power is in the collective will of the electorate. They elect members to the parliament and then approve its legislation, international agreements, and treaties by popular referendum. They go to the polls almost once a month. The cantons themselves have their own constitutions, fiscal autonomy, and full administrative authority, including over justice.

Swiss citizenship is conferred not by the state but by the commune of residence. The communes, of which there are over 3,000, also enjoy a great deal of independence. The system depends on considerable civic responsibility and a high degree of toleration, consensus, and trust among religions, languages, localities, political parties, and cultures. What in many countries would be an unworkable system is driven not by rules and regulations but by a code of social and ethical values. Solid principles go hand in hand with pragmatism and an acute sense of self-interest. Until 2000, bribes to persons outside Switzerland were tax deductible.

Compared with the rest of Europe the country remained virtually unscathed by the wars of the twentieth century. For this its people have to thank astutely managed neutrality, a well-trained and armed militia ready to take to their mountain fastnesses, and the need of belligerents as well as their victims to keep their money somewhere safe. In times of peace too a combination of political neutrality, banking secrecy, stable currency, and low tax rates has created an attractive place for private investors and multinationals' treasury departments. Other attributes include a highly developed banking sector, a reliable legal system, and an efficient bureaucracy.

In every aspect of Swiss life there are contrasts of scale. The country is the headquarters of most of the word's international organizations, including its own Red Cross, and many multinationals, both Swiss and foreign owned. In banking, insurance, and industries such as pharmaceuticals, chemicals, high technology, and specialized engineering, it is a world leader. The equivalent of one-third of GDP is represented by exports and same amount by imports. At the same time, life in Switzerland feels intensely parochial. About 75 percent of the labor force work for small and medium-sized enterprises and live in small towns and villages. To the newspapers, foreign news is what happens in the next canton.

In the international arena Switzerland espouses free trade and international economic liberalism. Its domestic economic system is built on cartels, price fixing, restriction of competition, fragmentation of markets, subsidized farming, and all the other sins against economic orthodoxy that wise men in Washington and Chicago urge emerging economies to stamp out. The US Department of State commercial guide to Switzerland describes agricultural subsidies and toothless laws against cartels as "anomalies." From a Swiss point of view there is nothing anomalous about preserving the independence and livelihoods of its many small businesses and communities.

Most trades are protected by corporations or guilds, which restrict the number of people allowed to practice and set high, mandatory prices for their services. The corporations are canton based and so there are usually 26 different corporations for the same trade, each with its own price structure. Retail businesses operate on low turnover, high margins with markups of at least 100 percent, and consequently high prices. There are virtually no barriers to imports and consumers can easily drive over the borders to shop. Yet retailers stay in business and there are few hypermarkets and other discounters. Why? Service, quality, and the Swiss conviction that Swiss is best.

A conservative, traditional, and regulated environment is not a bar to creativity and innovation. In the days when you had to wind up your watch, the Swiss watch industry at the volume end of the market was in danger of being wiped out by Asian competition. The industry was reinvented and now Swatch is a market leader. There are many similar stories of traditional companies transforming themselves.

In recent years the political and economic integration of Europe has made neutrality less meaningful. Switzerland's main trading partners are in Europe and globalization has entailed the integration of markets and institutions. Although voters have rejected joining the European Economic Area and the European Union, Swiss policy is to make its trading environment as compatible as possible with that of the EU while maintaining political and economic independence. It has made bilateral agreements with the EU or unilateral arrangements to eliminate trade barriers, including provisions for the free movement of labor.

Switzerland is not a woman's world. The honor of being the last country in Europe to give women the vote goes to Liechtenstein in 1984, but the runner-up is Switzerland in 1971. At the same time, it used to be socially unacceptable and legally impossible for a woman to own and operate a business. While women are now legal and enfranchised persons, the intangible barriers remain and few hold high-level positions.

Not least of the barriers to women in business is the male bonding created by military service. After basic training, most men between 19 and 42 serve a minimum of three weeks every other year. Often the ranks reflect the status in business, so it would be rare to find someone more senior than his boss. The military experience is a significant model for business organization.

Communication

First encounters among Swiss are formal and the transition to first-name terms will be slow, if it happens at all. Adept at dealing with foreigners, they may make concessions to more informal manners. Nevertheless, the sharp distinction between business and private life remains.

Swiss prefer modesty and understatement, which may appear forbidding to those from more expressive cultures. Apparent reticence does not imply vagueness or indirectness. They will interpret lack of clarity as insincerity, although it does imply control of emotion. The preferred negotiating style is open and based on problem solving and consensus.

Among German speakers, and to a lesser extent among French and Italian speakers, not much space is given in a business environment to small talk. Business is serious and humor has little place in it.

Relationships

Foreigners who move to Switzerland looking forward to getting to know the local culture and mix with the natives may well be disappointed. The international community is necessarily self-contained. This is true at all levels of society, especially the highest.

In a business environment, relationships are slow to develop and are the result of satisfactory dealings rather than personal compatibility. Socializing, primarily over lunch, is not uncommon, but nor is it a necessary part of establishing a business relationship. Nevertheless, long-term business relationships are valued more than short-term deals.

Leadership

Power in German-Swiss companies combines a clear and respected hierarchy with shared decision making and consensus. Senior people continue to avoid overt assertiveness and are discreet in the exercise of power. French and Italian speaking companies may be more Latin in their leadership styles, but are still closer to Swiss than to foreign counterparts.

Conflict avoidance is as much part of business as social and political culture. Strategies for arriving at a shared decision without confrontation include private briefing and lobbying. Before a decision-making meeting, for example, those concerned with a particular outcome will talk to each of the others individually before a meeting. Swiss avoid open discussion if they have not prepared for an issue that might lead to disagreement.

They are naturally cooperative and work well in teams, preferably under an acknowledged leader. Everyone concerned is expected to contribute. While decision making is the responsibility of leaders, they make sure that everyone affected will accept it. Decision making is consequently time consuming.

Organization

Punctuality in business and social life is exact and strictly maintained: Exact means to the minute. A strong sense of order and self-discipline imbues organizational—and social—life.

If conflict avoidance is part of the leadership culture, uncertainty avoidance dominates organization. Clarity and efficiency based on meticulously designed systems and assigned responsibilities are the primary goals. Innovation requires substantial research and planning. Flexibility is not a strong value and improvisation is a sign of poor planning. An aversion to uncertainty and risk means that timely actions whose consequences have not been thoroughly worked out will be postponed.

Meetings will have detailed agendas and consequent action plans. People can be trusted to follow through their assigned tasks. Contracts and agreements are expected to be met to the letter.

> **JAILBIRDS**
> Which country has the greatest proportion of its population in prison?
> Russia
> UK
> Portugal

CENTRAL EUROPE

Czechia

Since it became fully independent in 1993, the Czech government's preferred name for its country has been Czechia. Why numerous organizations persist in calling it by its more inconvenient adjectival name (the Czech Republic), especially when they are happy to call the Slovak Republic Slovakia or the French Republic France, is a mystery.

The geographic and cultural boundaries of what is now Czechia have fluctuated with the fortunes of larger and more powerful neighbors. In 1918 Czechoslovakia was carved out of the Austro-Hungarian Empire, uniting the western Slavs of central Europe. The Czech and Slovak union was always uneasy. Czechs were oriented toward Germany, Prague was a German-speaking city, and it was the most industrialized of the central European countries. Although the majority was Roman Catholic, there was a sizeable and active Protestant community. Before independence Slovakia had been ruled from Budapest; it was predominantly rural and more fervently Roman Catholic. The state survived independently for 20 years before being invaded by Nazi Germany. In 1945 it became a Soviet satellite. The nadir of its fortunes under Communism was the crushing by its Warsaw Pact allies of the "Prague Spring" of 1968–69, a liberalization that threatened Soviet economic and political hegemony.

In 1989 Czechoslovakia achieved independence again in the "Velvet Revolution," surviving four years or so before splitting in 1993 in a "velvet divorce" between Czechs and Slovaks. Czechia was left with a population of 10 million, the more viable and productive part of industry, a major cultural and economic center in Prague, and a sense of superiority over its central European neighbors, especially Slovakia, which was left with heavy industry, including defense, no natural resources, and a population of 5 million. Unusually for central Europe, Czechia has virtually no ethnic or linguistic minorities.

Much of the international image of Czechia as forward looking, independent, and somehow more "western" than other central European countries is due to the pivotal position of Prague in European literature, from Kafka to its brave and charismatic leader, Vaclav Havel. To those to whom European literature is a closed library, Prague is better known as one of the most popular "city break" destinations in Europe.

In the first decades of the twentieth century Czechoslovakia ranked among European leaders in political maturity, cultural sophistication, and industrial development. Its economy was based on processing industries and engineering, which exploited coal and lignite, metals, and other raw materials, and on a strategically useful position at the heart of Europe. All these advantages unfortunately made it a tempting target for the imperial ambitions of western and then eastern neighbors. Under Russian rule it concentrated on heavy industry, to the detriment of its strengths in specialized manufacturing.

After independence Czechia embarked with vigor on a program of privatization, industrial restructuring, and capital market reform. Industries such as light aircraft and automobiles compete successfully in world markets. It is now into the second consolidatory phase of capital market regulation, separation of bank and corporate ownership, bank privatization, and bankruptcy legislation.

Over 60 percent of foreign trade is with Germany and Germans account for 30 percent of annual foreign investment. Historical and linguistic ties combined with rapid westernization make it a useful base of operations for western development of other central European markets. It has a growing consumer market, competitive wage rates, and a relatively well-trained labor force.

Communication

The main difference between the Czech and Slovak languages is in the minds of those who wish to distinguish them for political reasons. For those who have neither, English will get you a long way with a younger generation and German with the rest. As with other central Europeans, children strove to be bottom of the class in Russian during the socialist era. Only those who do business with Russia admit to speaking it.

Humor should be used with discretion. While joviality goes with the introductory glasses of *slivovic*, a serious demeanor is reserved for serious discussion. Apart from the ever-present risk of its not being understood, humor can be seen as unprofessional.

Czechs are not typically open and plain spoken. Old-fashioned politeness can sometimes be mistaken for distance or even deviousness. More importantly, experience of totalitarianism over several generations leads them to conceal their true feelings from those whom they do not completely trust. Generations of survival as a vassal state of foreign powers, from the Habsburgs to the Soviets, have created a manner of dealing with foreigners that is outwardly congenial but inwardly defensive. If Czechs are not actively trying to get the better of foreigners, they are still careful to stop foreigners getting the better of them. In a more positive sense, they are confident about their own abilities and the superiority of the Czech way of doing things.

Leadership and organization

Team-based, participative management is a foreign import that comes with American business school theory and multinational company management training courses. As in other Slav business cultures, authority, accountability, and decision making are predominantly on a vertical axis. People at all levels are more competitive than collaborative. Managers nurture their status, discourage initiative, and keep a formal distance from their subordinates. Those with strong personalities and who are not afraid to exercise their power and authority are respected. Delegation and decentralization are alien to the core business culture. Authority is rarely questioned, even on trivial matters, and upward feedback is seen as threatening.

Formal hierarchy is very respected. Titles and last names are always used in business, and business cards religiously list all titles and qualifications. Meetings are for the manager to disseminate exhortations and instructions, not for sharing issues or decisions. There may be an agenda, but rarely is there an action plan. Meaningful interactions between manager and subordinate are on a one-to-one basis.

There is a reluctance to take responsibility: It is passed up the line to whomever feels secure enough to accept it, usually someone at the top. Self-motivation or initiative in a corporate environment is not a strong value. Your job description lists your duties and it rare to step outside them. It is not usual for people to keep to commitments, action plans, and deadlines without being reminded and cajoled. These attitudes are changing among a younger generation in the newer industries, however. They are prepared to work longer hours and demonstrate personal commitment.

On a corporate level, Czechs are uncomfortable with equal partnerships and look for a relationship, or try to create one, in which one side dominates.

They share with their German neighbors what is known in cross-cultural jargon as "uncertainty avoidance." Thorough analysis and debate precede decisions hedged about with provisos and fallback positions. Once made, a cautious decision will be implemented with equal thoroughness and tenacity. Flexibility and improvisation are to be avoided in preference to sticking to the procedures. Negotiated agreements are typically followed in detail. Requests for amendment or renegotiation may be seen not as a change in circumstance but as a breach of trust.

Foreign partners and investors should be reconciled to spending more time and effort than they are used to in to closing a deal or implementing the terms of a contract. As in most, if not all, of the recently independent central European countries, bribes and kickbacks are a not uncommon feature of doing business. They are commonly made to local politicians or bureaucrats for permits and authorizations, and many of their traditional western European counterparts are happy to oblige.

It is necessary to cultivate good personal relationships based on trust and experience. In an environment where commercial law and good business practice are still under development, one has to be sure of the person with whom one is dealing. Moreover, business people in all the countries that have recently converted to capitalism have been victims of the dreams and promises of well-meaning—and sometimes not so well-meaning—westerners, from international economic advisers to carpetbaggers. They have learned to take their time before making firm commitments. Personal relationships create obligations in business life that in more impersonal cultures would be considered nepotistic.

Hospitality and socializing are an important element in building these relationships and invitations should not be turned down. For one thing, matters that in some cultures are dealt with at the office are often discussed and decided at the restaurant.

DOG LOVERS
Which country has the most dogs per head of population?
> UK
> Poland
> Malta

Hungary

Ethnic Hungarians call themselves and their language Magyar and claim descent from the Asiatic people who settled around the Danube 2,000 years ago. Neither they nor their language are Slavic; 97 percent of the population of 10 million is Magyar. The rest are German, Slovak, Croat, Serb, and Romanian minorities, with a substantial Gypsy community. Three million Hungarians live as minorities in Romania, Slovakia, Ukraine, and former Yugoslavia. The flat, landlocked country is largely rural. While 2 million people live in Budapest, the next largest city, Debrencen, has a population of only 200,000.

The cheerful pessimism of Hungarians is associated with a tragic view of their history. The nineteenth century saw them struggling to break free from the Habsburg Empire. In 1867 they partially achieved this in the dual monarchy of the Austro-Hungarian Empire—the Emperor of Austria was also the King of Hungary. Austria controlled Hungarian external affairs, leaving it with substantial domestic autonomy.

The beginning of the twentieth century saw the dismemberment of the Habsburg Empire at the end of the First World War and with it the partition of Hungary, leaving substantial Hungarian minorities among their Slav neighbors. Hungary lost what was Upper Hungary, now Slovakia, to Czechoslovakia; Transylvania to Romania; and Croatia and Voyvodna, now part of Bosnia, to Yugoslavia. After a brief flirtation with communism in the Soviet Republic of Hungary, a nationalist right-wing regime, with aspirations to recover its lost territory and populations, ruled Hungary until its absorption into the Soviet sphere of influence after the Second Word War.

Hungary was an uneasy partner in socialism. The failure of the brave 1956 uprising was followed by more subtle forms of resistance. In 1968 it was the first Comecon (an association of communist states for economic cooperation) country to allow decentralization of the economy. As a result, its transition to a free-market economy has been among the fastest and smoothest of its neighbors.

Within five years of the collapse of communism over half of the economy was within the private sector. All small businesses are now in private hands, as are most of the larger former state-owned companies. The currency was pegged to the Deutschmark and the dollar. In 1994 the banking system was privatized and foreign-owned banks began to be established. Commercial and intellectual property laws have been reformed and adapted.

There is still work to do in the reform of public finance and the social security system, however. Corruption, while still a common problem where property development or official permissions is concerned, has been vigorously tackled.

As a result, Hungary has attracted half of all foreign direct investment into the former socialist countries, a third of which is from the US. Almost as much has been invested by Germans. Political stability has contributed significantly to its success. Power has changed hands several times without disruption of the fundamental policies of transformation.

Hungary is poor in natural resources other than bauxite and some natural gas. It relies especially heavily on foreign trade, which accounts for half of its GDP. Over 70 percent of exports are to EU countries, primarily Germany, Austria, and Italy. The river Danube is Hungary's main transport route. Since the opening of a canal linking the Danube to the Main in 1992, goods can be carried from the Black Sea to the North Sea.

Communication

The Hungarian language belongs to the Finno-Ugric group of languages, as do Finnish and Estonian, although they are mutually incomprehensible. It is a famously difficult language and apart from a few words of politeness, Hungarians do not expect foreigners to speak it. Despite the country's central position in Europe only a well-educated élite speak foreign languages. Older people may speak German, while those in their twenties are better versed in English.

The complicated syntax and grammar of Hungarian reveal thought processes different from European ways of expression. Clarity and brevity are not usually associated with Hungarians, even when they speak an international language. Politeness and circumlocution often conceal what is really meant. Humor can be used in business circumstances and is expected at informal occasions.

Hungarians address each other, and print their business cards, with the family name first, followed by their given names. Bartók Béla is how the Hungarian composer is known, for example. Titles, including professional and academic titles, are used extensively. In Hungarian the ordinary title comes after the name; if you hear *ur* and *kisasszony* they are not common Hungarian family names but Mr. and Miss. Married women have to put up with the suffix *–ne* on their husband's name and there is no equivalent to Ms. When a man greets a woman he waits for her to put out her hand first and then pretends to kiss it or, if not, says that he will. First-name terms are used at initial acquaintance only by an Americanized generation.

Hungarians never clink beer glasses when toasting, a custom dating back to the uprising of 1867 when Habsburg officers at an execution of Hungarian patriots did so at each volley of the firing squad.

Organization

In the past good personal relationships were an essential basis for a business relationship and personal relationships created obligations in business life. Among a younger, self-styled professional generation they are seen as less important, but remain far more significant than in northern Europe, for example. They are established and maintained with frequent and lavish hospitality and socializing, for which it is a challenge to pick up the bill if you are not Hungarian. Business discussions and decisions often occur in informal venues like a restaurant, but rarely in the evening. While pleasure overlaps with business, business is usually not allowed to intrude on pleasure.

Communism reinforced a strong sense of hierarchy that survives in all but the most advanced companies. Hungarians are adept at creating systems and procedures and even more adept at working outside them. A talent for improvisation and cutting corners, a necessary skill in the bureaucracy of the communist era, is seen as equally useful in a fast-changing and fluid business environment. They are motivated by getting the job done without undue concern for the process. They usually keep commitments and promises without being reminded and respect punctuality.

Leadership

Colleagues are naturally competitive and usually need strong leadership to work well in teams. Managers are expected to demonstrate charisma as well as competence. They keep a distance from the people they manage and it is anticipated that they will take all the responsibility for decisions. Meetings are controlled and dominated by the senior person present. Those managed are not expected to contribute more than information if it is requested. Consensus-oriented or participative management is an innovation that can be effective but sometimes requires patience to implement.

Education and the influence of multinationals is introducing a more western, that is to say American, way of doing things.

> **MEN OF WAR**
> Who has the largest standing army in Europe, after Russia?
> Turkey
> Poland
> France

Poland

The history of Poland is a saga of heroism, catastrophe, and renewal. At various times its neighbors have attempted to remove it altogether from the map of Europe. In 1795 they succeeded for a time when the country was partitioned between the Prussian Duchy of Poznan, the Russian Duchy of Warsaw, and the Austrian Galicia. In the turmoil of nineteenth-century Europe Polish language, religion, and culture were oppressed with varying degrees of brutality. In more recent times Nazi Germany tried to eliminate population as well as territory: 6 million Poles died in the Holocaust, half of whom were Jewish. In its periodic struggles for survival Poland has pinned its hopes on western allies from Napoleon to Churchill, and has always been let down. It now looks to NATO and the European Union.

Between the two world wars Poland enjoyed 18 years of independence from Russia, for five years of which it experimented with democracy. Led by the Solidarity movement, an alliance of trade unions and emergent political parties, in 1989 it became the first of the socialist countries of eastern Europe to re-establish independence. In 1990 Lech Walesa, leader of Solidarity, was sworn in as president. It was a sign of the maturity of Poland's democracy—albeit a nostalgic one for many Poles—that in the presidential election of 2000 Walesa gained only 1 percent of the vote and in the general election of the following year Solidarity did not get enough votes to be represented in parliament.

Under Stalin the territory of Poland was shifted westwards. Most of the former Prussian areas were recovered and substantial parts of the east were surrendered to Belarus, Lithuania, and Ukraine. Poland regained control of important cities such as Danzig, now Gdansk, and lost others long regarded as Polish, such as the great cultural centers of Vilnius and Lwow. German populations were sent back to Germany and Poles who did not become Soviet citizens removed. The result is a current population of about 39 million, almost all Polish speaking and Roman Catholic.

Ever since the partition of 1795 and the subsequent revolts and repressions, many Poles have found themselves involuntary residents of other countries or have actively chosen to emigrate. Over 6 million live in North America and there are more in Chicago than in Poland's second city Lodz. There are 2.5 million Poles in Russia and a million in France.

Despite the displacement, destruction, and reconstruction of more recent years, Poland has distinct regional cultures that reflect those of the occupying powers during the partitions of the nineteenth century. The west of the country and its main city Poznan are considered by the others to have a Germanic sense of order and a head for business, while lacking in imagination. Krakow and the Austrian south see themselves as more relaxed, less materialistic, and the cultural and intellectual heart of the country. Warsaw and the east were Russian and are viewed by the others as more disorganized, more unpredictable, and more self-important.

With a population of 39 million, Poland is the largest of the former socialist countries. It is also one of the most successful transition economies. The private sector is now responsible for 65 percent of GDP and provides jobs for 70 percent of the country's labor force. Small and medium-sized enterprises account for 99 percent of firms, employing 60 percent of the work force. A large and dynamic private sector and sound fiscal and monetary policies have produced one of the fastest-growing economies in Europe since 1994. Poland has overtaken Hungary as the leader in central Europe for foreign investment. The primary investor is Germany, followed by the US.

Agriculture is a different story. Poland is a rural economy with almost a quarter of the population still living on small, inefficient farms. The population of Warsaw is less than 2 million and that of Lodz less than 1 million.

Poles are proud of their achievements over the past ten years and are sensitive over the shortcomings that remain. Nevertheless, it has to be said that the economic infrastructure is undeveloped by western European standards. Transport and distribution, for example, appear chaotic. An inadequate and expensive telephone system means that internet penetration is only 15 percent. Legal and taxation systems are in development. There is an underlying sense of insecurity and self-invention in the business community as it pushes forward the transition to a fully fledged market economy. While income tax for 98 percent of the population is 19 percent, the social security tax (ZUS) deducts another 20 percent from gross salary. This is one reason for a vibrant shadow economy, estimated at around 20 percent of the official economy.

Frustration with the time it is taking to achieve full EU membership is a popular resentment cultivated by politicians. The main issue is movement of labor, with EU countries nervous of an influx of economic migrants and the impact of the large and inefficient Polish farming sector on the Common Agricultural policy. EU countries will have to decide whether to pay people to stay on the farm or live in their cities.

Communication

First meetings are likely to be formal. Among Poles it is customary to use a language mode even more formal than the French *vous* or the German *Sie*. The polite mode of address (*Pan* for men, *Pani* for women) on its own, with the last name or with a job title (*Pan Direktor*, for example) is employed. While Poles will accommodate to international, that is American, norms, they are nevertheless more comfortable with formality in initial encounters. Conventions of punctuality fall within the ten-minute limit.

Poles are fond of rhetoric and are not comfortable with open and direct communication, especially in a problematic situation or when a negative decision is called for. They prefer to postpone rather than resolve confrontation or embarrassment. They tend to suspect each other, and by extension foreigners, of ulterior motives, hidden agendas, and conspiracy.

Oral communication is more important than in most northern European countries. With their experience of previous times—of inefficiency as much as eavesdropping—older people mistrust telephone and other electronic communication and prefer to meet face to face. However, written agreements are carefully drafted and meticulously followed.

Overt humor is used only in informal circumstances. Nevertheless, in most encounters there is a constant undercurrent of irony and skepticism.

As in other postsocialist countries a networks of contacts (*siec*) is important. Among business people they are usually created out of university friendships. Former communist party colleagues are the backbone of the political class. However, close personal relationships are not necessary to begin a business relationship. Cold calling without personal introduction is acceptable and can be productive.

Socializing is not essential to developing good business relationships. While the western business lunch or breakfast is gaining ground, more in Warsaw than in the other cities, the customary Polish timetable is not amenable to such entertaining. Typically one starts with a first breakfast before beginning work between 7am and 8am, tops up with a second breakfast at mid-morning, and goes home at the end of the working day for the main meal at around 5. At the more senior levels it is nevertheless not unknown for deals to be done in individuals' homes or restaurants.

Traditional Polish organizational culture is not team based. Leadership is centralized upwards through a carefully cultivated hierarchy to the boss, usually *Pan Direktor* although women are beginning slowly to erode male domination. Taking initiatives and making critical or creative contributions is rarely seen as part of the subordinate's role. At meetings or other gatherings the senior person is expected to dominate.

Deadlines, action plans, and other commitments usually need frequent reminders and reinforcements if they are to be adhered to. Poles have a natural resistance to being constrained by systems and are bored by steady routine. The positive aspect of independent-mindedness is that insights and ideas can flourish if properly encouraged and channeled. They have learned to respond positively to volatile circumstances and are not disconcerted by unexpected change.

The influence of foreign multinationals on business culture is constantly increasing. The American style of management is seen as liberating. The strong

sense of self that preserved a distinct identity over centuries of foreign domination
and oppression also inures Poles against
any western influences that are not in their
evident self-interest.

JEWS

Which country has the largest Jewish community?

Czechia

Italy

France

Slovakia

Czechoslovakia was created in 1918 after the dismemberment of the Austro-Hungarian Empire. Slovaks had been ruled from Budapest while Czechs had been traditionally oriented toward Germany and Austria. Slovakia was agricultural, fervently Roman Catholic, and regarded as provincial by the sophisticates of Prague. They shared the brief and eventful decades of independence before the invasion of Nazi Germany and subsequent liberation by the Red Army. Slovakia shared in the "Prague Spring" of 1968–69, a liberalization that threatened Soviet economic and political hegemony and was crushed by the Warsaw Pact allies.

In 1993 Slovakia became an independent state after a "velvet divorce" from Czechia. This might have been peaceful, but for most of the population of Slovakia at least it was unwanted and attributed to the machinations of a minority of nationalist politicians on both sides.

The population of Slovakia is 5.5 million. Half a million live in Bratislava and Kosice is the second city, with 250,000 inhabitants. The other towns have fewer than 100,000. Around 10 percent of the population are Hungarians, who live mainly in the south and strive for greater educational and cultural autonomy. Another half a million or so—no one is quite sure—are Gypsies. There is considerable prejudice against them by people at all levels of society. Despite the association agreement, several EU countries have introduced visa requirements for Slovaks due to an increase in the number of Gypsies seeking asylum.

The general opinion outside the country, as well as among many of the citizens inside, was that Slovakia was doomed to failure. Insolvency was forecast within days, then months. The basic infrastructure was inadequate, the economy was based on outdated heavy industry and defense, and the Czechs had walked away with the light industry and service sectors of the former state.

Under the new government led by the populist Vladimir Meciar, there was growing international criticism of Slovakia's lack of respect for minority rights and general abuse of the democratic process. Slovakia chose gradual transition to a market economy instead of the "big bang" favored by Czechia. It retained strategic industry, particularly armaments, under state control. In 1998 Meciar's government was replaced by a coalition that introduced reform and austerity packages. The currency is now relatively stable, inflation was reduced, the economy is showing steady growth, and Slovakia has been accepted as an applicant for the second wave of EU membership extension.

After the Prague Spring, Slovakia became heavily industrialized under Soviet advice and influence. Some of these industries survive with state help, although half of the country's industrial production is now in private hands. About 80 percent of Slovakia's GDP is in the private sector, including one of the highest rates of privatization in the region. Small-scale privatization is complete. A motivated and western-oriented generation of professionals and entrepreneurs is transforming the business sector. Nevertheless, indirect state involvement in the private economy remains significant. Subsidies and postponement of social security obligations keep many traditional industries afloat. Employers and employees pay a combined payroll deduction of 50 percent of wages to support the pension, unemployment, and health funds.

There are still some structural challenges. There is scope for more privatization of large state-owned utilities; the privatization that has occurred was deliberately slow and clouded in an obscurity favorable to senior managers and former party bosses. Traditional industry is traditionally managed. Some large companies and industries are in need of radical reorganization, and unemployment, at well into double digits, is at an unacceptable level. The banking and financial sector requires substantial overhaul. Corruption is rife. In April 2001 the EU suspended aid payments to Slovakia because of concerns over the possible misuse of funds.

Czechia has a large share of Slovak trade due to historical ties and a customs union between the two countries. German and Austrian companies are close and have long experience in the Slovak market. Germany and Austria, followed at a distance by the US, are the leading foreign investors. The policy of the Meciar government to discourage foreign ownership of Slovak companies and to keep them away from the privatization process, coupled with the unreformed and corrupt business environment, has kept cumulative per capita foreign investment to less than 20 percent of that in Czechia.

Communication

Slovak is a Slav language closely related to Czech. That is the politically correct description—actually they are the same except for a handful of deliberately cultivated differences in vocabulary. Among the younger generation English is the preferred second business language, especially in Bratislava. Elsewhere and among older people German is still useful. Those who know Russian will find it helpful in understanding Slovak, although as a *lingua franca* it is out of favor.

It is essential to develop good personal relationships before expecting to get down to business. The Slovak business community is small and everyone knows each other. This does not prevent—some might say it encourages—determined rivalry between factions, cartels, and interest groups, however. It is a good idea before you do business to get to know who you are doing it with and how they operate.

Interaction is usually informal and on a first-name basis, especially if the conversation is in English. People are not usually plain spoken and direct but prefer to keep frankness for those they know well in an informal setting. They look for good humor rather than a sense of humor.

Oral communication is more important than written, phone calls and meetings more efficient than faxes and emails. However, the tradition of the protocol, written minutes of discussions signed by those present, is still common and is a useful way of making sure that there are no misunderstandings.

Leadership and organization

Leadership follows the Slav model, with responsibility, accountability, and power concentrated at the top. Decision making is restricted to a very few, if not only one person. Even relatively minor decisions may require the approval of a senior manager. Slovaks are uncomfortable in equal partnerships, either personal or corporate.

They are not natural team players. If they exist at all, teams need a strong leader and clear delegation of tasks. Consensus is not necessary. Meetings will tend to be dominated by the senior person present. Managers keep a distance from their subordinates.

While organizational structures may be overly bureaucratic, organization itself is based on personal relationships and mutual obligation and trust. Hospitality and socializing are an important part of building the relationships necessary to do business, starting at the first meeting of the day with *slivovica* (plum brandy) or *borovicka* (similar to schnapps). Northern Europeans are well advised to dedicate more time and effort to these relationships than they are used to.

People will follow commitments and stick to deadlines without being reminded. Efficiency is valued. People are generally punctual and meetings are normally systematic, with an agenda that is kept to and an action plan at the end.

NUDISTS

Where is the longest nudist beach in Europe?

Ireland

Netherlands

Romania

Slovenia

Although it was part of the Habsburg Empire and subsequently of Yugoslavia, Slovenia kept intact its unique language and cultural cohesiveness with a minimum of concessions to the dominant power.

During the communist era, Slovenia was Yugoslavia's most prosperous republic. It led the development of that country's unique mixed economic system. With one-twelfth of Yugoslavia's population, Slovenia produced one-sixth of its output and nearly one-quarter of its exports. After Yugoslav president Tito's death in 1980, Slovenia embraced democracy and the liberalization of its society and economy to a degree unprecedented in the communist world.

In 1989, the General Assembly asserted Slovenia's right to secede from Yugoslavia and in the following year 88 percent of the population voted for independence, which was declared by the Republic of Slovenia on June 25, 1990. Confrontation with Yugoslavia was brief and its army withdrew peacefully after ten days. Relations with Belgrade remain strained, particularly concerning the liabilities and assets of the former Yugoslavia.

The population is two million, of whom nearly 90 percent are ethnic Slovenes and predominantly Roman Catholic. Indigenous Hungarian and Italian minorities are represented in parliament. So-called right- and left-wing political groupings essentially derive from the former communist officials of the old days and the social-democrat independence movement. However, Slovenia is a small country and the real issues are less to do with policies than with personalities and economic interest groups.

Slovenia was the most productive of the Yugoslav republics and today is the most prosperous of the EU accession countries. While it was already further down the road to market capitalism than other socialist countries, many of its institutions needed substantial reform on independence. Foremost among these was fulfilling the requirements for EU membership and completing privatization. The legislative effort that this represented tested the political will of Slovenia's leadership to take on the vested interests that hindered reforms. These included especially changes in the financial sector, competition policy, and public procurement. The banking sector in Slovenia remains fairly rudimentary and lacking in innovation. Until the country adopts financial services legislation as part of its EU membership bid, the sector will continue to lack the dynamism necessary for larger-scale domestic funding of operations.

Other reforms concerned legislation and standards in commercial law, intellectual property, and foreign investment. The slow resolution of postwar expropriation claims tested the effectiveness of the legal system and also complicated the property acquisitions necessary for business expansion. Unusually for a transition economy, petty corruption is rare. Reasonable public-sector salaries are the main reason, along with the relative efficiency and transparency of bureaucracy.

Slovenian firms have responded to economic liberalization and ensuing European competition by specializing in mid- to high-tech manufacturing and reorienting trade from former Yugoslavia to western Europe. Germany, Italy, France, and Austria are the main trading partners. Even in socialist times Slovenian enterprises were relatively market oriented, and they have needed to adapt less than their equivalents in many other central European countries.

The former Yugoslav economic system was based on "self-management," in which management decisions were made at the enterprise level in response to market conditions. Firms were "socially owned," that is all employees and managers participated in control and overall management. In the course of privatization after independence, social ownership was converted to share ownership and worker management continued. In many cases companies have not been able to take adequate steps to respond to freer market conditions, for example in cost reduction or automation, and have been left behind by new or foreign-owned companies managed in a more conventional western manner. New family-owned companies led by dynamic entrepreneurs and without employee participation have become the fastest-growing type of enterprise.

There are more opportunities for women in prosperous and Catholic Slovenia than in the Orthodox and Muslim elements of the former Yugoslavia. They represent half of the labor force but less than a third of all managers, usually at lower grades than men.

Communication

Slovenian is a distinct Slavonic language written in the Roman script, although most people speak one or more of Serbian, Croatian, German, Italian, and English.

Unless they make concessions to Anglo-Saxon manners, people will stay on last-name terms or first names with the title. While neither would acknowledge any influence, etiquette in this respect is similar to Austrian.

Slovenes are typically cautious in revealing their true thoughts and feelings, which they cloak in geniality and politeness. Use of humor is sparing and subtle. As a general rule they will pay more attention to what is said than what is written.

Personal relationships

Slovenia is a small, closed society that depends on personal contacts and influence. Family ties, educational background, and home region create obligations—and rivalries—that are carried into the business arena. Faced with closer involvement with the west, this small and cohesive community has the challenge of being open while preserving its identity and core interests. Slovenes will cooperate as far as necessary, but outsiders will find it hard to penetrate the defenses of their self-interest. While it is difficult to break into the inner circles, it is an outwardly informal business environment in which socializing and hospitality are important to cultivate the required personal relations. Major agreements and decisions are as likely to be made in the restaurant as at the office.

Leadership

Slovenes work well in teams under a strong leader who takes responsibility for decision making and is clear about implementation. Bosses do not demonstrate that they are part of the team but keep a dignified distance. The Yugoslav model of decentralized worker-managed companies failed to create a participative and consensus-based management style. Decision making is focused on senior management and delegation of authority is poor.

Formal meetings are not an important part of the decision-making process. They are usually for information gathering or general discussion. If there is an agenda it may not be adhered to. A definitive result or action plan is not expected and followup is not always assured.

LIBRARIES
Where is the biggest state library in Europe (by number of books)?
        Moscow
        Paris
        London

LATIN COUNTRIES

France

France is Europe's largest country after Russia. It borders on six countries and has coastlines on the Mediterranean, Atlantic, and the Channel. With close on 60 million inhabitants, the population density is one of the lowest in Europe. The geography, climate, history, and culture are extremely varied, embracing regions as different as Brittany, Alsace, Provence, and the Basque country.

There is a strong attachment to one's home region and a reluctance to transfer between regions, the exception being a move to Paris. Even if people have worked all their lives in Paris, they will often consider themselves Parisian only if they were born there. True Parisians regard a transfer to the provinces as exile.

The north was originally populated by people of Germanic origin, with a system of customary law and speaking *langue d'oïl*. The south was populated by Mediterraneans, with a codified Roman law system and speaking a different language, *langue d'oc*. (*Oïl* and *oc* mean "yes." *Langue d'oïl* is the precursor of modern French, *oïl* becoming *oui*.) The boundary between the two civilizations runs very roughly from Bordeaux to Macon.

The north–south divide is complicated by differences between east and west. Western France from Brittany to Aquitaine has a strong Atlantic tradition that it shares with Britain and Scandinavia. Geographically, it is characterized by ports and long, navigable rivers, economically by maritime trade. It was primarily the west that supplied the sailors, merchants, and colonizers of North America. In contrast, eastern France belongs to continental Europe. It has strong historical and economic links with Germany, Switzerland, and Italy. This is the industrial heartland of France, based on coal and mineral deposits and the Rhine.

Some observers have added yet another dimension to the diversity of France, this one based on a central core surrounded by an outer ring. With its many borders and seaports, the outer ring has a mercantile, liberal, innovative, and outward-looking culture susceptible to external influence and change. Meanwhile, the inner core is rural, isolated, agricultural, protectionist, and traditional.

France is anything but a monolithic society, although it may appear so from Paris. In 1850 one in five French people could not speak French. A hundred years ago most French people spoke their own language or dialect in addition to standard French; many still do. French identity is based on territory and citizenship rather than ethnicity. It is a pluralist collection of economic, regional, and political interest groups that coexist in a sometimes uneasy truce. These differences are said to illuminate contradictory strains in French mentality and behavior. Newcomers should not assume that everyone conforms to a Parisian stereotype.

Centralism

If the cultural response to size and diversity is insistence on the universality and immutability of standard French, the political response is centralization. It derives not from the predominance of one powerful region suppressing the others—England, Prussia, Castile—but from the creation of an idea of statehood that transcends and absorbs regionalism and excludes any concept based on federalism or devolution. It is instilled from an early age in the education system that not only teaches but incorporates centralization into a national curriculum and examination system.

The chicken-and-egg question of whether centralization derives from a French mentality or vice versa can be endlessly debated. Nevertheless, it permeates French attitudes to all organizations, including economic ones. Centralized, ordered, legalistic, élitist, the political structure is a model for business corporations. Vertical administration, clear-cut divisions, ordered hierarchies, and central planning are features of companies as well as the state.

The basis of political centralism is a rigidly codified legal system, the *Code Napoléon*, established when rationalism was at its height. This is a monument to the belief that human reason can overcome the unpredictability of human behavior. A battery of regulations make up an ordered framework of existence imposed from above. It is an intellectual, artificial, regulated set of rules drawn up to anticipate every possible contingency. If there is a gap between principle and reality, it is filled not with improvisation but with ever more refined orders and regulations.

However, the real world does not follow regulations. The antidote is what the French term *Système D* ("D" standing for *débrouillard*, the art of overcoming obstacles, or beating the system). French ingenuity in creating formal systems is matched by ingenuity in evading them. This is a principle that applies equally well to the business environment.

Role of government

France has been a unified state with centralized political, educational, and economic systems for 200 years, one of the more durable in Europe. To be French is to adhere to a much stronger and homogenous set of values than is the case in countries in which a strong regionalism and a more recent national unity dilute a sense of national identity. There is a high degree of identification with the state. Concorde and the Channel Tunnel were more than commercial projects, becoming embodiments of national pride.

The government responds with political, economic, and social nationalism. Protectionism of industry, reaching down to small-scale industrial and agricultural enterprise, is a plank of economic policy. Direct and indirect intervention in industry is common. In many sectors the division between public and private sectors is blurred. Business expects government intervention in times of domestic crisis or to help ward off foreign incursion. Such intervention, unlike say in the UK where it is reactive and forced by circumstance, is centrally planned and administered. While privatization has returned some of the country's biggest companies to the private sector, the state retains major holdings in transport and communications. The state still spends more than half of GDP and employs a quarter of the workforce.

Although individuals are generally preoccupied with outwitting the government, especially in matters of taxation, the attitude of business is based on respect. Government may not always deliver what business asks for, but at least there will be a well-informed, reasoned answer that has the fundamental interest of business at heart. Civil servants are highly paid and enjoy social prestige. Government was traditionally regarded as politically motivated and manipulative but not dishonest. This view was severely shaken in 2002 by a corruption scandal involving the energy company Elf and senior politicians that allegedly touches President Chirac himself.

The links between government and business are personal as well as formal. Industry finds many of its leaders among the graduates of the *Grandes Ecoles*, which also supply the élite corps of civil servants. It is common to transfer back and forth between the two, the acquaintanceships thus formed being a vital ingredient of effectiveness in both spheres.

Foreign investment is closely controlled and monitored by the government. This has not prevented foreign multinationals from gaining control of about a fifth of French industry, concentrating on modern technologies. They own about 80 percent of the business machine industry, 70 percent of oil, and 60 percent of agricultural machinery. While some of these companies behave like natives, others have introduced predominantly American management systems and style.

State intervention and the attempt to create monolithic enterprises like Thomson or Bull has stifled not stimulated entrepreneurship. Despite its tradition of innovation, world-class research facilities, and a highly educated labor force, France has not produced a high-tech business sector to rival that of Germany or the UK. Small entrepreneurial companies, startups, and academic spinoffs are hampered by bureaucracy, social overheads, and one of the highest tax burdens in Europe.

Labor market

Only about a fifth of the workforce is unionized, the lowest proportion in Europe and lower than in the US. Unions are numerous and marked by a history of schisms, exclusions, and setting up new unions. The propensity for strikes in the public sector and large companies is more a product of competition between the unions and low membership than political activism.

The government's policies toward the labor market are conditioned by years of double-digit unemployment. Flexibility is not seen as an answer. French labor laws, for the most part assembled in a labor code, the *Code du Travail*, are extensive and comprehensive. The work contract, *contrat du travail*, is strictly regulated, as are the rules that protect employees in case of dismissal. The attitude to these and other formalities is one of compliance as long as they do not stand in the way of what management wishes to do.

If a company has more than 50 employees it is obliged by law to have a works committee, *comité d'entreprise*, chaired by the chief executive. Those with fewer than 50 employees often have one too. The number of employees elected to the committee ranges from three to fifteen in companies with over 10,000 employees. The role of the committee is not at the discretion of the chair but defined by law, and the chief executive is personally liable if he or she neglects to hold the monthly meeting. The formalities of the *comité d'entreprise* are rigorously adhered to and enforced. The annual financial statement, and any other financial information required by law, must be submitted to it and there is a legal requirement for the company to respond to any questions raised by it and to provide regular information on the general state of the company. It has a consultative role on personnel matters such as pay, benefits, working conditions, and terms of employment. The committee also operates staff social and welfare activities.

In small companies employee representatives on the committee (*délégués du personnel*) are elected by groups according to skill, seniority, or specialization. In larger companies they are nominated by their union and play a political rather than a corporate role. Their ostensible task is to relay complaints about conditions of work in regular meetings with the employer and the *comité d'entreprise* and to brief employees with information.

While the rules are rigidly adhered to and there is considerable value in an orderly mechanism for communicating information and complaint, up and down, the same comments apply to how it works in practice as to other apparently legalistic elements in the corporate structure.

Organization and structure

Limited liability companies can be either a stock company—*Société Anonyme* (SA)—or a private company—*Société à Responsabilitée Limitée* (SARL).The management of the *Société Anonyme* can take two forms:

❑   A board of directors comprised of elected shareholders (*conseil d'administra-tion*) whose chairman (*président*) is chosen by the board and has complete managerial responsibility. The board may appoint one or several managing directors (*directeur général*) to assist the chairman.

❑   A dual management system consisting of a supervisory board (*conseil de surveillance*) and a management board of two to seven executives (*directoire*). These executives are appointed by the supervisory board and manage the company under its control. The management board votes by majority.

A SARL is usually small, with a maximum of 50 shareholders who appoint one or several managers (*gérant*).

French institutions of whatever size are highly centralized. Beneath a powerful chief executive—*président directeur général* (PDG)—is a strict hierarchy of executives organized on functional lines with rigid chains of command. There are typically many more layers of middle management than in, say, a German or a Dutch company. All lines of communication and authority run vertically to the boss. Staff functions are there to advise the boss and not the line managers. Matrix management has had its day in most business cultures, but in France it hardly saw the dawn. Interdepartmental liaison is cumbersome and wherever possible flows through the center.

This means that when things go well they go very well indeed. The problem comes when things do not go well and a response to changing situations is needed. Traditional French authority structures are unresponsive to varying conditions. Problems tend to be pushed further up the line. Change in French organizations, as in French society, tends to be spasmodic and radical.

If corporate life were generally as formal as it appears on the surface, it would be far more rigid and stifling than it is in practice. Rules and procedures are rarely broken, but they are constantly distorted, manipulated, and ignored if they do not serve the purpose for which they are intended. A plea for a special case—*le cas par-ticulier*—is invariably acceded to. Beneath the apparent structure of the organization there is usually an invigorating subculture based on informal networking and characterized by flexibility, skepticism, and energy.

Le plan

Among capitalist countries France was the leading exponent of economic planning and did it better than any of the so-called centrally planned economies further east. Corporate strategic planning among companies is also far-reaching and detailed. The larger the company, the more elaborate it is and the longer the time horizon. Nuclear power, high-speed trains, and the electronics industry are typical of long-term strategic investments carried out over many years according to a rigorous plan unaffected by changes in government, the economy, and, some would say, external circumstances. This is one reason that French industrial policy sometimes seems out of phase with that of other countries.

Planning tends to be deductive. It is a question of an intuitive vision for the future rather than a prediction. The PDG decides on the direction in which he or she wants to go and hands the detail over to specialists who draw up the plan. An inductive process, where ideas and data are gathered by line managers who partic- ipate in planning, would be alien to the authority structure. The result is usually that managers do not own the plan and have no commitment to its implementation. Newcomers should find out what the plan is, but not be surprised if their colleagues are getting on without it.

Le patron

The PDG is expected to be a strong authority figure with a high degree of technical competence. In a recent survey of European managers, one of the questions was: "Is it important for a manager to have at his fingertips precise answers to most of the questions that subordinates raise about their work?" Of the French people sur- veyed, 60 percent said it was, the highest percentage along with Italians.

French PDGs show much more attention to detail than equivalents in other countries. Bosses naturally behave in a way that in other countries would be con- sidered dictatorial. It is difficult for them to admit that they are ignorant about something. Even in private, diplomacy is needed to change their opinion. Likewise, bosses will rarely open their mind, much less their heart, to subordinates or share problems with them. At the same time, subordinates will feel free to criticize and argue to a greater extent than in many other countries.

In dealing with subordinates it is better to err on the side of the directive as long as one's position is well founded and logical. This is sometimes misinterpreted by outsiders as a need for autocratic leadership. Along with logic in the French mental- ity goes a deep and healthy skepticism. They are happy to be led, but only in the right direction and for the right reasons. Respect for authority is based first and foremost on respect for competence. Strength of personality is rarely enough on its own.

Delegation

Job descriptions are usually a detailed list of tasks and reporting lines. Supervisors are expected to follow up and chase progress. In keeping with the nature of hierarchy, more emphasis is placed on supervision than on control systems.

The practice of regular performance appraisals is being introduced in France, but progress is slow. They are usually trait based—considering punctuality, reliability, and so on—rather than performance based. In an environment where performance is inextricably linked with the personal qualities of those doing the performing, appraisal implies personal criticism. Performance standards and targets are avoided as much as possible because they are potential weapons. Appraisal based on objective and collaborative target setting and feedback would require a considerable change in conventional working relationships.

A high degree of analysis, control, and technical knowledge of operations is required of line managers. They are expected to provide precise answers to questions, not approximations.

Teams

The concept of a team is a collection of specialists chosen for their competence in a given field under the command of an unequivocal leader. Professional relationships between colleagues are founded more on rivalry than collaboration. This begins in the highly competitive school environment, which is based on getting over a series of ever higher hurdles. Learning to collaborate to solve problems is not an educational goal.

In business, competitiveness is fostered by strong vertical hierarchies. Far from refreshing, people find it disconcerting when others do not compete. They will not wait for a group consensus before taking an initiative. To those from more participative cultures this can appear deliberately provocative. Foreigners used to a team approach will usually have to adjust their expectations of working relationships.

Meetings

Meetings called by the manager will follow an established format with a detailed agenda. Their purpose is for briefing and coordination rather than to be a forum for debate or decision making. People will come well prepared for the contribution they are expected to make and ready to fend off objections if they arise. Usually they will not expect to be seriously contradicted. In the public forum of a meeting, to question a proposal or an idea is to question the competence of the person who put it forward.

Getting together at a meeting to kick ideas around, floating a few trial balloons, or sorting a problem out together is not common. There is too much personal risk and too great an opportunity to unleash the competitiveness that characterizes relationships between colleagues. A carefully drafted report objectivizes ideas and reduces the chances of authors laying themselves open to attack.

If the input of others is needed, it is most likely to be secured with the individuals concerned before the meeting takes place. Interaction between them is through the medium of the boss, whose contribution will probably have been made before the meeting and given prior approval. If the boss calls proposals into question in public it is taken as a sign of displeasure. A meeting, and any other "public" occasion, is above all an opportunity for the boss to assert authority. Consensus is not a major objective. The primary purpose is clarification and assent.

Meetings may not be a spontaneous interchange, but they are less time consuming than in team-oriented cultures and what they propose and discuss tends to be better thought out. Spontaneity and creativity take place at the lower level of communication, in informal discussion between people who believe that they can trust each other.

Meetings where there is not an established senior figure as chairperson are less structured. Participants will feel free to leave the meeting, conduct side conversations, and interrupt. There is little of a collegiate atmosphere. Contributions are assertive to the point of being combative and phrased to beat back opposition. If a decision is to be taken and some of the relevant people are missing, it will be taken anyway and the others will be informed. However, the likelihood of their going along with it will be diminished.

Communication

As in most business cultures, writing memos, letters, and minutes is more often for self-defense than communication. However, studies and reports are a significant element in decision making. Oral presentations and discussions for disseminating information or gathering input for decisions are Anglo-Saxon innovations. Circulation of reports for individual study and comment is more important. For this reason, a high value is placed on reports being comprehensive, clear, well structured, well written, and well presented.

This is not to say that communication in France is invariably stiff and formal. It happens on two levels. On the surface business relationships are conducted in what is considered to be a proper, orderly, and professional way, uncluttered by personal relationships. This is what is meant by *sérieux*. But beneath this there is a complicated network of personal relationships, alliances, and factions through which things actually get done. Off-the-record, informal contacts are very important. The skill of bosses in engineering them with their subordinates, despite the hierarchical barriers in their way, makes a major contribution to effectiveness.

Upward mobility

At the summit of the educational system are the meritocratic *Grandes Ecoles*, which provide the civil service and industry with its élite. They are practical and scientific, and competition to get into them is very high. They provide not only an education but entry into a powerful and pervasive alumni network.

Considerable importance is attached to professional qualifications, not only at the recruiting stage. The most prized discipline is mathematics, in which French schools and universities excel. One senior French manager said that he would dearly like to employ more British mathematicians because they worked so well in teams, but they did not have the technical ability to hold their own. Whatever this says about the relative worth of British and French mathematics, it is certainly illuminating about his priorities.

There is a bias toward purely academic qualifications as opposed to apprenticeships or on-the-job training. Technical qualifications, for example engineering, carry the highest status, followed by law and finance. Sales and marketing used not to attract the intellectually gifted, but an increasing number of *Grandes Ecoles* and regional business schools are producing high-caliber marketing graduates. Accountants have a lower status than in Anglo-Saxon countries and the finance director might not be a board member.

Job hopping for experience or promotion is still unconventional. The predominant ethic is to remain with one company. This is reciprocated by a mixture of paternalism and the legal and administrative hurdles in the way of dismissing someone for anything other than gross misconduct.

There is a high degree of company loyalty. The company is a social unit in which each member has a well-defined part. While French people like to feel individualistic and self-reliant, they also need to feel part of a caring social unit. Family centered in private life, they are company centered in business life. The cliché, beloved of chief executives, that their staff are a family is more applicable in French than in Anglo-Saxon companies. Given the high proportion of family businesses, it may well also be factually true.

Promotion is usually on the basis of seniority tempered with educational qualifications and competence. In organizations based on vertical hierarchy and specialization, it is rare to be promoted to different departments unless you are obviously being groomed for the top. In a large company it is difficult to work your way to the top from the back office or the factory floor. These positions are usually reserved for family members or graduates from the *Grandes Ecoles*. It has been estimated that three-quarters of the senior managers of the 200 largest companies are the sons of wealthy families, compared to a quarter in Germany and a tenth in the US.

For outsiders the first requirement for acceptance is professionalism. New ideas and techniques are welcomed as long as they are well researched and logically argued and have conceptual rigor. Their implementation depends primarily on personal relationships. Respect for the messenger is as important as that for the message. It is unwise for outsiders to join in the internal politics of the organization, but they should make every effort to get to know their colleagues well, and be known by them, before instituting change or asserting authority.

Attitudes and behavior

"Intellectual" is not a term of abuse in France as it is in some other countries. French people enjoy abstract thought, theory, formulas, and a degree of logic and analysis that often seems impractical to pragmatic thinkers like the British or Dutch. Eclecticism is not an important element of mental discipline and there is a mistrust of pure pragmatism. One embarks from a central axiom and moves logically to a conclusion. The French have been accused of preferring clarity to truth, words to facts, and rhetoric to knowledge. They can be very stubborn and inflexible when confronted with the necessity for change unless they see an overall logic to it. They will tolerate impracticability more easily than inconsistency, an approach more suited to radical restructuring than gradual reform.

Despite a reputation for chauvinism, the French are not hide-bound by traditional ways of doing things. They are open to borrowing manners or style from anywhere as long as it is useful and, above all, elegant. They embrace novelty with enthusiasm, whatever its source. French homes and offices are full of gadgets. Interactive video telephones and high-speed trains cause excitement, not scandal.

Women

French women are increasingly represented in the management of retail and service industries and in areas such as law, finance, and personnel. There remains considerable bias against them in industry and outside Paris.

Etiquette

Etiquette among colleagues varies according to generation, gender, the business the company is in, and whether they are talking to Anglo-Saxons or have adopted an American style. Colleagues on about the same level tend to use first names in private but go back to last names in public or in front of the boss or at formal meetings. In more traditional companies last names are the rule all the time and for everyone. Among younger people the old formality is rapidly changing, however.

Dress codes are variable, reflecting status or the type of business, Paris or the provinces. Often the most formal wear is reserved for visits to head office, while out on the road or in a branch office style is more relaxed. Everybody shakes hands on meeting and parting, however well they know each other.

Language

The French love of elegance applies above all to language. National pride increases sensitivity to incorrect use of the language, but people also find it genuinely jarring to hear it being massacred. While this is a reason to learn to speak it well, it is not an excuse for not trying. It is more of a compliment to make an effort than an offense to speak it badly.

It may also be a necessity to speak French, however poorly. The French are almost as notoriously bad at languages as the British and Italians and for the same reason: They are badly taught in school. As far as English is concerned there has been a noticeable change of attitude in recent years. Soon French children will begin to learn English at the age of seven and the syllabus is being made more practical.

They are less tolerant when French is written badly—and there is less excuse for making mistakes. It is worthwhile persuading typists to overcome their inhibitions about contradicting *le patron* and making corrections. Even slight memos and notes are written in a mandarin style that in other countries is the preserve of senior civil servants. You will rarely find colloquially written memos and reports in the recorded speech style favored by Anglo-Saxons. This is partly a concern for professionalism and partly an emphasis on correct grammar and usage in school. To write correctly is a sign of education and breeding.

Punctuality

Punctuality depends on the social circumstances and the importance of the person to be kept waiting. About 15 minutes is the average slippage. The French will change their timetables at short notice if subsequent engagements are more important.

Humor

French people prefer wit to the belly laugh. They tend not to sit around swapping jokes. Their humor is more likely to be intelligent and satirical and at someone else's expense. The political jokes that are the forte of Latin and Slav humor are more common in the south.

At work, humor is rarely used on formal occasions or meetings. It is not usual for the PDG to warm up an audience with a couple of stories or sprinkle a presentation with jokes. If they do, these must be intelligent and dignified. Similarly at meetings, even relatively informal ones, humor is rarely used to make a point or release tension. It would be regarded as flippant. It is not that business or money are too serious to be made fun of; they are treated with a healthy disrespect, not to say cynicism, outside the office. But to do so at a business meeting is not *sérieux*. The personal remarks that pepper Anglo-Saxon conversations with colleagues, however friendly or amusing, are regarded as aggressive and rude and should be avoided.

Socializing

Lunch with a superior is rare and formal. Bosses do not socialize with their subordinates at work or after hours. Getting together over sandwiches in the boardroom or going out for a beer or a game of golf would be very unusual. Senior managers socialize with those of equivalent status in other companies.

The traditional two-hour lunch break to give people time to go home to eat with their families has been undermined by a commuter style of living imposed by bigger cities, industrial developments, and office parks. Even if you cannot get home, lunch is still regarded as "private time" and food as deserving the main attention. While a sandwich at the desk or a quick hamburger round the corner is becoming more common, lunch is usually for relaxing at length on one's own or with friends. The working lunch and even the fashionable working breakfast are now more widespread, but they are innovations and are more of an intrusion on personal life than they are, say, in Anglo-Saxon countries.

This applies also to home entertaining. Foreigners who are used to sharing meals with colleagues should not feel slighted if it does not often happen. The exception is in companies large enough to have staff restaurants, the more innovative being single status. These will be used by everybody except the most senior managers.

More paternalistic companies will also organize social events for the staff through the works committee. Christmas parties and presents for children, summer camp, or excursions abroad for workers are usually paid for or subsidized by the company. More senior managers may make a token appearance, but among themselves will keep their personal life separate from business relationships.

Office parties are rare and usually confined to celebrating transfers and promotions. Company loyalty is valued highly, so leaving parties are not normal and are paid for by the leaver, off the premises.

Personal relationships are regarded as important for their own sake. The French believe that there is more to life than the job. Hard work is admired, but workaholism is not. While the affectation of regularly working late is creeping into Parisian working habits, there is a clear division between private and business lives.

Weekends and vacation days, sport, cultural activities, and family life are very important. Colleagues are expected to be lively and interesting companions, well informed and appreciative of the good things of life as well as successful at their jobs.

DEATH ON THE ROAD
Where are you most likely to die in a car accident (deaths per 100,000 of population)?
Italy
Germany
Greece

Italy

The unification of Italy began in 1870 when King Victor Emmanuel put an end to foreign domination for the first time after the Goths and Vandals invaded the Roman Empire. Since then the reconciliation of rival cities, regions, and interest groups has been painstaking. Many people still speak Italian in public and their own dialect at home. The Tuscan version of the original Latin predominates because it was the written language of Dante. If the economy is the German's principal source of national pride and the monarchy the Briton's, cultural achievement is the Italian's.

While each village and town asserts its individuality, some broad distinctions can be made. The officially recognized division is between the industrialized north and the underdeveloped south, the *mezzogiorno*, which officially begins just to the south of Rome. Northerners say that it includes Rome. The two regions have markedly different attitudes to life and business. The stereotypical northerner is pre-occupied with work and money, the southerner with power and the good life. To northerners the southerners suck their profits away in subsidies and handouts. To southerners the northerners are money grubbers who exploit the labor force and divert their savings for their factories.

The fact remains that massive subsidies and the political and criminal interests that have preserved the status quo for the last half-century or more have condemned the south, especially Sicily, to underdevelopment and continuing economic and social poverty. Unemployment is 5 percent in the north and 22 percent in the south.

Families

Italy is a matrix of interests and loyalties. Horizontally divided into regions, it is vertically partitioned by factionalism. All aspects of Italian life are dominated by rival interest groups: political parties, public and private sector, employers and unions, church and state. Affiliation to at least one interest group is helpful. Belonging to a political party, the church, a trade union, a Masonic lodge, a trade association, or a village is not a sociable association of like minds or like interests, but is economically useful. The most important affiliation is to family. Family ties remain more important than in any other European country with the possible exception of Spain, and are the basis of the large number of self-employed and small businesses.

Affiliation, and the rights and obligations that go with it, replaces what passes for a wider social awareness in countries whose political and social institutions are more universally accepted. There are national policies in abundance, but they do not percolate to the level of ordinary life.

Political framework

The political stability of Italy is habitually dependent on a balance of tension between rival interest groups who through tradeoff or collusion arrived at a *modus vivendi*.

On paper there is a well-structured democratic system based on a comprehensive written constitution, an active presidency, and two elected houses. However, the balance of power between them is so finely calculated that legislation can be batted between them for years. Add a multiplicity of parties, proportional representation, and a sophisticated lobbying and sponsorship system of economic and regional interest groups, and the result is what is euphemistically described as a stable coalition and is in fact a permanent standoff.

Really important issues bypass the logjam by means of national referenda. Another solution to central government inertia is decentralization. There are 20 regions with considerable autonomy in health, education, and police. In addition, elected local authorities in the numerous *comuni* have significant spending power, although Rome keeps control of funding.

Government is popularly viewed as a group of separate cliques working for themselves. It is sometimes said that this attitude results from centuries of foreign rule through cumbersome bureaucracies. The payment of taxes is seen not as a duty to the community but as an exaction to be evaded. This is perhaps a rationalization of something that goes deeper into Italian social values, namely a healthy mistrust of formal institutions of any sort, even ones in which people directly participate. At the same time there is a genuine enthusiasm for the EU. Brussels is a remedy for ungovernability, just as Vienna and Madrid had been, only this time Italians can have their share of the power that goes with it.

The influence of political parties extends deep into economic and daily life. They exercise considerable power through their control of appointments to a wide range of jobs, from cabinet minister to municipal employee to middle management of state-owned companies. Patronage, or *raccomandazione*, along with the trading of favors and influence and votes and other inducements, is a normal part of business life in the public sector. Private business has the same ambivalent relationship with the tentacular public sector as the individual has with government.

The political environment not only affects the conduct of business but also exemplifies attitudes that pervade the business environment. Virtually nothing of importance is done by the book. As for corporate loyalty, the idea of working to make money for an impersonal organization without extracting as much personal benefit as possible is not widely held.

Business sector

Italy claimed at the end of the 1980s to have taken Britain's place as the fifth largest economy in the world, behind Germany and France. Now the UK economy is said to be a third bigger—but how do the Italians know? Up to a third of economic activity is in the "gray" or black market and by definition outside the scope of official statistical departments. Like so much that purports to pass for hard fact in Italy, it is an estimate. No statistic, including those in this book, should be taken as more than an approximation.

Extensive privatization has considerably reduced the direct role of the state in industry over the past decade. Italians are much less directly dependent on the public sector for their livelihood than in most northern European countries. Only one in five employees is in a public-service occupation as opposed to just over one in three in the UK and just under one in three in the US and Germany. The indirect role is still considerable. Government spending as a proportion of GDP is the highest in the EU. This is mainly in the form of social security and similar transfer payments.

The private sector is dominated by a small number of family-owned companies of international standing such as Fiat, Olivetti, and Benetton. Controlled by the *salotto buono* of business families and industrialists like Berlusconi, Agnelli, Pirelli, and De Benedetti, they are more like family companies on a large scale than professionally managed, widely held corporations. They are diversified conglomerates. The Agnelli family, for example, has controlling interests not only in Fiat but in sectors as diverse as telecommunications, construction, and publishing. Cross-holdings between families discourage political intervention and foreign takeover. The power of big family groups is gradually diminishing, even if it still remains considerable. In recent years they have been joined by a new generation of professionally managed entrepreneurial companies such as Bulgari, Luxottica, Natuzzi, and Parmalat.

The backbone of the economy is the thousands of small and medium-sized private firms in the north. Their owners resist amalgamation partly for independence and partly for financial realism. It is more profitable to keep things in the family and to stay small enough to employ the officially self-employed, to avoid social security charges, to pay workers in cash, and to use outworkers to keep out of the hands of bankers and unions. Productivity in this sector is several times greater than in the state sector and strikes are a rarity.

For similar reasons, large sectors of the economy remain artisanal and dispersed in small independent workshops. These exercise economic power and benefit from economies of scale by belonging to cooperatives, professionally managed and with substantial investment in plant and equipment. The retail trade, agriculture, and construction industries are dominated by cooperatives, themselves grouped into consortia.

Industrial relations

All companies in Italy with more than 15 employees are obliged by law to have a works committee, the *consiglio de fabbrica*. This has the right to monitor conditions of work, investment plans, and so on, as well as being the channel for grievances.

About 40 percent of the officially calculated labor force is unionized. Unions are highly politicized and membership is on political rather than craft or industry lines. The relationship between management and unions is confrontational. Both unions and employers are strongly averse to the idea of worker participation. In addition to the three largest unions—Christian Democrat, Communist, and Social Democrat—there is a host of smaller unions and workers' committees that bedevil industrial relations, especially in the public sector. It is these smaller unions that are mainly responsible for the high rate of strikes. That the unions have failed in their essential mission is evidenced by the inequality of earnings. The differential between the highest and lowest paid is over a third greater than in Germany.

There are two labor markets. The official one is highly regulated with a strong bias in favor of the employee in the areas of recruitment, redundancy, and dismissal, although the traditional jobs-for-life environment has been seasoned with realism and declining union power. The unofficial labor market, in which an estimated 25 percent of the workforce is engaged, is by definition unregulated.

Financing

Risk capital is in short supply from institutional sources. New ventures are based on private funds and expand through retained profits. Banks dominate the financing of industry under the control of the Banca d'Italia, which has the distinction of being free from political interference and suspicion of corruption.

Banks are highly regulated. They are not allowed to participate in the ownership of commercial companies. Short-term banks that provide retail services and working capital finance are prevented from making medium-term loans. These are the preserve of the medium- and long-term credit institutions.

Even so, there is no unified banking system and the largest banks are heavily oriented toward their home regions. Every region, town, and often village has its own, made viable by protectionism and the highest savings rate in Europe. Banking services from funds transfer to medium-term loans are fragmented, esoteric, and complicated.

Business organization and structure

Regulation of business is minimal and, where it exists, open to manipulation. Italians created the art of accountancy in the fifteenth century and have been creative with it ever since. Independent auditors should not be confused with statutory auditors of joint-stock companies who, on behalf of the directors, report to the shareholders that accounts follow the prescribed format. They have no powers to verify that they conform with the books of the company. Accounts of smaller private, unquoted firms should be treated with circumspection, remembering that their primary purpose is not to provide a full and fair picture to shareholders but to form a basis of negotiation with banks and tax authorities.

The board of directors (*consiglio d'amministrazione*) is headed by a *presidente*. Under him there is usually a managing director (*amministratore delegato*). *Direttori* are department heads. Other titles, whether functional or status, are meaningless. If there is an organization chart it it will have been drawn up for a purpose other than clarifying the organization, perhaps for showing to foreign business partners.

In large companies a conventional hierarchy in the sense of clear reporting lines from superior to subordinate is only to be found at the lower levels of organization. At middle to upper levels the true hierarchies are built on personal alliances between people in different parts of the organization who trust each other and rely on each other to get things done. People have the power to influence and make decisions outside the apparent organizational structure. Finding decision makers is an art, especially in a subsidiary of a holding company, where they may be in a different part of the organization.

In public and private sectors, conglomerates are heavily decentralized. Within the same holding company there is a wide diversity of management styles among individual subsidiaries. The age and education of senior management and the age, size, technology, and market of the companies determine how they are run. The key word in describing the Italian approach and the primary attribute demanded of a manager is "flexible."

Flexibility means routinely ignoring procedures. Protocols, rules, and organization charts may well be drawn up and defined, but they will be ignored as a matter of principle as well as practice. Making sure that things are done properly and well is a question of personal supervision and trust in the competence and reliability of individuals. These key elements of control and trust are easier to ensure in paternalistic family companies than in large corporations.

The disorganization apparent to someone from a more systematic background is, in the highly competitive private sector at least, illusory. For these companies flexibility means concentrating on what is essential to get a job done without getting bogged down in principle. Pragmatism and a talent for improvisation are more than a substitute for orthodoxy.

Planning

There is rarely a written strategic plan in an Italian company. It may be in the mind of the owner or the senior decision makers, but it is unlikely to be promulgated. If it is written there is a purpose other than planning behind it. There is a strong temperamental aversion to forecasting and planning, especially to grandiose schemes on an industry or national level. At the same time, there is a keen entrepreneurial sense based on recognition of new opportunities in the market.

Italian companies thrive on ambiguity and risk. They will identify and exploit a niche without waiting for an in-depth analysis. This can affect the quality of joint ventures with longer-term objectives. While Italians are alert to the opportunity of short-term gains, there is a bias against long-term strategic positioning. A business association lasts only as long as it is consistently profitable.

Leadership

The traditional leadership model derives from the family company: the boss as autocratic father figure, the sons as senior managers with the ear and trust of the boss, the employees as faithful retainers who do as they are told and are well looked after. This works fine in family companies, but is less effective when it is translated to a large and professionally managed organization.

The single most important management issue I came across among Italians involved the characteristics of effective leadership. It dominated all the conversations. (For non-Italians the predominant issue was the decision-making process.) For a number of reasons, including technological demands, social pressures, and economic pressures for larger business units, there was a strong feeling that traditional leadership styles are no longer appropriate. The head of a socialist cooperative, whose ideas on management were indistinguishable from the most ardent capitalist's, made a fine distinction between *autorità*, *autorevolezza*, and *autoritarismo*: authority, authoritativeness, and authoritarianism. The distinction is important in any culture, but vital in one in which impersonal organizational mechanisms have low credibility.

Authority derives ultimately from the owners of the firm and the chairperson or the managing director who represents them. However, it is not transmitted systematically through the organization; it is delegated personally to individuals who can be trusted. Authority is attributed by employees to those whom they know have the personal confidence of the owner or senior manager. These do not necessarily have a corresponding place in the organization. Title or position in the organization is not always a guide. For example, a major marketing decision need not necessarily be made by the head of marketing, it may be taken by the boss with the company lawyer. Alternatively, the head of the marketing department is not always the one most qualified by training or experience in marketing, but someone with whom the managing director can best work.

Authoritativeness is based as much on personal qualities as technical competence. Another manager in the public sector, this time a Christian Democrat, made a Catholic distinction between formal and substantive management behavior. On a formal level the boss is expected to be *simpatico*, charismatic, and creative and to demonstrate that he (or occasionally she) is the boss. He should make a *bella figura* as a manager as well as in other spheres of activity. On a substantive level, consistency and reliability were the traits most often mentioned. This is not to say that technical expertise counts for nothing. While role playing comes naturally to most Italians, they are equally adept at sensing if there is a solid basis of competence behind the façade. The high quality of Italian engineering and design does not come from networking skills. The status of technical people, as opposed to finance or marketing, is consistently high.

Authoritarianism is the trap into which Italian managers are most likely to fall when they leave the environment of the small family company. To behave in a rough, dictatorial way, to expect and exact deference, is a common enough role model in small businesses where relationships are close. Nevertheless, it does not work among subordinates who have a purely utilitarian relationship with the company. They do not feel obliged to cooperate simply because of their position in the organization or because it is written down in their contract of employment.

The most important part of the leadership role is not planning or decision making but implementation and control. To attempt to achieve either with clear instructions and procedures alone may lead to disappointment. Italians generally feel that they can do the job better than their bosses and do not readily take instructions unless they feel a personal commitment to what they have to do. It is essential to achieve a consensus first and to obtain the commitment of people who are expected to carry out a task, otherwise it will not get done. It is not enough to gain a verbal agreement, which may be given out of politeness. Persuasion, insistence, and followup are essential. However, once commitment is obtained the energy, flair, and creativity applied to executing it will be extraordinary.

Delegation

Delegation in an Italian company is on the basis of giving responsibility to trusted individuals. It is rarely defined in terms of goals or accountabilities, which are often imprecise. This extends to job descriptions. Where they have been instituted they are for the record only and are usually put away in a desk and forgotten. People may be appraised by their bosses and notes put on the personal file, but it is rare that these will be shown to, or discussed with, the individual concerned. Formal personal appraisal is very difficult for either side to manage, as is any direct criticism, unless it is in the context of a recognized personal relationship. The informal "godfather" relationship, which some American companies attempt to institutionalize, is common in Italian companies and part of the informal hierarchy system.

Formal control systems concentrate on essential and pragmatic indicators, such as turnover, cash flow, and gross profit, and are rigorously monitored. More subtle management information systems, full of allocations and ratios, are usually seen as time wasting.

Teamwork and competition

Italian business relationships are based on mutual dependence and a sense of mutual obligation most easily satisfied with members of the extended family. The most successful organizations in Italy are the family or those modeled on the family. A purely salary-based, contractual relationship is not enough; it does not create the right bond. It has to be in the context of a relationship based on honor.

Once a relationship has been established, based on a common purpose where everyone will visibly profit, there will be total cooperation and commitment. If the relationship has not been created, colleagues will be highly competitive to the point of undermining each other.

For a team to work well it should have a respected leader capable of managing personal relationships. Teams composed solely of peers are difficult to maintain as there is no concept of power being shared equally by a group.

Meetings

Any process of open decision making in Italy is illusory. Decisions taken and agreed in formal meetings, minuted and scheduled for implementation, may never happen. Meanwhile, a different decision will have been taken by someone else and implemented by their subordinates and allies.

Meetings are usually unstructured and informal. The smaller the meeting, the more unstructured it is. They may start with three or four people, a few more may come in, others may go. It may not always be clear why some people are there at all. Sometimes it feels like meetings are merely social gatherings to reinforce a sense of togetherness. You may get the impression that nothing is happening or a dozen things all at once. The purpose of meetings is to enable the decision takers to evaluate the mood of the others, to sense supporters and test the water, not usually to make decisions.

It is difficult to impose an agenda, although it is always worthwhile trying if you are in a position to do so, otherwise discussion may be interminable. There is a tendency to overanalyze and split hairs—*spaccare il capello in quattro*. A large proportion of meetings end without a satisfactory conclusion, in which case they are always reconvened.

A meeting is often a stage for exhibiting eloquence, personality, and status, and is consequently a free-for-all of opinions, comments, and ideas. Everyone is entitled to make a contribution, is listened to and apparently agreed with. The weight of the idea resides not in the idea itself but in the importance and influence of the speaker. Newcomers or junior people will be paid the courtesy of a hearing, their contribution welcomed and accepted but somehow left out at the end.

If a proposal is to be put to a meeting it is often advisable to clear it with each of the participants beforehand. Then they will react constructively. If a new idea is sprung on a meeting everyone will automatically object.

Opinions must not be imposed but agreed to. Making a decision on a vote is rarely a good tactic unless you know it will be unanimous. While people will not publicly go out on a limb to fight for a minority view, they will not submit to a majority decision either. They will abandon the group or undermine its work from the inside. The guiding principle is not to offend the *dignita* of a dissident, but give him or her time to change opinion and to save face. If there are signs of entrenched positions a skilled chairperson will often adjourn the meeting. When it is reconvened, after some subtle lobbying, the objections will have disappeared.

Communication

Most, if not all, of the examinations that a university student takes to graduate are oral. From an early age Italians learn to acquire and impart information orally. If Northern Europeans have the patience to listen carefully to what seem to be rambling speeches, they will notice that Italian contributions to meetings and discussions are as carefully constructed as a memo. Conversely, the memos they send to their Italian counterparts will be ignored.

While rhetoric and also politeness are important, when necessary they can be direct and assertive, except when it comes to saying "no." This is less to spare the other's feelings than to leave the door open for future possibilities.

Communication channels are tortuous and complicated. Informal contacts are vital in every aspect of Italian life and information is one of the ingredients. There is never a shortage of opinion, but facts are usually in short supply. They are secretively guarded and traded on a transactional basis. The word *dietrologia* sums up the belief that behind every event there are sinister, powerful personalities or organizations, manipulating everything. The simple explanation is that because there is less emphasis on making clear goals and targets, companies are less transparent. Things get done without apparent reason, others die silently and nobody seems to know why.

Formal presentations are not common in the Italian business environment and if called on to make one an Italian may be uncharacteristically pompous and professorial, unless he has an American training, in which case he may include the obligatory labored jokes.

Upward mobility

Relatives, connections, influence, and membership of the right political party were, until recently, important considerations in making a career. In a *British Social Attitudes Special International Report*, Italians were reported as believing that the most important factors in getting ahead were education, knowing the right people, ability, hard work, and political connections. Ambition came sixth, lower than in the other countries surveyed. The thrusting high-flyer is more a figure of fun than a role model.

Nevertheless, while being a cousin or *raccomandato* by a politician may get you on the bottom rung, it will not necessarily get you much further up the ladder. There is a strong and growing professional managerial class in the private sector. It is especially active in private companies which have outgrown their original family based structures. Status, pay, and opportunities exist in the private sector even for a person with no direct connections.

There is no recognized educational élite in Italy, although many managers in larger companies are graduates of business schools.

There is a strong degree of company loyalty based on being closely acquainted with a group of people. Job security is important, reinforced by the difficulty of firing people. There is little job hopping except among foreign multinationals. If there is a fast track it is based on nepotism. There is not yet the breed of professional manager who moves from company to company, and those who do may find themselves squeezed out.

Attitudes and behavior

Italians display intense rectitude and loyalty in personal relationships, especially with family but also with anyone else who comes into the private sphere. This is parallelled by what outsiders may regard as amorality in relationships with institutions. To Italians ethics principally apply to personal relationships in which they are scrupulous, the inverse of cultures where civic responsibility outweighs personal morality.

They are receptive to fresh ideas and new solutions. Inventiveness and imagination are prized. They have a talent for improvising solutions—*pensiamo al rimedio*. They will willingly cooperate with others as long as they get a chance to demonstrate their own skills.

To describe someone as *un tipo furbo*—sharp—is not a compliment; it is much better to be *in gamba*—smart. At the same time, it is important to demonstrate intelligence and education. Being cultivated is not a social grace but a social necessity. When I was researching this book the most mundane of conversations about business were peppered with references to sources ranging from Aristotle to Umberto Eco, Adam Smith to JK Galbraith. At first such name dropping may seem pretentious to those from backgrounds where familiarity with literature and the classics is considered unbusinesslike.

Women

While there are some very successful individual businesswomen in Italy, there are relatively few women in managerial positions and the professions, although their numbers are increasing. The exception is in family companies, where their status as family members outweighs their sex. There is no more perceptible male chauvinism in Italy than in other countries with a greater proportion of women in positions of responsibility, but there is considerably less feminism.

Etiquette

Italian etiquette is based on an easy formality in which considerateness is more important than formulas. Whatever the relationship and whatever the rank and social class, courtesy and good manners are important.

The polite third person, the *lei* form, predominates, especially with senior people or in companies with a strong sense of hierarchy, for example most public-sector organizations. The informal *tu* will only be used where there is a relationship based on something more than a business association. In newer companies with an open style of management, in small family firms and among younger people, colleagues use first names and very quickly get to the *tu* form. Even then you will often probably call the boss and older colleagues *lei*.

If the *lei* form is used then last names will be the rule with *Signor* or *Signora*. *Signorina* is for young and junior women, but *Signora* is the safest. Professional titles, most commonly *Dottore*, are often used. *Dottore* is for any form of graduate and it will not be taken amiss if wrongly used. However, there is no sense of stiffness or exclusion. Italians are very open people, curious and tolerant of other ways and other manners. If you are late, for example, it will not be held against you as long as you are genuinely apologetic. There is a high tolerance of inefficiency and genuine mistakes, but a low tolerance of arrogance or rudeness.

People dress formally for business. Making a good impression matters deeply. The excellence of Italian taste and design is an expression of the Italian desire to make a *bella figura*. This is not superficial. It extends to social graces and courtesies, the kind of conversation you make, the kind of person you are.

It is not done to throw your weight around, although neither does it pay to be modest and retiring. Be dignified but do not stand on dignity, authoritative but not authoritarian. The further north, the more seriously and soberly one behaves.

Punctuality

The attitude to punctuality is often misunderstood by meticulous northerners. Deliberate lateness is seen as sloppy. Taking others for granted by keeping them waiting is rude. Twenty minutes is about the limit of acceptability; after that there must be a good reason and an apology.

Nevertheless, time is an artificial framework designed to get people more or less at the same time in the same place, but it ranks lower in priority than what you do within the framework. If something intervenes to make you late—a meeting running over time, a surprise visit from someone important, or an unexpected telephone call— then it is understandable. While it is impolite to arrive late for a meeting, it is even more impolite to break off the previous one because it is overrunning. If the appointment is more important than anything else, everyone will be meticulously on time.

In these circumstances an ability to juggle each other's appointment schedules is second nature. You are equally likely to be invited in to the tail end of a host's previous appointment as to be kept waiting outside. If the ensuing conversation is promising the two meetings may be rolled into one, someone else steps in, and you all end up going out to lunch together. The end result is not in the timetable but may be more useful than anticipated.

Humor

Italians value wit, humor, and good spirits. It is important to enjoy life and work, and not to treat the latter as a burden or take it too seriously. They do not often tell jokes as such, with the exception of political ones, but are fond of irony and the humor of the incongruous. They can be self-deprecating and there is much good-humored banter. At the same time, they will be very aware of public dignity. When playing the institutional role, especially in public, the tone will change to formality and seriousness.

Socializing

The long lunch hour is common only in the south, where people are able to get home. In the urbanized north a 9–6 routine is now the norm, with a brief snack at noon. In private companies managers are expected to work until 9 or 10 in the evening. Large companies provide some sort of canteen facility or luncheon vouchers as a fringe benefit.

There is no recognizable pattern about socializing during or after work, no customary "happy hour" or drink in the pub afterwards. Groups of people will have parties and celebrations, including leaving parties, which will include people at all levels of seniority. Everyone is very approachable and there is no standing on ceremony.

Outside immediate working hours there is very little mixing. There is a sharp differentiation between work and private life. Taking work home or being telephoned at home or on holiday are unusual. Spouses are not often involved in entertaining, either at home or in restaurants, and will rarely meet other colleagues' spouses.

Drinking without eating, other than an aperitif at a café, is rare. Even mild intoxication is ill mannered and the hard-drinking executive is a rarity. The usual form of entertainment is dinner in a restaurant. This is primarily a social not a business event, to find out if you each think the other is the kind of person you wish to know. Those readers whose eyes glaze over when they are expected to talk shop after seven in the evening will find this to their liking. Those who believe that social occasions are an extension of the business day and like to talk about business on every possible occasion will find that they get fewer and fewer opportunities to do so.

SOLAR HEATING

Which country has the biggest solar energy collection per head?

    Cyprus

    Germany

    Spain

Malta

The islands of Malta—Malta itself, Gozo, Comino, and uninhabited Kemmunett and Filfla—have a population of about 380,000. Their ethnic and cultural composition derives from their position in the Mediterranean between North Africa and Sicily and their strategic importance to Britain when it was a Mediterranean power. Almost all the population is Roman Catholic. English and Maltese are the official languages. The Maltese language has a North African basis heavily influenced by Italian and Sicilian. English is also widely spoken.

Malta's industries are tourism and light industry, mainly textiles and clothing for export to Europe, predominantly France, and the US. There are close economic links with Libya, which has invested heavily in property and commerce as well as supplying most of the oil for the islands' energy needs. The Maltese government is the dominant economic force and the economy is highly regulated.

Voters are perfectly and vehemently polarized between the Nationalist Party and the Malta Labor Party. However, the oligarchic nature of the ruling groups, including opposition members, in a network of interconnecting family relationships means that personal connections are absolutely essential.

A relaxed, Mediterranean communication style is combined with a pragmatic and direct approach to meetings and negotiation. Socializing is an integral part of business life, whether over a long lunch or dinner.

SATELLITES
Who owns Europe's biggest orbiting satellite?
Turkey
Ireland
France

Portugal

Portugal is an Atlantic not a Mediterranean nation, and it is an error as well as a social gaffe to lump it with Spain. Until the 1974 revolution the country's orientations were toward Africa, where it had a colonial relationship with Angola and Mozambique, and South America, where trading links with Brazil are still strong. The exception was a strong connection with the UK, through the port wine trade. One thing it does have in common with Spain is a marked about-face toward Europe following political change and membership of the EU.

Trade patterns have now changed, with other EU trading partners edging out the UK. Over the past two decades Portugal has undergone extensive modernization of its infrastructure and industrial base. The manufacturing sector is dominated by the textile and footwear industries and automobiles, which account for 15 percent of total exports. Portugal's economy was traditionally agrarian and 25 percent of the labor force is still employed in agriculture.

The 1974 revolution was followed by nationalization of banking and industry, consisting primarily of textiles, chemicals, and shipbuilding and repair. This was reversed by a privatization program begun in 1989. The state maintains a golden share in some companies, although others are in 100 percent private ownership. A new generation of entrepreneurs challenged the hegemony of a dozen families who hitherto had dominated the private sector. In the past few years there have been an impressive number of new ventures, many of them in IT, telecommunications, and other high-tech industries. With dynamic and professional management they compete on the world market.

Organization

The traditional corporate structure of a public corporation, *Sociedade Anonima de Responsabilidade Limitada* (SA), contains a board of directors, *conselho de administracao*, and a board of auditors, *conselho fiscal*, which is composed of shareholder representatives. More modern companies have a management board, *direccao*, made up of no more than five directors appointed by the general board, *conselho geral*. The latter is elected by a shareholders' meeting. A shareholder is also appointed as statutory auditor, *revisor oficial de contas*, whose responsibilities should not be confused with that of an independent auditor.

A *Sociedade por Quotas de Responsabilidade Limitada* (Lda) is managed by a director appointed by the owners. There are no other boards or officers. There are workers' committees empowered to inspect and comment on financial information and terms and conditions of employment.

While the revolution changed many aspects of Portuguese social and political life, it left the civil service and its methods virtually intact. The large state-owned companies are compartmentalized and bureaucratic. Smaller and private companies have the more unstructured style of a family company.

As a result of the accelerated economic and social change of the past 20 years, business behavior is less uniform and depends on both the age and social background of the business partner and the size and characteristics of the company. There is a growing professional managerial class, many of whom are educated abroad or at local business schools. Smaller privatized companies, multinationals, and especially the recently created high-tech organizations have a radically different management style and forms of organization to traditionally managed companies. They aspire to a more team-based, participative management style than is customary.

Traditional Portuguese organizations are based on a vertical personal hierarchy under strong control from the top rather than a systematic division of responsibility. Leadership is essentially directive, with a concentration of power at the top of the organization working through a chain of command based on personal loyalty, not systematic delegation. Delegation is to the person one trusts rather than to the position they hold. Subordinates are given little power or responsibility, even extending to the secretary's control of the diary.

Organizational procedures tend to be vague and negotiable and there is what outsiders may regard as a cavalier attitude toward delivery dates and similar commitments. Management information systems and financial budgeting tend to be rudimentary. Sales volume and cash flow are the key indicators.

Communication

Spanish speakers will be understood in Portugal, although they should be prepared for one-sided conversations as replies in Portuguese will be very difficult to understand. It is a language rich in phonics as well as literature. There are 13 vowel sounds associated with the letter *a* alone.

Portugal is the self-styled country of *brandos costumes*, soft customs. People are quiet and understated. They are uncomfortable with the assertiveness that is expected in some other cultures. They may appear to outsiders as overly polite, even diffident. They are not known for saying clearly and directly what they think. If a Portuguese says "no" it is often less a refusal than an invitation to restate your case.

Nevertheless, oral communication is more significant than written. It is more effective to talk than to send an email or memo.

Humor is not a noticeable ingredient in business conversations and the more aggressive forms of irony, sarcasm, and banter will not be appreciated or even understood.

As well as the titles *Senhor* and *Senhora*, Portuguese make indiscriminate use of *Doutor* to anyone suspected of having a university degree. They also use the titles *Engenheiro* and *Arquitecto* when appropriate. There are familiar and polite forms of address, *tu* and *voce*. *Tu* is only used with people who have more than a business relationship and are equal or close in status. There are several possible combinations of *tu* and *voce* with first and last names and titles, deriving from a refined sense of hierarchy. The deferential *o Senhor* and *a Senhora*, without a name, are then used. The most important thing to remember is to avoid *tu* with subordinates and junior people unless you have known them a long time.

Dress for men is based around the jacket and tie and varies in formality with the seasons. There is little distinction between dressing for work and for social life.

Normal working hours begin at nine although many Portuguese are late starters, turning up nearer to ten. They are also late finishers. It is increasingly common to work until eight or later and in the more modern companies this is expected. Timekeeping generally is on the relaxed side, with late arrival and last-minute cancellations not uncommon.

The day is punctuated with long lunches and numerous coffee breaks and may end up with dinners at restaurants. The habit of going home for lunch is waning and colleagues will eat out together. Otherwise they do not meet socially. However, evening meetings and telephone calls at home are common and often necessary to compensate for missed appointments during the day.

Leadership and organization

Organizations are primarily built on networks of personal contacts and relationships. They are maintained through frequent socializing and informal meetings, which are not just for small talk. Serious matters are often dealt with and issues resolved outside of the formal office environment.

Portuguese organizations are not characteristically team based. Teams need strong leaders and team roles are not always well defined. Managers do not look for consensus among their subordinates and maintain their superior status. It is more important to appear decisive and authoritative than participative. While people prefer to avoid confrontation, they are individually competitive and wary of losing out to their peers.

On a corporate level equal partnerships are uncomfortable. The expectation is that one side will take the lead.

Meetings are for briefing and discussion. They are not considered an appropriate forum for decision making or delegation, nor is a clear, decisive result anticipated. As with most appointments, meetings are unlikely to start on time. There will be an agenda but people will not feel bound by it and may leave for other pressing business. The formality of making contributions through the chair is not generally widespread.

Unless a senior person is present, who will automatically dominate proceedings, everyone feels free to make a contribution. The aim is not to find common ground but to express a point of view as emphatically as possible and preferably in contradiction with everyone else's. People are flexible and collaborative in private, but the public forum is for competitive self-assertion. If agreement or support for a proposal is required at a meeting it is essential to have lobbied the participants in private beforehand. Otherwise they are likely to disagree on principle. Action plans and other commitments may be agreed on but are unlikely to be followed unless rigorously enforced.

MUSLIMS
Where is the largest mosque in Europe?
London
Rome
Paris

Spain

Radical change in Europe has not only happened in the former socialist countries. In researching this edition of the book I asked respondents to read the chapters about their own country in the previous editions and to say what had changed. The most numerous, detailed, and passionate replies came from Spaniards. Highlights include radical social and demographic change, a transformed economy, the privatization of most of the companies owned by the former state-owned holding company INI, Spanish multinationals in the Fortune 500, a new generation of managers trained at business schools in Spain and abroad, and above all the rejection and replacement of old social attitudes and business practices. Whether or not the changes are more profound than those in other countries, Spaniards certainly feel more excited by them than any other nationality with which I corresponded.

Old Catholic Spain, dominated from Madrid, its face turned away from Europe to Africa and its old colonies in the New World, dominated by church and state and bankers and bureaucrats and old families who counted their names—that is no more. It has by no means disappeared, but is inhabited by an increasingly superannuated generation bewildered by change. The combination of the collapse of traditional authority systems of family, church, and state and the transition to a pluralist democracy, membership of the EU, economic deregulation, a wave of foreign investment, and the fifth largest market in Europe opened the floodgates to a generation anxious to rebuild a European Spain. Spain has not lost its involvement in the New World, however, in that its multinationals dominate Latin American markets. And not all of these changes are comfortable. Immigration, for example, is a new and troubling phenomenon for many Spaniards.

Regionalism

A quarter of Spaniards speak a language in addition to, or instead of, Spanish, the language of Castile, of which Madrid is the capital. The most important are Catalan (Barcelona is the capital), Basque (Bilbao), and Galego (the language of Galicia, similar to Portuguese). These are languages in their own right and are widely spoken in their home territory. The aspirations for autonomy of Catalans, Galicians, and above all Basques were ruthlessly driven underground in the Franco era, although they resurfaced before the ink was dry on the 1978 Constitution, which established a system based on autonomous communities.

It was not only the above three *nacionalidades historicas* that achieved self-government: 14 others claimed it or had it thrust on them with varying degrees of enthusiasm. There are now 17 regions, each with its own capital, flag, and legislature. Their responsibility and powers and—for Spaniards the most important—their authority to raise taxes vary. Basques collect their own taxes, control their own police, have their own television channel, run their own schools. Other regions are independent from Madrid virtually in name only.

Euskadi, the Basque region, is probably the most notorious of the *nacionalidades historicas* outside Spain through the activities of ETA, a terrorist group claiming to fight for Basque independence. It arouses similar emotions among Spaniards, including many Basques, as the IRA does in Britain. Members of ETA are accused of being Spanish Talibans, Stalinists, Mafiosi only interested in money making and arms dealing, the terrorist wing of the nationalist party the PNV, and so on.

Euskadi's economic importance lies in the iron and steelworks of Bilbao, once the wealthiest part of Spain but then the victim of the same blight that affected most other European centers of heavy industry: disinvestment, pollution, and outdated technology. It has tried with some success to regenerate itself as a service and cultural center around the focal point of the Guggenheim museum.

Galicia is less well known to European business people and will probably remain so. Green, wet, and windswept in its Atlantic climate, its economy has suffered with the collapse of its fishing industry.

Catalonia is the most thriving of the three. It has managed to retain its individual character despite the large number of immigrants from the rest of Spain attracted by its economic prosperity. Barcelona thinks of itself as more cosmopolitan, forward looking, and industrious than the rest of Spain.

Southern Spain is in sharp contrast with these northern regions. Andalucia is the Spain of flamenco and Moorish arches and is more concerned with the quality of life than its earnest and solid northern counterparts. The inhabitants of neighboring Murcia have a similarly unfair reputation in the rest of Spain—comparable to that of the *mezzogiorno* in Italy—idle when they are at home and cheap labor when they are not. The Spain of Don Quixote—Castile, La Mancha, and impoverished Estramadura—shares the vast, high, arid central plain between north and south. Madrid is in the middle, an island of prosperity aloof from the surrounding areas. The popular *hidalgo* image of Spaniards as superior and reserved derives more from Castilian manners than the relaxed and unpretentious style of the rest of Spain.

Despite regional loyalties, economic circumstances foster a high migration rate both externally and internally. Yet companies who need to transfer employees between regions are careful about local sensibilities.

Attitude to government

Since the restoration of democracy to Spain there has been remarkable continuity and stability of government oriented around the center. Extreme right- and left-wing interests, feared in the early years, have been marginalized. A new breed of more representative legislators has in many Spanish eyes not enhanced the credibility, competence, or honesty of government. There is as much deep mistrust of officialdom as ever. That regional government brings the administrators closer to their constituents has not made them any better disposed toward it, especially as taxes have increased to finance it. Two-tier government means two pairs of hands in the till.

As in Italy and Greece, attitudes to government, especially in respect of taxes, are sometimes explained as a hangover from days when the government was an occupying power. In Spain's case, especially if you were a Catalan or a Basque, the alien power was Madrid. The argument seems pretty tenuous in a democratic society that elects its own government. There is a deeper reason, to do with a conception of what constitutes a community. In Spain and other Mediterranean countries a community is based on personal and family ties. What may appear to be favoritism and corruption is the exercise of mutual obligations. In the less family-oriented countries of northern Europe a community is based on a more abstract idea of common interest. Whether this derives from accidents of geography, climate, history, or anything else is open to debate. The fact remains that foreigners used to an equitable relationship between governors and governed should be prepared for a different attitude to the authorities.

Business sector

The business élite of Spain are the bankers. Banco Santander Central is Spain's biggest company, followed by Banco Bilbao Vizcaya in fourth place. Although the stock exchange has grown significantly in importance in recent years, not least because of the privatization of the state sector, for most companies banks are the principal source of long- and short-term finance to the private sector. Although many banks belong to industrial groupings and have direct shareholdings in companies, there is no concept of a "house" bank. Because of lending limits, to guard against fickle withdrawing of credit and to maintain secrecy a company will usually have as many banks as it can. As a result there is fierce competition among the big commercial banks and the savings banks and bank lending is rarely unsecured.

The private sector is dominated by former state-owned companies in the energy, utilities, and construction sectors, notably Telefonica, Repsol, and Endesa.

There are an ever increasing number of publicly owned companies quoted on the stock exchange. Foreign investors such as Volkswagen have a significant presence, although the greater part of total business turnover is still accounted for by family-owned small and medium-sized enterprises. In the 1990s many of the larger companies invested substantially in Latin America.

Much effort has been devoted to increasing the level of professional management skills. Universities and vocational training schools have business-related courses and the dozen or so business schools set up in the late 1980s have matured into successful institutions of an international standard. They have brought American management techniques to Spain. Many people finish their higher education abroad, usually in the US or the UK where they can perfect English language skills.

Business organization and structure

There are two forms of company: the stock company, *Sociedad Anonima* (SA), and the *Sociedad de Responsabilidad Limitada* (SRL). They can have as few as one director. Companies with more than 500 employees and two directors must have an employee representative on the board. Those with over 50 employees need to have a works committee.

The business school generation is trained in basically American management and is part of the global management class that can be found in every country in Europe. Decentralized, team based, target centered, quality focused, functionally specialized—these are all characteristics that are to be found in the larger companies and newer industries. As these people gain in seniority, take over their family companies, or set up their own ventures, their methods and style will permeate all levels of business.

However, at present they cannot exist in a vacuum. They derive from and co-exist with a more traditional style of Spanish management still thriving in older-established companies and family firms. Even if readers are dealing with the global class, an acquaintance with the former ways may explain otherwise inconsistent aspects of their corporate culture.

In this style highly compartmentalized, bureaucratic, and authoritarian organizations are built on the concept of personal hierarchy. An organization chart, if there is one, is a social rather than a functional system. Instructions from the top pass down a recognized chain of command. The purpose of demarcation is not to enhance operational efficiency by a division of labor, but to enhance control by senior management. The concept of a team is one of individuals working independently under a strong leader. Rules, systems, and mechanisms are seen as a last resort to stop things falling apart. The reluctance to trust in systems means that there is a constant atmosphere of crisis and emergency. To be good at coping with it is a source of pride and is felt to be much more enjoyable than being a cog in a machine.

Planning

Forecasting and planning are not salient features of traditional Spanish business practice. Fixing a strategy is the responsibility of the chief executive or the owner. It will be based on intuition and business sense rather than systematic study. If it is communicated at all, which no one expects, it will be in the form of vague hints and admonitions. There is no taste for intellectual schemas and grand designs. The preference is for the tangible, the practical, and the opinions of people one trusts. Information gathering is a question of talking to as many people as you can without letting on what you are trying to find out. In a business environment where numbers of any sort are unreliable, this is the only tactic. In a more modern company, if there is a formal, written plan it is likely to have been put together by strategic planning consultants for the benefit of senior managers. Nevertheless, translating it into specific action plans may be beyond the experience or inclination of middle management.

A traditional family company is unlikely to have sophisticated financial plans or budgets. The key numbers are turnover and cash flow. Unless they are declining, other figures are unimportant. Accounting systems are designed not to enlighten but to conceal financial information from tax authorities and banks. This is rapidly changing, however, under the influence of foreign investors and business partners who demand what they consider to be proper reporting. The stock market also exerts pressure for accounting standards and independent auditing. Spanish investors have been wary of investing directly in companies and prefer to use the intermediary of investment funds, which spread the risk and benefit from better intelligence than the individual can hope to gain.

Leadership

The archetypal leader is a benevolent autocrat. Outsiders who are used to a more participative style are best advised to reserve it until they have established themselves as firm and decisive. The quality most admired in a leader is to be courageous, *valiente*. Sharing decision making with subordinates may be interpreted as weakness and is more likely to generate insecurity than commitment. If subordinates have a problem, they expect the boss to solve it; if a question, the boss should know the answer. This by no means precludes explanation of decisions and seeking opinions and comment, as long as it remains clear who is in charge.

Authority does not automatically go with status but is determined by the quality of personal relationships with subordinates. A rigid adherence to protocol and insistence on proper channels of authority and communication will alienate them. Loyalty is to people and not institutions.

As in most directive cultures, the problem is not in making decisions. Lines of authority are clear and decisions are passed up the line until they stick. The problem is in getting a commitment to implement them.

Delegation should be concrete and specific, based on realistic short-term targets and detailed instructions on how to reach them. The written job profile is an innovation among larger companies. Spanish employees of the old school might feel slighted if they were given written instructions. If these do exist they are a general list of responsibilities with little advice on how to get the job done.

Appraisal systems of any sort are an innovation. Spaniards are used to criticism in the sense of being reprimanded by the boss, *jefe*, for something they have done or not done, without right of reply. This is expected. It is a privilege of the boss to assert authority. Criticism is an exercise of rank rather than a constructive or meaningful piece of feedback, and the person reprimanded will certainly not admit that he or she is in the wrong. People are surprised by positive feedback and are not as anxious to know how they are doing as they are, say, in Anglo-Saxon cultures. It implies a dependency that they would rather not acknowledge. The presumption is that they are doing fine and, if not, it is someone else's fault.

A general review of performance, especially if it is backed up by objective fact, takes on a more personal tone and is resented. Spaniards also resent criticism by people with whom they have a more informal relationship. You can criticize a subordinate without mincing words, but it is a much more delicate matter to point out something to a colleague.

Control

Operating plans have the same status as forecasts and are usually not much better developed. Where they exist, they are interpreted as instruments of control over individuals rather than blueprints for action. They will tend to be understated to minimize the chances of recrimination. Schedules, budgets, and forecasts tend to be rough guides. Delivery dates are often approximations not to be taken literally. Outsiders who believe that installing sophisticated reporting systems is a first step are correct as long as they realize that it is not the last. Making it work by personal negotiation with the people responsible is also required.

One barrier to the enhancement of internal control and audit systems is that they are interpreted as a lack of trust. Large customers who try to impose detailed schedules and quality checks are resented.

Meetings and teams

The Spanish like to be independent and make decisions on their own. Theirs is not a culture of meetings. The traditional function of meetings, if they occur at all, is to communicate instructions. Managers who try to use them constructively complain that the necessary participative skills do not yet exist. With the wholesale introduction of American methods and philosophy, this has begun to change. Social and political developments have also affected the expectations of employees about their role within organizations. While individual accountability is still the basis of organizational life, automatic assumptions about authority are being questioned and participation increasingly demanded at all levels. This leads to complaints by older-style managers that meetings are too frequent, too long, and ineffective.

Spaniards may say that they do not work well in meetings, or in teams generally, because they are individualistic and "jealous." There is certainly a streak of anarchism in the Spanish mentality that is used to justify authoritarianism in many spheres of life. However, the attitude also derives from a conception that collaboration has more to do with voicing opinion than arriving at decisions or, still less, implementing them. This leads to a concept of the meeting as a forum to express ideas of which one will be chosen. A contribution to a debate is seen to further the aim of the meeting less than the personal goals of the person making it. Participants are protective of their own idea, which they will be more inclined to defend than amend. The most senior person present is seen as the arbiter. If he or she makes a proposal, then the purpose of the meeting is to obtain the others' agreement to it.

The idea that a meeting can be used to decide on an action plan, allocate responsibilities, and coordinate implementation is therefore a novelty. Those who are used to collaboration producing a result to which everyone has contributed something, and in which everyone shares responsibility, will find this frustrating. People will feel free to raise ideas and objections, but in the end they consider that it is the boss's neck that is on the line. Unless the chair constantly pulls the subject back to the matter in hand, the agenda—if there is one—will be rapidly abandoned.

At the same time, it is important to force agreement out of others because they will criticize and undermine later on. It is not usually advisable to ratify a decision on a majority vote because the outvoted minority will feel slighted. Consensus is most easily reached by getting everyone to agree with the chairperson rather than with each other.

Communication

The need to communicate to subordinates or colleagues anything other than what is strictly necessary to do the job is an innovation in Spain. Management keeps a closed door, especially if they are talking to someone else. There is plenty of one-to-one communication with the boss, as this is the conventional way for decisions to be made and instructions given, while everyone else wonders what they are talking about. Except in the largest companies there is a marked absence of correspondence, memos, and staff noticeboards. Communication is predominantly oral and preferably face to face.

Upward mobility

People try not move to a different locality for promotion. The extended family remains the basic economic unit, source of security, and social framework. Family ties prevail and migration is still a symptom of desperation, not ambition. In all cities a regional accent is the mark of the laboring not the managerial class and is an impediment to promotion.

Education is seen as the key to progress and there is a thirst for training of all kinds. Some foreign companies, in an attempt to get off the wages spiral, offer training or education subsidies as an incentive to prospective employees. There is no educational élite, other than the best business schools. Some point to one or other of the Jesuit universities or the Opus Dei University in Navarre, but, as is the case with the Masonic order or any other secret society, the practical influence of the latter in everyday business life is hard to gauge.

In many Spanish companies, family is still more important than intelligence in recruitment. Family connections will have gained access to the better universities, or paid for a foreign education if this was too demanding, and will guarantee an appropriate standard of breeding and manners.

Personal loyalty, friendship, and ability, in that order, are the most important qualifications for promotion. Intelligence, in the sense of cleverness, is a quality that Spaniards rate lower than character and breeding. There is not the admiration of cleverness, sly quickwittedness, that is implied in the Italian *in gamba* or the Greek *exipno*. *Listo* is the closest, meaning sharp and not altogether trustworthy. *Inteligente* implies solid and boring. *Bueno*, as in *un tipo bueno*, is the best compliment. It implies being clever, honorable, and *valiente*.

Competitiveness

While relationships in Spain are familiar or even jocular, there is little sense of collegiality. Working relationships are vertical rather than horizontal. The word most used to describe feelings about peers was not rivalry or competitiveness but jealousy. To have got ahead is probably because you have insinuated yourself with the boss or are related to him, not as a result of effort. Promotion is more often seen as a step up to privilege and an easy life rather than greater responsibility. The successful are expected to flaunt their achievement. It is highly desirable to be seen to be making good: a German car, an expensive house, good clothes, a retinue of assistants and secretaries and other hangers-on.

Women

Women have made significant inroads into the professions. A woman lawyer is no longer a rarity. Women managers have in the past been associated primarily with family-owned companies where there is no male line. Women with professional qualifications are, according to both men and women, accepted in their own right. The problems come from unqualified men who feel threatened by technocrats of either sex.

Etiquette

Spanish business and social behavior, in all but the most elevated circles, is very informal. Familiarity is a basic facet of Spanish life. You call the maid and the doorman *usted* and your colleagues and the boss *tu*. This is confusing for Latin Americans, for whom it is the other way round. It is very important not to call your subordinates *usted* because that puts them on the same level as domestic staff. With everybody you get very quickly on to first-name terms. In the south of Spain, where manners are slightly more formal than in the north, it may take a little longer to get on to *tu* terms.

In the office, at meetings, and at restaurants it is common for men to take off their jackets and even loosen their ties. On a very formal occasion, with strangers, or if there is a wide mix of ranks, it pays to be circumspect and see what the others do. Even then, manners are based on an easy and relaxed informality. Human relationships are very important. A good working environment does not mean pleasant surroundings but rewarding relationships with colleagues. The best reference you can give another person is: "He is a good friend of mine." This does not mean a penetration of the privacy barrier, as in Germany or the UK, but an easy relationship based on trust deriving from a personal sense of honor, *orgullo*, and reinforced by respect.

Modesty is valued over assertiveness. Demonstrating superiority, intelligence, or ability is not highly valued. With people like the Italians or French, to whom selling yourself forcefully, clearly, and rationally is part of the game, Spaniards appear understated. With opinionated people like the Germans and British, who try to give the impression that they know best, they may appear diffident or vacillating. When they speak a foreign language Spanish understatement is exaggerated, since often they are wary of being ridiculed for speaking it badly.

Spaniards feel a great sense of personal pride and honor. Anything that diminishes or impinges on that will spoil a relationship. Nevertheless, it is important to know what they are proud of. Technical ability, professionalism, or competence does not concern a Spaniard as much as pride in personal qualities. What may sometimes be interpreted by outsiders as intolerance of other people's opinions is from their point of view a strong sense of self-reliance and personal worth.

Punctuality

Procrastination and delay are endemic. In the kind of business environment in which readers of this book will be operating, it would be wrong to associate this with indolence or obstructionism. It is more likely to be attributable to an attempt to cram too many things into too short a time. The popular conception of the *mañana* attitude is to be found in the stifling bureaucracies of the state sector and not the bustling private firms.

Humor

In public or in formal situations senior people cultivate a serious and dignified image in which joking is out of place. On all other occasions it is important to be amusing and entertaining and good company in and out of the office. This does not imply that work is not taken seriously, but that it is not necessary to be solemn about it. Humor is often bantering and personal, but is not characteristically biting or sarcastic about other individuals and is not used as a weapon. Foreigners as a class or people from other regions are fair game. Catalans have sleepy Andalucian jokes and Andalucians have miserly Catalan jokes. Self-deprecating humor would be at odds with the strong Spanish sense of personal dignity and is rare.

Socializing

The working day starts later than in northern countries, 9am at the earliest, and ends later, after midnight if dinner is involved. It is common for colleagues to have lunch together, but not for ranks to mix. In any case senior people will be lunching with outsiders. Canteens are single status, although the boss would rarely eat there. Social life outside work tends to be with people of the same level in different companies.

Going out for coffee, lunches, and dinners is a vital part of business life. They are used to establish a personal relationship, to see if the chemistry is right and if each can trust the other. This is done by discussing everything except business until coffee is served, when the host will bring up the specific subject of the meeting. Until then one is not expected to bare one's soul nor to remain distant and formal. The strength of a business relationship depends less on a community of interest than a community of feeling.

STAINED GLASS
Where is the largest stained glass window in Europe?

    Norway
    France
    Czechia

BALKAN COUNTRIES

Bulgaria

Bulgaria's population of almost 9 million is mainly ethnic Bulgarian, with a Turkish minority in the south. For 500 years it was part of the Ottoman Empire. With Russian assistance it extricated itself from Ottoman rule in 1878, although it continued to tussle with Turkey, Romania, Serbia, and Greece over Macedonia and Thrace until 1945. The primary goal of reclaiming these two territories led it to ally with the losing side in both world wars. Under communism, central planning, collectivization, and state planning were rigorous and thorough.

After Soviet withdrawal from eastern Europe in 1989, political parties were re-established, confiscated property restored, and privatization started. A new constitution was enacted in 1991, which is the basis for Bulgaria's parliamentary democracy and legal system. The Communist party continued to rule as the Socialist party and to the best of its ability, under a cloak of superficial democratic and free-market reforms, carried on business as usual.

Between 1989 and 1997 there were eight governments, all promising much reform and delivering little except economic collapse. Unwilling and incapable of carrying out the necessary fundamental changes, the *nomenklatura* was more concerned with preserving its political and financial status. So-called privatization was in fact a handout to party *apparatchiks* in league with managers who ran their new assets down and kept them going with soft loans. The banking system almost collapsed in 1996. There are still several conglomerates and interest groups with suspect origins and business connections that wield considerable influence in the Bulgarian economy and among political groups. However, since 1997 the government has taken steps to curb the more blatantly corrupt practices and increasingly enforced legislation.

Ordinary Bulgarians were condemned to another ten years of growing poverty, until in 1997 they took to the streets. A coalition government headed by the center-right United Democratic Forces came to power with promises of urgent reform. It moved quickly to stabilize the economy with a $500 million standby agreement with the International Monetary Fund (IMF) and set up a currency board to reduce 500 percent inflation and peg the currency to the Deutschmark. After a painful period of austerity, the economy and the standard of living of ordinary Bulgarians began a recovery that more or less continues as they tread the stony path of IMF orthodoxy toward western market capitalism.

Per capita income is still officially around $1,500 per annum, but this does not account for the unofficial market where many people make a living. It is estimated that the unregistered market represents an additional 20 to 30 percent of GDP.

Most of industry and agriculture has been privatized, trade liberalized, and the fiscal and banking system reformed. A large and productive agricultural sector has helped to cushion the fall in living standards. Large state-owned cooperatives have been broken up into small privately owned farms. In the process of Bulgaria's joining the EU and faced with the increased competition of global markets, they will doubtless have to be merged back again into larger, more productive units. The retail sector is dominated by small businesses, whose apparent prosperity is an indicator of the importance of the unofficial sector of the economy.

It is therefore not surprising that foreign investors have not been beating a path to Bulgaria as they have to central Europe. Russia remains the country's main trading partner, accounting for about one-third of the total. It supplies the country's oil. About half of international trade is with the EU, notably Germany, Italy, and Greece. Germans and Belgians are the biggest investors. The Kosovo crisis was a setback in that it interrupted the country's overland and Danube river trade routes with western Europe.

Doing business in Bulgaria requires more flexibility on the part of northern and western Europeans than perhaps they are used to. It is not an easy place for outsiders. A sense of isolation, poverty, social collapse, and a decade of mismanagement have created what a Bulgarian respondent calls an "inability to understand the big world looking through the prism of a tiny country." People are defensive, cautious, and looking for short-term gain, very often personal. For many people business behavior is based on strategies for survival.

The foundation of business relationships is the personal relationships that underlie them. You should not rely on abstract conventions, agreements, contracts, and procedures, unless you are sure that they bear the personal commitment of the people with whom you are dealing. Like its Balkan and Black Sea neighbors, the fabric of Bulgaria's society is woven from family, extended family, and personal associates. What northerners see as nepotism or cronyism is the normal and accepted way to get things done. It is perhaps not surprising in this business environment that Bulgarians overwhelmingly see personal contacts and luck as the most important factors in a business career and hard work as the least important.

Communication

English is the second language of a younger and professional generation, while French and German are more current among older people. Russian can be useful.

Bulgarian is a Slavic language. It is written in a variation of Cyrillic and is worth acquiring to find your way round. However, important communication is oral not written. Those from cultures where things acquire significance only when written down are advised to practice their listening skills and to get out of the habit of sending memos and emails if they want to achieve their aims. Instead, pick up the phone or meet for coffee.

Bulgarian conversational style is not characterized by openness and sincerity. Things may be said to test a reaction, or for rhetorical effect, or to disguise the true intention of the speaker. Plain speakers are advised to confirm and reconfirm what they first understood and to restate their own message, which may have been regarded as an opening gambit to be built on or revised later. All of this will take place in a warm and good-natured atmosphere in which humor flourishes. Once a basis of understanding is reached, the relationship will remain solid and dependable however circumstances may change.

Hospitality and socializing are vital to establish the necessary relationships of cooperation and trust and to set up the informal communication channels through which people get things done. Indeed, decisions are often taken outside the office in an informal environment.

Leadership and organization

The overriding first impression of Bulgarian business behavior is informality. People dress casually, try not to look busy, and are very friendly. Outsiders should not fall into the trap of concluding that they are disorganized, it is merely that their organization is different—informal, fluid, and reactive.

Traditional corporate culture is anything but team based. People look for strong leadership and the assertion of authority from bosses, who maintain a separate status from their subordinates. Management styles are highly personalized. Information flows, decision making, and reporting are vertically oriented and usually centered at the top of the organization. People are reluctant to commit themselves and take responsibility unless they are very sure of their ground.

Meetings are not a forum for analysis, debate, or decision making. They are more to reconcile the personalities involved in an issue than to resolve it. The systematic conduct of meetings with agendas, minutes, and action plans is found only in the more westernized companies. Unless specifically given tasks by their boss and forcefully reminded, people will not follow undertakings, commitments, or deadlines.

MOBILE PHONES
Which country has the greatest and which the smallest number of mobile phones per head of population?
> Ireland
> Finland
> Germany

Cyprus

The political and commercial importance of Cyprus outweighs its size. Its recent history and current political status have an impact not only on its own future but on Turkish–Greek relations and the future of Turkey in Europe. Commercially it is an important offshore base for banking, shipping, and trade with eastern Europe.

The recent history of Cyprus cannot be understood without reference to Greece and Turkey and superpower interests in the region. The bare facts are that until 1974 it was a unitary state whose independence was guaranteed by the UK, Turkey, Greece, and Russia. The population of around 850,000 was 80 percent Greek and 20 percent Turkish, mainly in the north of the island. In 1974, for reasons too complicated and disputed to summarize here, the Turkish army invaded Northern Cyprus and divided the island. Populations were exchanged in lamentably traditional Aegean fashion and Turkey unilaterally declared the Turkish Federated State of Cyprus.

In 1983 this became the Turkish Republic of Northern Cyprus, with its capital in Famagusta. It is recognized only by Turkey, which maintains a sizeable garrison there. The population, severely depleted by emigration to the UK, has been boosted to 200,000 by immigration from the mainland. There is effectively no traffic of goods or people between the two halves of the island across a frontier policed by the UN. Cyprus is by no means the only issue that causes constant procrastination over Turkey's accession to the EU, but it is an important one.

For the rest of this chapter Cyprus refers to the Republic of Cyprus, the ethnically Greek state whose capital is Nicosia. It is this state that has been accepted as an applicant for EU membership.

A population of fewer than a million is mainly occupied in services, primarily tourism, and agriculture. The cornerstone of political and economic policy has been structural transformation to meet the demands of EU membership, coordinated by the Government of Cyprus Planning Bureau. This includes legislation to liberalize foreign investment, competition, price control, exchange control, and banking law. It has resulted in increased domestic competition and the dismantling of the protection that enabled the economy of Cyprus to recover so dramatically after partition.

Students of globalization will be less interested in the travails of the domestic business person than in Cyprus's role as an offshore entrepôt and financial center. For adventurous tourists, financiers, and traders, Nicosia has developed over the past ten years into a crossroads of the eastern Mediterranean. While adhering to all European and international norms and standards, Cypriot legislation and control of offshore banks and companies is as favorable as possible to them. Thanks to generations of British rule and emigration to the UK, English is widespread as a second language. Education tries to embody the best of Greek and British. Add that to a strategic geographic location, tax incentives, and a modern infrastructure, and Cyprus becomes a convenient place for companies and individuals to do business with the Middle East, eastern Europe, the former Soviet Union, and north Africa.

For example, the US is one of the leading originators of exports to Cyprus, three-quarters of which are cigarettes re-exported to eastern Europe. (Where they go from there is another story.) There are other goods and commodities that benefit from a convoluted paper trail. Of course, the Cypriot authorities make determined efforts to combat money laundering and other iniquities of international trade.

Communication

English is widely and fluently spoken in Cyprus. Humor is freely exercised in all but the most formal circumstances. Cypriots share with other Mediterranean people and some native English speakers a belief that conversation with acquaintances is to entertain, to persuade, to solicit information, rather than to reveal outright one's thoughts and feelings. This is reserved for those who know each other well. Northerners should not assume that what is first said is the last word on the subject.

Nevertheless, or perhaps because of this, it is an oral culture in which what is said is taken more seriously than what is written. A written proposal or agreement is seen more as a starting point for discussion than a conclusion.

Personal relationships go hand in hand with business relationships. Socializing and hospitality are a necessary part of business life. Personal contacts are not always required to begin business—a trading mentality accepts dealing with strangers—but will often result from it. And business is as likely to be done in an informal setting as at the office.

Confidence in their own views leads to what more than one Cypriot respondent termed obstinacy. They are more accustomed to dialectic, which pits one opinion head to head with another, than with a search for common ground. This is one reason why they do not see themselves working well in teams.

Authority, accountability, and decision making are concentrated in individuals. Delegation and implementation are on an individual basis. While leaders will make every effort to persuade their subordinates as to the rightness of a decision, ultimately it is theirs alone and active participation or consensus is not required. They keep an authoritative distance from those that work for them and take the dominant role in meetings and discussions. Even senior managers have a hands-on approach, believing that people have always to be reminded of commitments such as delivery promises, deadlines, and action plans.

TOURISM

Which country has the greatest and which the smallest number of hotels per 100 inhabitants?

> Denmark
>
> Italy
>
> Austria

Greece

For a country with such an ancient and revered past, Greece has a propensity for constantly remaking itself. The latest transformation over the past few decades is from an underdeveloped Balkan backwater on the fringes of Europe to a modern mixed economy sufficiently well managed to qualify for entry into European Monetary Union.

Greece still has some way to go, however. With the tightening of fiscal policy and reduction of budget deficits inflation is at record lows, but official unemployment is around 10 percent. The public sector still accounts for half of GDP and privatization is retarded by the opposition of unions and other vested political interests. Nevertheless, the statistics do not reflect the evident affluence and dynamism of a private sector that avoids to the greatest extent possible any official record of its success.

Despite a tradition of political and economic crisis, it would not be accurate to say that confidence in government in Greece is damaged; it was never very high to begin with. The government's primary role is seen as redistributing money and whether you are on the giving or receiving end depends on your ingenuity.

Outsiders should be careful not to confuse what they regard as civic irresponsibility with lack of patriotism. This is embodied in religion and language and a strong sense of history. Although they are happy to play along with the romantic notion that they are descendants of the Ancient Greeks, their true antecedent is Byzantium, which they have kept alive in institutions and customs throughout centuries of foreign domination. Constantinople not Athens is the real spiritual home.

While Greeks are rightfully resentful of what they perceive as outside interference and blame their misfortunes on outsiders, whether Turks, Russians, or Americans, they are anything but chauvinistic. Aptitude and necessity have given them an international outlook. The worldwide shipping industry, trading communities in every continent, and prosperous emigrant communities bear witness to an immensely enterprising and adaptable people.

Greek life as well as language is demotic. Social hierarchies sit uneasily on its society. The basic social unit is the family, closely followed by the *xorio*, or village. This is not a geographic or community concept but a close network of family alliances that survives even in the context of the Athens conurbation, where almost half of the Greek population lives.

Business environment

The traditional backbone of Greek industry had been large conglomerates run by dynastic families and closely associated with the banks, notably the National Bank of Greece. Second in importance is the multitude of small family-owned companies. Nimble and entrepreneurial, these companies have learned to be opportunistic and flexible, if they have survived the record number of bankruptcies in the past few years. Some have been replaced by new businesses set up by entrepreneurs returning from abroad. Foreign investment has been targeted on tourist-related industries, such as hotels and food and beverage companies. Tourism remains the most buoyant sector, with as many visitors each year as there are inhabitants.

Industrial relations are politicized, confrontational, and unstructured. The ministry of labor actively controls the pay structure by fiat. In order to compensate staff for performance and discourage them from leaving, companies have to resort to perks, bonuses, and subterfuge. These are also used to induce people not to take two jobs, a common practice that is partly to earn money and partly to build up the personal business to which most Greeks aspire.

Corporate structure is based either on the French SA model, *Anonymi Eteria* (AE), or the limited company, *Eteria Periorismenis Efthinis* (EPE). An AE has a board of at least three directors elected by shareholders. The chief executive is either the general manager, *genikos dieftindis*, or the managing director, *diefthinon simvoulos*. The former is usually associated with an SA and the latter with an EPE, although sometimes the two positions can be found in the same company.

In a traditional company the titles and positions are irrelevant. There is one boss, the *effendikos*, who takes all responsibility. He is the owner or has the owner's trust. Below him is a narrow and vertically oriented hierarchy of subordinates who are delegated specific tasks and have little responsibility.

This approach works better in small and medium-sized family companies than in large or state-owned companies. Unless they have trained or worked in a large company abroad, Greeks are uncomfortable in that kind of environment. Greek and Italian mentality should not be confused, but their attitude to corporate life is very similar. Organizations exist solely for the benefit of the individuals within them.

Banks are instrumental in introducing management discipline. The cash-flow forecast is the most important piece of financial information, coupled with a one-year or 18-month operating plan. They expect to see a proper management structure and a realistic organization chart. Some multinationals and a few of the state-owned companies have introduced other American-inspired practices. There is a growing number of young people educated in business schools in the UK and the US, emigrants returning from Australia, America, and Europe, who bring back with them new attitudes and practices.

Upward mobility

The major consideration for preferment is whether the person concerned can be trusted rather than qualifications, expertise, or performance. This is the basis of the nepotism, political affiliation, and personal influence, known in Greek as *messon*, that permeate the fabric of every Greek organization.

The technocratic ideal of rising to the top on merit and performance alone is honored in the breach in all European cultures, but rarely more so than in Greece. Trust is the basis on which outsiders are also judged. They are genuinely welcomed as a source of new ideas and expertise, international contacts and influence, but any suspicion that they are exploiting the relationship or attempting to dominate it will be detrimental. It is unwise to join in the politics, even if there appear to be factions or individuals who want you on their side. Greeks are world champions at such matters and in the end the loyalty of Greek to Greek is stronger.

Compared with most European countries there is little discrimination against women. They are well represented in the professions and in politics and their opportunities in business, like those of the men, depend more on their connections than their gender.

Communication

The Greek language is extraordinarily rich and difficult and further complicated by the alphabet. Knowing other languages or Ancient Greek is not much help. Greeks are well aware of this—even a smattering reaps richer rewards than in other countries and will be treated with infinite patience.

There is a subtle range of formality in the way Greeks address each other, but this need not be inhibiting to an outsider. Any attempt to address them in Greek will be regarded as a compliment. *Kyrie* or *Kyria* can be used with the first or last name (or on their own) and the polite plural or informal singular can be used with either. First names are employed between colleagues of similar age and status and sometimes last names. The formality of first acquaintance will rapidly move to informality. If in doubt ask, but you will probably have been told first.

Personal contact is important in the smallest matters. Only when it is impossible to meet face to face will the telephone be used, and then at great length. Information and gossip are hoarded and swapped on a transactional basis.

There is a distrust of written communication. The recipient of a letter or memo will ask not what it says but why the sender wants a permanent record. In addition, written Greek is difficult, even for Greeks. Until relatively recently there was a separate written language, *katharevousa*. Letters and memos still tend to be stilted and formal and there is a great deal of snobbery about how well you write. Orally, however, there are no constraints. In today's populist environment simple, demotic Greek is preferred and regional accents are acceptable.

Humor is as frequently enjoyed in business as anywhere else. It is witty, satirical, and pointed, especially where government is concerned. Among people with a close relationship it can be uninhibited and personal. This applies not only to humor; pretentiousness and standoffishness are not appreciated. Even comparative strangers may quiz you about family circumstances and personal finances.

Greeks are skilled debaters and employ a whole gamut of verbal and physical expressions. To outsiders used to a more restrained mode of expression, what appears like a full-blown argument may be a quite innocuous exchange of views. The time to beware is when your interlocutor becomes quiet and withdrawn.

With the exception of the banks, dress is more informal than in most other European countries. It is also a poor guide to status. The only consistency is that it is not usual to dress up to go to work or dress down to enjoy oneself.

The official working day starts early and ends at lunchtime when most people go home, although large companies are increasingly changing to northern European hours. Breaks for coffee and snacks are a seamless part of the day. Lunchtime entertaining is usually for business guests.

More formal occasions at the office, such as the ceremonial cutting of the New Year cake, are attended by most people but are not occasions of social mixing. Larger companies may organize social events for those lower down in the organization. Out-of-hours mixing among colleagues results from social compatibility and not business reasons and there is little mingling among ranks.

Leadership and organization

Traditional leadership styles are highly directive in that individual rather than group responsibility is paramount. Greeks work best in teams with a strong leader, who ultimately takes all decisions and is then careful to make sure they are carried out.

Individual leadership coexists with a preference for collective action. *Parea*, companionship, is an essential feature of Greek life. In a country where reading a book or going for a walk on one's own is viewed as deplorable eccentricity, individual action is rare. This by no means implies unanimity. To be a member of any group, formal or informal, carries with it the obligation to make a distinctive contribution. This combination of extreme individualism and collectivism can be confusing to outsiders. It can be very productive in a small and paternalistic environment, but frequently leads to factionalism in larger organizations.

The meeting is a forum for the dynamic expression of strong personal opinions, preferably contrary to everyone else's. Each person has their turn and will be
listened to and energetically argued with. Formal meetings are arranged only for
important issues. Frequent informal coordination and briefing meetings constitute
a valuable method of finding out what is going on when information systems are
crude and unreliable. There is seldom a formal agenda and rarely are there formal
minutes, other than the ones that individual participants take.

While procedural mechanisms may be drawn up they are not always adhered
to, especially if they run laterally rather than vertically across the organization. The
quality of cooperation between departments depends largely on the personal relationships of those concerned.

Forecasts and plans are the preserve of
senior management and remain subject to
constant amendment. The plan is a tool for
negotiating with banks and shareholders
rather than a management device. Time
horizons are short and there is a preference
for opportunistic, reactive policies.

UNMARRIED PARENTS
Which country has the largest and which the
smallest proportion of children born to unmarried
parents?
    UK
    Denmark
    Greece

Romania

It is important for Romanians that they are considered a Latin people. By race, history, and above all language they claim affinity with western Europe, primarily Italy and France. Seeing themselves as the easternmost outpost of western European culture enables them to maintain a sense of identity different from their Hungarian and Slavic neighbors, especially Russia. It has also been useful for reformers to explain the transition to democracy and a free-market economy not as an alien imposition but as a return to western values, and in particular to the liberal political, economic, and legal systems of the western-style constitutional monarchy of the 1920s and 1930s.

At the same time, Romanians can look back on a history inextricable from the rise and fall of Byzantine, Hungarian, Ottoman, Austrian, and Russian empires. Their religious culture is Romanian Orthodox. Those working in Romania may draw conclusions from their own experience as to whether the most formative influences have been western or eastern European.

The population is 23 million, 90 percent of whom are Romanian Orthodox. The rest, mainly in Transylvania, are Catholic and Protestant. There is a large and uncounted Gypsy minority who do their best to remain unintegrated. Some 30 percent of the population is engaged in agriculture. Bucharest has two million inhabitants, while none of the other major cities has more than 350,000.

There are three distinct and at various times in their history independent regions: Moldavia, Wallachia, and Transylvania. There are about seven million people in Transylvania, of whom two million are Hungarians and close on one million belong to a variety of ethnic groups, the largest of which is German. The mythic power of Transylvania goes far beyond Count Dracula. At different times in the pasts of Hungarians and Romanians it was the embodiment of their national independence, aspirations, and culture. It has changed hands between them several times, each transfer adding to recrimination and bitterness. Neither side speaks objectively about the other.

A fourth area inhabited by Romanians is what is now known as the Republic of Moldova on the other side of the Prut river. Those who have labored over nineteenth-century European history will recognize it as Bessarabia. The eastern part, known to Russians as Trans-Dniestria, is of great strategic importance to Russia. At the end of the Second World War the USSR incorporated this territory and created a separate republic, asserting that Moldovan was a language different from Romanian, which clearly it is not. After the breakup of the Soviet Union Russia has ensured that it remains independent from Romania.

The name Romania dates back to 1862 when a semi-autonomous monarchy was created within the Ottoman empire, uniting the thrones of Wallachia and Moldavia. In 1877 it became fully independent. 1918 marks the beginning of modern Romania, when Transylvania and other smaller territories were acquired with the defeat of Austria-Hungary. At the end of the Second World War, in which Romania had fought on both sides, Romania fell into the Soviet sphere of influence and by 1948 the monarchy had been abolished and a communist government installed.

Romania's communist history is dominated by Nicolae Ceaucescu, who came to power in 1965. Although he never broke with the Soviet Union he won popular support for his political independence. He adhered closely to communist orthodoxy at home and used the secret police, the *Securitate*, to clamp down on any political, social, or economic dissent. Ceaucescu had bold plans for modernization and development. Over one-fifth of central Bucharest was demolished to make way for grandiose construction. Massive industrial schemes were designed to make Romania self-sufficient in industry and agriculture. His most disastrous policy was paying off the foreign debt incurred by the industrial projects by exporting so much agricultural and industrial production that the country was driven from a state of relative economic wellbeing to near starvation.

Ceaucescu's nepotistic and destructive rule became too much even for fellow party members. They were plotting to replace him when they were preempted in 1989 by a popular uprising and military mutiny that started in Timisaora and spread rapidly to the capital. His reign ended before a firing squad. Iliescu and his National Salvation Front quickly took over, ensuring a continuation of the old system.

Romania has been prosperous in the past and there is potential for it to be so again. It has a wide range of natural resources, including a fertile agricultural base, oil, gas, and coal. The Danube and the Black Sea are convenient trade routes. Not all of industrial development is unviable and Ceaucescu's legacy of a relatively low foreign debt gives scope for modernization. However, the National Salvation Front and its successor governments avoided necessary economic reform. Even if they had the will to break free from socialist convictions, they feared the social costs and political upheaval of inflation, rapid unemployment, and a fall in an already minimal standard of living, especially their own. Commercial law, competition law, intellectual property law, labor and social security law, banking law, and tax law were reformed on the French model, but although much legislation was enacted, little was done to implement it. Admittedly the country was starting from a lower base. Under Ceaucescu the economy had remained resolutely centralized with none of the reforms and modifications that enabled individuals, small businesses, and farmers in other countries to maintain a modicum of capitalist expertise.

A new coalition government in 1996 pledged to accelerate reform. It focused on eliminating price controls, freeing the exchange rate, eliminating subsidies, encouraging foreign investment, and pushing forward with privatization. Some progress was made, although it again ground to a virtual halt. An economic crisis and a hard line from the IMF were necessary to get it going again in 1998. The state sector continues to account for 70 percent of industrial production and many large state-owned enterprises are still awaiting privatization or liquidation.

Uncertainties in the business climate and delays in genuine reform have kept away foreign investment. Despite the existence of the legislation needed to operate a market economy, Romania remains a difficult business environment. Government red tape and bureaucracy, including local municipal administration and other regulatory authorities, are extensive and obstructive. Special interests continue to make specific projects difficult to implement, especially when providing competition to ingrained economic institutions. Commercial and fiscal legislation is sometimes unclear and Romanian justice continues to be slow and bureaucratic. There is a perception, unfounded or not, that the legal system does not treat companies equally. Corruption is a major problem despite high-visibility but ineffective anticorruption campaigns. A national commission to combat organized crime and corruption has been painstakingly ineffective.

Shortage of capital, limited collateral, and lack of experience channel new entrepreneurs toward activities where initial investments are low and returns can be made rapidly, such as trade and services. Despite investment in education and training, there is still a serious skills shortage and the level of exposure to western business practices has been low. Foreign investors must be willing to provide extensive training to their partners and employees. It is also important for foreigners to understand the working environment in which their colleagues worked until recently, and in many cases, notably in the state sector, still do.

Communication

Romania has 14 linguistic minorities, the highest number in Europe, representing most of the Black Sea peoples and its exiles. Romanian uses the Latin alphabet. It is considered a Romance language as much of the vocabulary and some of the grammar derives from Latin, although there are also important Thracian and Slavic elements. Those who go to Romania expecting to communicate in Italian will be disappointed. Even words that are recognizably Latin when written have a Romanian pronunciation.

Until recently French and Italian were the foreign languages most likely to be spoken. In some parts of the country German is a useful language. Nevertheless, these are being eclipsed among professional people by English.

Romanians find their language melodic and beautiful and enjoy speaking it, sometimes to the detriment of getting the point over clearly and concisely. To an

outsider unfamiliar with stylistic conventions they seem to skirt around issues, especially if they are disagreeable. Humor is rarely used in a formal business context,
being reserved for the restaurant afterwards.

In societies that were formerly secretive and closed, where hard facts were in
short supply, and information was designed to influence and not inform, old habits
die hard. Information is a commodity to be traded and a source of power and
status in an organization. Frank and open discussion occurs at a later stage in a
relationship.

Business relationships remain formal. First names are for relatives and friends.
In a business environment people use last names or professional titles, or simply
Domnul (sir) and *Doamna* (madam) when addressing one another. First names are
used among younger people and in business with English-speaking partners,
however.

As in other eastern European countries, old-world courtesy is one of the social
devices for excluding women from the man's world of business. Many of those who
succeed in breaking in go to lengths of flattery and deference that western liber-
ated women would find insufferable.

It is the custom if you are a guest of one of the more traditional and state-
owned companies to be offered a glass of plum brandy, regardless of the time of
day. By all means refuse it politely if you wish. It is a gesture of genuine hospitality
that also reflects the status of the host. He needs to have attained a certain level in
the organization to be able to do so. It is also a sign of things to come if business
begins to develop. Socializing and hospitality during the day, in the evening, or at
weekends are an essential part of cementing the necessary personal relationships
on which business relationships are based. Serious business may be done on these
occasions away from the protocol and formality of the office environment.

Organization

In business and outside, Romania is a society of insiders. The basis of organizational
life is personal networks. Those who do not succeed in creating the necessary relationships find more difficulties and obstructions in their path than those who do.
Newcomers without introductions or other personal credentials may find it difficult
to break in.

The attitude to time in Romania lacks the urgency that some outsiders feel
necessary in business. Little value is placed on strict punctuality. The rhythm of
working life is relaxed and orchestrated around recuperative breaks.

On a more elevated level negotiations, decision making, and implementation
are anything but hasty. While final decision making is concentrated at the top of the

organization, the due process of clarification, analysis, and approval is distributed over several levels, each of which gives their assent and approval.

Organizational structure in traditional companies is far from lackadaisical. They are organized along strictly systematic and hierarchical lines. The lower down the organization they are, the less people are willing to diverge from their allotted duties.

Private companies, especially smaller ones, have developed more streamlined processes and are prepared for the greater flexibility necessary in changing and volatile markets. Nevertheless, the processes can be just as opaque and decision making is still concentrated at the top.

Leadership

Romanian leaders are very aware of their responsibility to lead and the social status that goes with it. At all but the highest levels of organization people have been accustomed to instructions, not empowerment. It is not a team-based culture.

People at meetings are expected to be respectful of protocol and the authority of the person in charge. Those in lower-level positions will keep their counsel and wait to be addressed. As the meeting is usually intended to provide evidence of clear leadership rather than being a forum for discussion, there is unlikely to be an agenda other than that in the leader's mind or a comprehensive action plan. Instructions are relayed down the line on a one-to-one basis and an experienced manager will follow up closely to make sure that they are being carried out.

> **MUSLIMS**
> Which country has the largest Muslim community?
> > UK
> > Germany
> > France

Turkey

Modern Turkey was created out of the ruins of the Ottoman empire after the First World War. It was a new and independent country, predominantly Muslim, western oriented, confined mainly to Anatolia, with a democratic and secular government run by ethnic Turks in the capital, Ankara. In all these respects it differed from its predecessor, the despotic, oriental regime of a multicultural European and Asian empire based in Constantinople.

The leader of the new Turkey was Kemal Atatürk. He took his name in 1935 when all Turks were obliged for the first time to take a family name as well as a given name. It means Father Turk, or Father of the Turks. His biography is essential to an understanding of Turkey, if only to explain why his picture is in every public space and many private homes too. His vision, ruthlessness, and force of personality still inspire the Turkey he created.

Atatürk first came to prominence in 1915 as the victor of Gallipoli against superior Allied forces. In 1919 Greece, with the support of French and Italian armies, invaded Anatolia with its big idea of a new Greek Empire based in Constantinople. Atatürk and his revolutionary government reformed and reinspired the shattered Ottoman army and a demoralized people and ultimately expelled the invading armies. They relocated the capital in the Turkish heartland away from the multi-cultural, internationalist, western-dominated Constantinople and its successor Ottoman government. Within ten years of its founding in 1923 the new republic adopted a western-style constitution and legal codes, Islam was superseded as the state religion, polygamy abolished, women were given the vote. Arabic script was replaced by a western alphabet, Constantinople was renamed Istanbul, and wearing a fez became a capital offense. It remained a single-party democracy until 1945 when other parties were permitted.

Atatürk's vision is still not fully realized. Turkey is a country of polarities. European–Asian, secular–Islamic, urban–rural, traditional–modern are among the opposing forces at the heart of Turkish society. In business or social situations it is sometimes difficult to decide which tendency one is dealing with at the time, and not only if you are a foreigner. Turks themselves acknowledge tensions and uncertainties in their own sense of identity.

In many respects—not all of them comfortable—Turkey is heavily engaged in Europe. It is a member of the EU customs union and an applicant for EU membership. It has been a member of NATO since 1952. It is inextricably involved in Cyprus and has interlocking, frequently conflicting interests with Greece. Turkish *Gastarbeiter* in Germany make up the largest immigrant community in the EU.

Yet in the past the country has been reluctant fully to embrace European social and political values. In addition to purely economic factors, for example rampant inflation, progress in EU membership has been impeded by human rights issues, the role of the army in government, and the curtailment of democracy exemplified by the suppression of Islamist political parties.

2002 may have been a watershed, however. Capital punishment was abolished, restrictions on Kurdish human rights relaxed, and freedom of the press restored. A free and fair election threw out all the MPs of the previous coalition and brought to power a moderate Islamist party. Whether this is a temporary wobble of the army's hold on affairs or a permanent shift remains to be seen.

Meanwhile on the European side there are misgivings ranging from specific issues regarding Cyprus and Greece, through fears of migration, to racism and prejudice against Islam. These are weighty matters, but the key issue will not go away whatever the near future holds: Does a Muslim country on the continent of Asia belong in a European community?

Turkey is fully engaged in Asia. The population outside the major cities and the Mediterranean seaboard has a standard and style of living that has more in common with the East than the West. Turkey is an important regional power in the Black Sea and the Middle East. Its neighbors include Syria, Iraq, Iran, and the troubled states of the Caucasus. It has taken the lead in forming the Black Sea Economic Cooperation region (BSEC). A quarter of the population of Turkey is Kurdish, of whom half live in southeast Turkey and an unquantifiable proportion sympathize with those of their kin in Iraq and Iran who wish to create an independent Kurdistan.

Almost all Turkish people are Muslims. They are by no means a heterogeneous community, including orthodox Sunni and unorthodox Aliyeh, fundamentalists who wish to set up an Islamic state and those who support the secular democratic state. To a greater or lesser extent all Muslims are faced with the dilemma of accommodating to the western values that increasingly dominate their lives. While it is deeply rooted in Turkish culture and society, in the business environment Islam is no more perceptible than other faiths in western countries.

In the political arena Islamist parties have been repeatedly formed and suppressed on the grounds that they conspire to bring down the secular state. Their adherents regroup under another name. These represent a minority of Muslims, but are in no sense marginal. When permitted they win a substantial number of seats in parliament and in the past have gained power in the ruling coalition. Their suppression creates frustration and alienation that sometimes spills over into violence.

The Turkish army is the largest in NATO after the United States. Military spending is 12 percent of the national budget, the highest in NATO. The army was the founding force of the republic and still considers itself to be the guarantor of a unitary state and the secular republic. It provides half of the members and most of the policies of the National Security Council. While ostensibly concerned only with security, the influence of the National Security Council pervades all government departments. If the army feels that the state is under threat it is prepared to dismiss the government, suspend the constitution, and rule directly, as it has done three times in 1960, 1971, and 1980.

In eastern Turkey there is a continuing state of emergency to combat the insurgency of the Kurdistan Workers' Party, otherwise known as the PKK. This has led to curtailment of human rights, eviction of communities, and a considerable drain on the national budget. Kurdish language broadcasting and education are banned.

Since 1945 the country has had a succession of weak and unpopular governments based on fragile alliances, uneasy coalitions, and shifting political loyalties, interspersed with periods of military rule. Popular support is undermined by blatant corruption and economic mismanagement. Periods of accelerated growth are punctuated by financial crises. There are persistent high levels of inflation, often rising to over 80 percent, caused by large fiscal deficits for which subsidies, grants, and a swollen public sector are largely to blame.

With a population of 65 million, Turkey is the third largest country in Europe after Russia and Germany. Some 9 million live in the commercial center Istanbul and 3.5 million in Ankara. The administration is highly centralized. The 73 provinces are ruled by governors appointed by Ankara and locally elected authorities have little autonomy. Istanbul is the country's commercial center, followed by Izmir and Adana, while Ankara is for those interested in government-sponsored infrastructure projects.

Around 40 percent of the population is engaged in the agricultural sector. Turkey is self-sufficient in food and exports commodities such as cotton, tobacco, fruit, and vegetables. Tourism dominates the service sector. The dynamic private sector is the engine of the economy, even though its contribution is understated as much of it operates in the "unregistered" economy. Textiles and clothing is the most important manufacturing sector and accounts for 40 percent of exports. In recent years, the pattern of Turkish trade has shifted from the Middle East to the EU. Germany, Italy, France, and the UK are the principal trading partners. Turkish contractors and developers are very active in central Asia and other neighboring countries such as Russia.

Political uncertainty and the volatility of the economy dominate the business environment. Turkish business people are used to working with unpredictability. As in other emerging markets, short-termism, reactivity, and undercapitalization prevail. Some large companies and multinationals may indulge in strategic planning and long-term investment, but in general these are not for the majority of Turkish companies.

The financial sector is overbanked and underlent, preferring to dedicate its resources to government securities. Loan portfolios are concentrated on companies with close corporate or personal relationships. Part of the reason for doing business only with those you know well is that accounting practices are neither at commonly-accepted world standards nor evenly applied.

In a fast-changing environment, where information is unreliable and elusive, personal contacts are essential. Those who are used to looking on a screen for company information, credit checks, market data, economic forecasts, and so on are better advised in Turkey to pick up the phone to a friend. The fabric of Turkish society, including the business sector, is built on personal relationships. These start with the extended family and spread out to ethnic and religious affiliations, school and army friendships, and so on. They are the basis for recruitment and promotion, and business partnerships and alliances. Looking for a job? Looking for a finance director? The first call is not to the recruitment consultant or the appointments page but family and friends.

While they cannot hope to become members of these exclusive clans and networks, outsiders should understand their importance and make every effort to forge loyalties and alliances with the individuals with whom they work. This begins with first meetings in which, from a western point of view, an inordinate amount of time may be spent on what seems like gossip and small talk.

There are many managers, often the younger ones, who have the same education, training, outlook, management style, and competences as anyone you may meet in a western multinational. Others, usually but not always older, have a traditional Turkish way of doing things, matched by the expectations of their employees. What follows is a description of this more traditional culture.

Communication

Turkish is not readily accessible to speakers of European languages. Above all, they will find tense forms and sentence construction alien to their way of thinking. English is spoken by the educated classes and French among older people. Otherwise your chances are better with German, especially outside the main cities.

The traditional form of address, which remains common among older and senior people, is the given name followed by *bey*: John *bey*. The modern form is the last name preceded by *Bay*: *Bay* Mole. Despite the spelling difference they are pronounced the same. Women are *hanim* or *Bayam*.

Formal meetings in an office environment are interspersed with informal meetings in cafés and hotel lounges. Both kinds are unstructured and discursive. In a business environment humor is subtle and infrequent. Turks are not usually direct speakers and are reluctant to say "no." It is more important to be polite than informative and to find agreement and compromise rather than to clarify contrary positions. This creates a positive but often clouded atmosphere.

It would be wrong to describe the Turkish way of analysis and problem solving as circuitous. Rather, it is inclusive and multifaceted. Turkish education is based on principles different from those of the West. It does not emphasize questioning, logic, and dialectic, but acquisition of knowledge and learning by heart. The questioning of authority, of teachers and what they teach, is not encouraged. What has been called "emotional intelligence" is cultivated and feelings are closer to the surface, even in a business environment, than they are allowed to be in most western European cultures. Those who are not used to this conversational style may find it beneficial to confirm and reconfirm what has been said and to cultivate a sensitivity to the nuances of expression and language used by their partners.

Turkish is an oral culture in which what is heard and said carries more weight than what is written. Most business is done according to verbal agreements and written commitments are difficult to obtain. Legal contracts and agreements are not reliable, since bringing a case to court is usually very time consuming.

Leadership

Turkish concepts of leadership are based on vertical hierarchy under a single decision maker. Obedience to authority and respect for a strong leader are strong values in all aspects of life, including business. For a manager to gather advice, ask for help, or otherwise demonstrate uncertainty or ignorance is seen as a weakness.

Bosses keep a distance from their subordinates. They expect neither initiative nor questioning nor constructive criticism from those they manage. Decision making is concentrated at the top of the hierarchy. Delegation of authority is not an important managerial competence and is rarely practiced. As a management tool for decision making or problem solving, the team meeting or staff meeting is rarely used. Unhampered by consultation, decision making is usually fast and intuitive. Implementation is time consuming, requiring a high level of elaboration and control.

Subordinates try to avoid responsibility and rarely make suggestions or commitments, especially if there is a risk that these may backfire on them. They are especially reluctant to voice problems. Foreign managers will need time and patience to clarify their expectations and establish the necessary trust if they wish to develop a team-based and collaborative approach.

The inhibition of upward flows of information and feedback is compensated for by informal networking skills that are much more developed than among western counterparts. Information generally is regarded as a commodity and a source of power and is traded rather than disseminated freely.

Organization

Turks are skilled at developing comprehensive systems and procedures and, once these are in place, at finding ways round them. Flexibility and improvisation are considered more effective than sticking to the rules.

This is reflected in standards of punctuality. Slippage in timekeeping and last-minute changes of schedule are less signs of inefficiency than a talent for doing several things at once and fitting as much into the day as possible. It is more important to do what seems significant than to stick slavishly to a timetable.

Since the value put on keeping to procedures and systems is lower than in many western countries and concepts of empowerment and personal accountability are different, a higher level of direct control and hands-on management is expected. Turkish managers instinctively keep a continual check that their instructions are being carried out.

Forward planning based on numerical analysis and projection is not highly developed and is seen as irrelevant in a volatile environment. In any case, neither the necessary internal management accounting system nor the external market information will be sufficiently reliable. Similarly, performance management based on standards and quantified targets, whether applied to the company or individual employees, is a technique that has still to find a widespread following. Cash flow and gross margin are the main, if not the sole, performance criteria.

HIPPOPOTAMUSES

Where will you find the biggest herd of hippopotamuses in Europe?

Netherlands

Spain

Norway

Russia

When I first went to the Soviet Union on a package tour we were advised to take our own rubber plugs for the wash basin and bath. We came up with various explanations for the deficit—the inefficiency of central planning; a rubber shortage; theft; neglect of personal hygiene—whether as a cause or a consequence of the plug deficit. But whatever the explanation, it was sure to be condescending.

Some years later, a Russian business partner came to the UK. I asked him what struck him most. Top of the list was having separate hot and cold taps so far apart that you had to wash in either very cold or very hot water. Patiently I explained about putting the plug in the hole and filling the basin with water. He was horrified that we washed in stagnant water. Russians always wash in running water, which is why they have mixer taps and not much use for plugs.

The temptation to jump to condescending conclusions about Russians is even stronger than with other Europeans. The Soviet Union lost the Cold War and its economic and political systems have proved inferior to capitalism, for example. We are victims of two generations of our own propaganda, kept alive by the stories that western media seek out and their interpretation. Those who wish to understand and do business with Russians have to make a greater effort than with other Europeans to put smugness and prejudice out of their mind and assess reality as they experience it.

A lot of country...

The Russian Federation is vast. It covers 11 time zones and stretches 6,000 miles from the Baltic to the Pacific. Its area is over 30 times bigger than Europe's largest country, France, and almost twice as big as the US. It spans frozen tundra in the north and a balmy Mediterranean climate in the south. There are 20 republics and 55 regions. Like Americans, Russians think big.

...for not many people (relatively)

However, for its size the population of Russia is small, about 150 million, compared with about 340 million in the EU and 265 million in the US. About 80 percent are Russian, a proportion that is steadily decreasing as they have a lower birth rate than ethnic minorities. The country as a whole has a negative population growth; in other words, more people are dying than are being born. There are some 95 minorities, most of whom do not speak Russian as their first language. Tatars, a Turkic-speaking Muslim people, are the largest minority with 4 percent.

The distribution of the population is very uneven. Vast territories of Siberia have no constant population at all. There is considerable migration from the northern regions to the central ones following the collapse of ambitious programs aimed at the development of the far north and far east. These are the lucky ones. Many are trapped in their temporary homes in the Arctic with no money to move back south. There was also an exodus of ethnic Russians from former Soviet republics, especially from the Caucasus and Central Asia. The statistics are unreliable because not everybody registers.

Moscow is an international, cosmopolitan, and imperial city. While there is less reason now for non-Russians to come to Moscow, there is a host of ethnic types whom one rarely sees in the west. Mongols and Tartars, Tajiks and Uzbeks, Chechens and Azeris mingle with the new flood of westerners. Russians are sensitive about race and in private can be politically incorrect in their observations about minorities, whether Russian or western.

An urban society

The days of the Russian peasant are long gone: 75 percent of the population is urban, about the same proportion as France. Since it is primarily the younger generation that migrates to the city, rural areas are populated largely by elderly people. Moscow has 9 million inhabitants and St. Petersburg has 5 million, compared with 10 million in Paris and 7 million in New York and London. There are 14 cities in Russia with populations of over a million. More than a third of the population live in towns with a population of more than half a million. The geographic and administrative isolation of these large communities in a vast and for much of the time inhospitable hinterland fosters wide economic and cultural diversity. Many cities and their surrounding regions are economically and politically self-sufficient. Several regions and republics in the Russian Federation aspire to independence. There is a very real fear of further fragmentation of the Federation and for the security of Russia herself.

Every city has its distinct character and its own approach to reform. Russia's third city, Nizhnii Novgorod, a large inland port on the Volga, is furthest down the road to free-market capitalism, while a couple of hundred kilometers away there are secret cities only known by number that are still in the iron grip of the defense establishment.

A fragmented society...

Fragmentation is not only geographic. In the old days Soviet society was far more heterogeneous than westerners were led to believe. Industry was highly vertically integrated and horizontally divided. A large company would own not only its factories but the entities that built them and the machinery inside, the apartment buildings that housed its workers, and the farms that fed them. Nevertheless, it would have had very little contact with other companies in similar businesses. In closed cities companies could be in the same business and supplying similar products while remaining completely ignorant of one another's activities.

It has been said that because there is no word for privacy in Russian the spirit of collectivity is deeply ingrained in the Russian psyche. (I am unconvinced by this argument. There is no word for privacy in French either. Or for entrepreneur in English, unfair in German, foot in Greek—but does it mean that the natives don't have these things?) Certainly, collectivism and collectivity have been imposed on Russians since long before the October Revolution, but this seems to have had little impact on the fundamental fissility of Russian society and the competitiveness of individual Russians. There have always been distinct and self-sufficient social hierarchies based on education and profession. There are still self-perpetuating oligarchies in politics, diplomacy, industry, science, education, and the arts whose children follow in the family business. It is still hard to be a journalist if you are not the son of a journalist or a diplomat if you are not the son of a diplomat, and harder still to make a successful career if you do not have the right contacts.

The fundamental social unit is the extended family, including networks of close friends. However, outside this unit there is as much rivalry and competition, ambition and status seeking as in any western country. The only large social institution where social mobility, lateral and vertical, was possible was the Party. Now the surest path to upward mobility is through private enterprise.

...but a strong sense of self

Russians have the misfortune to think of history as periods of relative calm punctuated by crisis. They talk of "before the crisis" and "after the crisis." Outsiders may be forgiven for wondering which crisis, as there have been so many. They probably mean the economic crisis of August 1998 when the currency collapsed and many people lost their livelihoods and savings. Unfortunately, it may not be the last of the political and economic crises that are a feature of transition economies, especially those as large as Russia's. The majority who do not enjoy the blessings of the New Russia can be forgiven for looking back with nostalgia to the certainties and relative calm of socialism.

A sense of confusion about the collapse of the Soviet system often results in simultaneous displays of self-deprecation and pride. There is a regret for the loss of the empire, especially those states with large Russian populations. The loss of the Crimea is particularly resented. At the same time there is a sense of "good riddance," especially toward the Central Asian Republics, which were a net drain on Russian resources. Russian Independence Day is celebrated, albeit to the amusement of some Russians who wonder from whom they have seized independence.

Russians have a natural resistance to change born of bitter historical experience. Change has usually been imposed from above and its consequences have normally been more hardship and misfortune. Losing the Cold War was a blow to Russian self-esteem and many feel threatened by it. It is not a matter for congratulation by westerners and even less of self-congratulation as moral and economic victors. The dismantling of the empire, which may not yet be over, and of the socialist economic system has brought material benefits to only a small minority.

There is a similarly ambivalent attitude toward recent history. Stalin is revered among the generation that remembers the Second World War—or the Great Patriotic War as Russians call it. Russia lost 20 million dead and there is scarcely a family that was not touched by it. The defeat of Germany is seen as a Russian victory and Stalin as its architect. Yet in the next sentence he can be excoriated for the purges.

Nevertheless, it is as well not to join in the self-criticism—or even to advocate western solutions for Russian problems. Through it all is a strong sense that however much it borrows, Russia is different from the West. Sooner or later an iron curtain slams down—"We Russians are different" or "This will not work in Russia" or "We have our own way in Russia"—and the topic is closed.

The business environment

The commercial environment makes obligatory practices and behavior that in western Europe would be considered unsavory. Tax regulations have not caught up with changing conditions. The taxation system is geared to catch evaders with the result that it encourages evasion: If everything were put properly through the books the effective tax rate of profit, personnel, and VAT taxes would be well over 100 percent. It also encourages rampant bribery of tax officials.

Tax is payable in advance. While in theory overpayment is reclaimable from the government, in practice refunds are considerably delayed, sometimes indefinitely. For some years tax concessions were available to companies employing people with disabilities. The consequence was a phantom disabled labor force on company payrolls, similar to Gogol's *Dead Souls* (a novel about a conman who bought for next to nothing the titles to dead serfs so that he could raise mortgages on them). This loophole has now been closed, but there are many others that it would be unpolitic to reveal. It should be pointed out that western accounting companies have been as creative as Russians. An effective dodge featuring shell companies in Cyprus is colloquially named after the international accountancy firm that invented it.

Law

The basis of Russian law is the *ukase* or decree, administered and enforced by the state. In the old days it originated from the Politburo and now it comes from the president's desk. The constitution bundled through in the fear and uncertainty after the storming of the White House effectively emasculated parliament and gave the president more individual power than the pre-revolutionary czars (or emperors, as they are more correctly known. You were a czar of Moscow but an emperor of Russia).

The idea that a *ukase* incorporates the will or even the acceptance of the people under its rule or that a judiciary should be independent is alien to Russia. The law is regarded a coercive instrument of the state. In the Soviet era laws did not even have to be promulgated. There was a body of secret laws whose existence only came to light when you broke one of them. Not only was ignorance no excuse, it was a prerequisite.

Contracts and written agreements are no less important for Russians than for westerners, but they have a different significance. They are clarifications of working relationships rather than legal endorsements of them. They are not expected to be used as the basis for litigation. And because circumstances change, they can be brought up for renegotiation at a later date.

The legal status of many companies is in doubt. Title to assets that were formerly the property of the state is unclear. Many companies and their land, plant, and buildings were simply appropriated by managers without payment or legal sanction. Many new companies were incorporated under the law of the Soviet Union, which no longer exists. Laws and regulations are under constant review and revision and it is common practice to make them retroactive.

In the end, the effectiveness of any body of law relies on the ability to enforce it. Commercial law is untested in Russian courts. Indeed, there is no judicial system as it is understood in the West. Westerners who invest in the Russian stock market should understand that its legal framework is rudimentary and untested in court. There cannot be many major markets in which agreements are made purely on a basis of trust and mutual self-interest and without any legal underpinning worth the paper on which it is written. As some safeguard for those engaged in international trade, it is often possible to transfer assets and intellectual property offshore and to domicile agreements under western law.

The overabundance of bureaucratic regulation left over from the previous regime creates a fertile ground for inducements and corruption. The lack of a viable legal system makes the enforcement of contracts and the collection of debts a matter for the Mafia rather than the courts.

Mafia

There is Mafia and there is mafia. In the sense of organized crime plying the traditional trade of protection, drugs, gambling, and prostitution, Russians have a long history of their own and little to learn from the West. The benefits of reform for the Mafia are the same as for other big businesses. Profits can now be laundered, legitimized, and displayed and activities internationalized through expansion and alliances. The Mafia dominates retail and transportation business in the large cities. Any business that generates large amounts of cash is especially at risk. The crime explosion and the collapse of policing create a genuine need for "protection," what is called a "roof." The cost of the roof is up to 10 percent of turnover, payable in cash.

Overlapping but distinct is mafia with a lower-case *m*, describing any group of people colluding for their mutual benefit. This too was a characteristic feature of Soviet professional and private life. The economic system could only work on the basis of informal networks of managers and bureaucrats trading favors, goods, and services. These "families" are even more important after the breakdown of more formal structures.

Getting on

Russians put a high value on education. Competition for places at the leading universities and academies is fierce. In the past nepotism and political favoritism played a role in getting into the right schools and even gaining the right grades. Nevertheless, the system was as meritocratic as any in the West.

Money has now become the primary passport to a good education. Practical lessons in entrepreneurship are common at secondary schools, both to raise money directly for the school and to enable students to earn enough to pay the fees. On a broader level, intellectual and artistic attainments are now valued for what they will fetch in the market.

Because of the nature of Soviet society, middle-class social structures and values are the inverse of the West's. The best and brightest in the class were steered toward pure science, where they were rewarded with the best education, pay, benefits, and social status. Academicians occupied the pinnacle of society at the same level as senior party members. Applied science and technology ranked slightly lower. Writers and artists were also valued. The dullards and underachievers gravitated to law and accountancy. Both of these professions were regarded as little more than clerical functions. Whatever the field, academia claimed the brightest.

With free markets and a civil society, the role of lawyers and accountants has changed dramatically and they are bubbling to the top of the social brew, meeting the scientists and artists on the way down. Out of necessity, many scientists have turned to commerce and proved to be remarkably successful. Westerners should not be put off to find a rocket scientist running a trading company. Motivated and extremely intelligent, they come new to a new game without the old habits and ways of thinking. Brought up with a respect for truth and accuracy, they are very good to work with. The old Soviet managers and specialists in trade find it hardest to accommodate to new conditions and are the least satisfactory to deal with.

Biznesmyen

Given the size and scale of the challenge, privatization has been remarkable: 85 percent of formerly state-owned businesses are now privately owned. Not that they are exposed to the full rigors of the free market. Owners and employees are a powerful political lobby and they continue to be feather-bedded by the state with soft loans and a favorable fiscal policy. In addition, entrepreneurial ventures have mushroomed. The people with whom readers work are likely to support the democratic and free-market movement. They have done best out of reform and do not necessarily represent a majority view. The contrary view, one held not only by nostalgic communists, is that privatization was a disaster for the economy. The majority of Russians are worse off in every respect than they were in Soviet times.

In the old days *biznesmyen* was a euphemism for criminal. As most forms of private enterprise were illegal, this was technically correct. With plummeting standards of living after *perestroika*, getting into business became a necessity for those trapped by rocketing prices and fixed incomes. For many *biznes* is synonymous with Mafia, corruption, and the indignity of peddling on the street. For a few it is a liberation.

Business is as much a means of self-expression as an opportunity to get rich. Not that getting rich is underestimated. In a society where egalitarianism was enforced in private life, the rewards of success were reflected in corporate benefits rather than homes and cars. The perks of the most senior managers were concealed in secluded *dachas* and foreign trips. Conspicuous consumption is now allowed to validate success. New Russians build fancy villas, take vacations in the West, and send their children to English boarding schools. Moscow is purported to be a primary market for Mercedes, BMW, and Rolls-Royce. This is not a general phenomenon throughout Russia, however. The affluent new Russians are mostly to be found in Moscow, with others in commercial centers like St. Petersburg, Nizhnii Novgorod, and Vladivostok.

Attitudes to the West

Russians have a distorted vision of the West. A drive through a British inner city will usually modify their conceptions of western affluence and give them comfort that they are not as far behind as they thought. It takes longer to modify their preconceptions about how business works. Russian managers, especially those who are hired by western companies, are surprised to find that they have a far greater degree of freedom than their counterparts in the West. Westerners at the highest level are far more constrained by procedures, reporting lines, and accountability. Russians can thus easily doubt the seniority and status of western associates who need board approval for all but the slightest commitment.

Thanks to a concerted effort by academics and consultants, both western and Russian, most Russian business people are well versed in the basic theories of western business management. They are therefore surprised when they find out that market-driven strategies, quality programs, strategic planning, team-based management, financial analysis, human resource management techniques, and the rest of the business school core curriculum are underutilized by all but the largest companies.

The one exception is the annual budget. This is the most important management tool to explain to Russian colleagues—especially since for many western companies it is the only one. Once they appreciate the tyranny of the budget and the process for setting it, they can begin to understand the rationale for day-to-day decision making.

For example, Russians are puzzled that when westerners go to Russia they can spend the equivalent of a Russian's annual salary in a hotel and take them to an expensive restaurant, but balk at giving them a fax machine so that they can communicate more effectively. It has to be explained that there is a line in the annual budget for travel expenses but not for providing partners with capital equipment. Russians are advised to find out when their western partners begin to work on next year's budget and lobby hard for what they want at that time.

It is as well to concentrate on explaining western methods rather than prescribing them to Russian colleagues. Immensely self-critical about their own circumstances and constantly looking for ways to improve them, the barriers come down when outsiders pontificate.

Leadership and organization

Note: In this section do not read "she" for "he." There are only "hes."

The blame for the inefficiencies and idiosyncrasies of the business environment today is often attributed to 70 years of communism. It is instructive to read the memoirs of western businessmen who traded in Russia before 1918. Without underestimating the dire effect of state socialism and central planning on the economy and the structure of society, it is remarkable how little effect Marxist-Leninism had on the values and behaviors of people in business and public life.

The autocrat is the dominating cultural role model for Russian leaders. The organizational icon is not the pyramid but the Christmas tree. The ever-widening branches are connected not to each other but to a central trunk of resources, communication, and instruction in direct control of a strong and autocratic boss, the "star" on the top.

Decision making, from the long term to the day to day, is highly centralized. One of the biggest compliments you can pay a Russian manager is to say that he has "the power of the telephone"; in other words, to get something done all he does is lift the receiver. Lower down the hierarchy the effectiveness of managers in having their proposals and recommendations listened to depends on their skill in getting into the boss's office. This is the single biggest reason for delay in getting decisions. The traditional advice to outsiders to find the decision maker is nowhere else more valid. Spending time with subordinates, aides, and associates, however qualified and plausible, is usually a waste of time. The information and requests you make will only be fed up to the boss if he asks for them.

Delegation, as opposed to giving instructions, is an underdeveloped skill. The ability to keep half a dozen conversations going at once with people sitting in his office and on the phone is essential. There is usually a strong contrast between this frenetic activity and the indolent calm of the secretary's office outside, where the most used item of office equipment is the television.

It is the role of the chief executive to make plans and set targets on his own responsibility. The strategic planning horizon does not usually extend beyond the next 12 months. Given the tumultuous changes in the environment, there is little incentive to do so. Paradoxically, the dominance of central planning in Soviet times meant that managers were absolved from this task. There was also no concept of market forces or demand. Planning, forecasting, and budgeting are new skills for Russian managers.

The *ukase* is the archetypal management tool. Because it is the result of the deliberations of one person, with perhaps a small group of close advisers, untested by debate and unsupported by analysis or systematic input, it can appear arbitrary to those in the organization. Managers who wish to be more participative face an uphill task. Their employees are uncomfortable with open discussion and debate.

The formal meeting is rarely used as a means of discussion, debate, or information gathering, much less decision making and implementation planning. These activities are done one to one or informally. There is no equivalent of the board meeting, the management committee meeting, the staff meeting. Meetings are for assembling with outsiders or rubberstamping previous decisions.

Yet managers are well aware that they need information, feedback, and consensus from those they manage. In the absence of formal mechanisms for doing this it is garnered informally. The manager will gather a small group of intimates and confidants to be his eyes and ears. This cannot be termed a team, in the western organizational sense. Russians work together not so much in teams as in groupings. The roles are undefined, their operation unstructured, and responsibility and accountability remain always with the senior person. The model is repeated down through the organization. Networking, personal relationships, consensus building, and trading information and favors are as essential for Russian managers as is the power of the telephone. This extends to their western business partners. In a chaotic and lawless environment, a solid personal relationship based on loyalty and trust is the basis for a profitable working relationship.

Language

Russian has now become an important international business language. In the Soviet era one dealt mostly with professional negotiators from government agencies who were fluent in European languages. Travelers were confined to a few cities nominated on their visa and provided with an interpreter. Now in the newly independent states as well as Russia you can travel virtually anywhere and deal with private businessmen who perhaps have no English and for whom Russian may even be a second language. *In extremis*, people from central Europe, even Poles and Balts, will speak Russian if they have no English or German.

Unless they already speak Russian, most readers will not have time to learn it properly, although a smattering will go a long way. On the difficulty scale for Anglo-Saxons it is harder than German and easier than Greek. Many commercial and scientific terms are borrowed from English, French, and German. At the very least, knowing the Cyrillic alphabet is essential if you visit.

Fifteen minutes on the Moscow metro are enough to illustrate that in the mix of oral, visual, and literal communication, Russians favor the oral. It is very important not to rely on letters and faxes and reports to get the message across but to confirm with a conversation wherever possible. Conversely, those from more literal cultures, such as northern Europe, should pay closer attention to what their Russian partners say than to what they write.

Nevertheless, Russians make frequent use of what they call "protocols." These are minutes, memos, or action plans that clarify decisions and agreements but are expected to be more elaborate than their equivalents in many western countries.

As with any nationality speaking International English, it is wise to check and recheck the meaning of words and phrases. If you say to Russians "You're not going to the office today?" they will say "no" if they are going and "yes" if they are staying at home. Words we take for granted may have a different interpretation, especially technical expressions to do with accounting and banking. It is wise to make sure that everyone is using the same definition of "profit," for example.

Russian is a flexible and figurative language and Russian speech is full of proverbs, catchphrases, and imagery gathered from sources ranging from the Bible to twentieth-century writers like Ilf and Petrov. While humor is not associated with formal occasions such as meetings or presentations, it is never far from the surface in a business or a social context.

There is also a Russian slang, called *mat*, which will be of interest to more proficient Russian speakers. It is based on the many taboo words and phrases with sexual connotations. Operating with about four basic nouns and a couple of verbs and numerous derivatives, it can be heard at all strata of society and in all situations from the street to the boardroom. Russians tend to be more proper and prudish than westerners, which makes *mat* that much more expressive.

Like many British people, Russians are given to understatement. The equivalent of "not too bad," meaning "good," is *normalna*, normal. The phrase of which I am most wary is "no problem." It usually means that the speaker has given the matter little thought. "This will be very difficult" is much more promising of success. Nevertheless, in general Russians are more prone to speak straight than to clothe their statements in diplomacy and fudge.

Behavior and etiquette

When speaking Russian and to each other, Russians are meticulous about appropriate forms of address. Name and patronymic is the most formal. In the western translations of their business cards the patronymic is replaced by an initial and foreigners are not expected to follow the convention. Titles such as Doctor and Professor are widely used. Probably the most prestigious title in Russia, reflecting social priorities, is Academician, one of the 200 members of the Academy of Sciences. Unmarried women are called *devushka*, miss. *Gospodin* and *Gospaja—Monsieur* and *Madame—* are usually used for westerners and in places such as restaurants.

Colleagues refer to each other by their last names. First names are usual among colleagues of more or less the same status. Every first name has a score of variants, each of which represents a different level of intimacy.

Russian etiquette is generally relaxed and informal. Toward women it is unreconstructedly old-fashioned. There are many traditional little rituals and customs. The one westerners are mostly likely to contravene is never to shake hands over a threshold.

On first meeting Russians sometimes appear gloomy and forbidding, mainly because the conventions of body language are different. For example, a smile is only used for greeting among personal friends. Smiling is not respectful on formal occasions. Smiling for no reason is a sign of idiocy, not geniality.

Conventions of listening are different. In common with Nordic peoples, Russians are brought up to listen attentively without interrupting and without the encouraging signs and gestures and interruptions to which westerners are accustomed. When the other person has finished speaking it is polite to let what they have said sink in for a second before replying. Westerners used to the cut and thrust, parries, and *non sequiturs* of their own conversational style may have a constant suspicion that they have said something wrong.

In many western countries a tangible distinction is made between home life and business life. In Russia this distinction does not apply. I recently discussed a contract with Americans in the US on a Saturday evening after a ball game. We left the host's house and drove five miles to his office to sit round the boardroom table. The following week on a similar occasion with Russians in Moscow, we left the office and went home to thrash things out round the dining room table. At night is when the most serious telephone conversations take place. One need have no inhibitions about phoning a Russian colleague at any time before midnight.

For those who have access, the sauna has a special place in Russian business life. In Soviet times the sauna was where agreements and decisions were confirmed if not made. Men trust each other more when naked. It was yet another impediment to the advancement of women. Those who find the discomfort of saunas unpleasant need not shirk them in Russia. The ill effects are more likely to come from the food and drink. In a six-hour sauna most Russians spend less than half an hour in the hot room and the rest of the time around the table. Nobody minds if you put in only a token minute or so in the heat room. State-owned companies were the only institutions that could afford to maintain saunas. New Russians do not have time and are as likely to prefer tennis for exercise.

Restaurants remain vital in developing business relationships. The standard menu is a wide assortment of *hors d'oeuvre* followed by main course, dessert, tea, and cake. While predictable in their content, meals are unpredictable in their timing. The above menu is as likely to be served for breakfast after getting off an all-night train, complete with vodka, brandy, and wine, as for dinner late at night. The same is true in private houses. People eat when they are hungry and when it is convenient.

The rest of the day's timetable can be as fluid. Those with a meticulous sense of routine and punctuality might as well put it in suspension. Early risers might have to be patient too: Russians start work well after nine.

Westerners are often warned that in Russia they will have to function in a haze of smoke and drink. This is not my experience with youngish middle-class professionals in the private sector or in science. The majority of my associates are non-smokers and a few teetotal; one is even a vegetarian. At meals and parties it is more often westerners who get drunk—not because we are less used to it than Russians but because we drink more. If Russians want to get drunk they are more likely to do it privately with a couple of friends than on a formal occasion. One tip is to imitate the Russians and drink only at the toasts. In between, drink the fruit juice that is always on the table.

This is not to deny that smoking and drinking are favorite Russian pastimes and solaces. Among the New Russians they are not universal, however, and it is not at all compulsory for westerners to join in. Fortunately, Russians are among the most tolerant of human weakness (it is human malice that goes unforgiven) and over-indulgence is unlikely to be a cause of embarrassment the next day.

JEWS

Where is the largest synagogue in Europe?
Budapest
Ljubljana
Berlin

Americans in Europe

American management theory and practice pervade European business. This is partly a consequence of the high level of direct investment. In many countries and industries Americans are the leading foreign investors and may even dominate domestic interests. Their influence is compounded by international consulting and accountancy industries, imbued with US ideas and methods.

Indirect influence is also pervasive. Much European business education is modeled on American theories and teaching methods. For example, many of the core theories of people management taught at European business schools are based on original research carried out in the US in the first half of the twentieth century. The resources available to American business academia are much greater, and its status much higher, than in many countries in Europe. In the more popular domain, the gurus who sell the most books and claim the biggest audiences are American.

The motivation for looking at the American example is that, at least until Japan provided an alternative, the American way was the most successful. With success goes *chic*. Just as Europe adopted English dress, manners, and jargon at the end of the nineteenth century, so it adopted Americana in the twentieth. In every European country those managers who seek an alternative for their traditional style look to the US. It is also neutral. It is more comfortable for most Europeans to follow the American model than, say, the German, which has had comparable success.

American business culture is much more varied than European preconceptions allow. Our direct experience is mainly limited to multinationals and their expatriate employees, not necessarily typical of either the parochial or the entrepreneurial sectors of their domestic environment. The following remarks are limited to those aspects that create the greatest misunderstanding between Europeans and expatriate Americans.

Organization

The influential theories associated with the term "scientific management" originated in the US and are based on the belief that organizational processes can be systematically analyzed and improved. All of the processes of the organization, down to minor reports and decisions, are subject to detailed quantitative analysis. Planning, both in the sense of budgeting and also wider strategic planning, is detailed and taken seriously. Areas of management that in Europe would be left to qualitative assessment, for example human resource management, are subject to systematic analysis. To Europeans this can seem unnecessary or impractical, but Americans view unsubstantiated and unquantified assertions with skepticism.

As the environment changes, so the organizational functions necessary to cope with it are very quickly changed too. The immediate reaction to a development in the business or technological environment, or to a change of management, is to change the organization. A characteristic of US corporate life is constant upheaval in which social hierarchies and relationships are repeatedly disturbed.

Organizations exist independently of their members. The needs of individuals are seen as subsidiary to the needs of the organization. Each member has a well-defined function to carry out and if that particular function no longer has any part to play, then neither does the person doing it. The readiness of companies to fire surplus or underperforming employees, and the corresponding readiness of employees to change companies in order to further a career, are part of an arm's-length relationship between an individual and an organization. While the immediate feelings of "terminated" employees may be as bruised as those of a European counterpart, there is no more rancor than in the case of a blue-collar worker who is laid off. It is accepted as the way things work. If the organization's needs change again, those people may be hired back into the company at a later date. However, while a person belongs to an organization he or she is expected to identify with its goals and to demonstrate dedication to it. Loyalties may be temporary but not less than whole-hearted.

Power in an American organization resides with the chief executive officer and is exercised through a small operating or executive committee of senior executives. Whatever other titles or position the person may have, the only one that matters is CEO. The board of directors, of whom several may be outside directors, is more like a German *Aufsichtsrat* than a British board of directors. The American board's main task is to appoint the CEO and it has little influence over day-to-day operations. The CEO's power and accountability are rarely shared. He or she appoints the executive committee and they are delegates rather than colleagues. There is much less feeling of collegiality than in a German or British corporation and little concept of shared responsibility. It is more akin to the French pattern. Vertical reporting lines are more important than peer relationships, which tend to be intensely competitive.

Beneath the level of senior management, accountability is rigorously defined and meticulously reported, wherever possible in terms of profitability or some other financial yardstick. Americans are used to transparent organizations and are uneasy with the ambiguity and hidden hierarchies that characterize many European companies. However closely organizational values are adapted to suit the indigenous culture of the host country, the key disciplines of system and control are kept firmly in place.

Leadership

While the reality of the American leadership style may not match up to the self-image of rugged, dominating individualism, at least not in the context of conformist business organizations, it is firmly based on the concept of individual accountability. The role of the boss is sometimes described as a "coach," but in its sporting rather than educational sense. Football and baseball coaches are considerably more directive than consultative. To carry the analogy further, coaches in American sport continue to manage and direct their players during the course of the game.

American bosses are not generally skilled or experienced in dealing with argument or open disagreement from their subordinates. They would tend to regard it as insubordination rather than constructive criticism. Conversely, it is sometimes hard for European superiors to evoke vigorous comment from American subordinates.

The outward egalitarianism of American manners is deceptive. Within a business organization there is a well-defined and rigorously observed hierarchy. Your position in the hierarchy has little to do with seniority or status or influence or any other "social" determinant. It concerns how much power you have. Power is measured by the degree of the business under your direct control. The way this is evaluated varies from business to busines—it may be the number of people reporting to you, the amount of profit generated, or the amount of earning assets.

Status is communicated by sophisticated titling systems, in which rank is coupled with function: vice-president finance, for example. Equally sophisticated is the salary and perks system that goes with it—the type of office, furniture, computer, country club membership, credit card, the quality of hotel in which you are entitled to stay, eligibility to use the corporate jet, and so on. Since cars are not tax efficient and are usually privately owned, they do not feature in the status system.

Americans may lose patience with the participative, committee cultures of some countries. They do not look for consensus, in the sense of collective responsibility for a decision jointly arrived at, but for wholehearted commitment to a course of action for which one person carries total responsibility. Any vestigial notion of shared responsibility evaporates completely if it goes wrong.

Meetings are primarily a communication tool for imparting or gathering information, supported by the appropriate numbers or other hard facts. They are also the forum for the formal presentation of proposals for examination and ratification. An in-house presentation to a small group, or even one's boss, demands a professionalism more usually associated with a board presentation or a sales pitch in a European context. The object is not to make a decision—this will have been previously lobbied or be subsequently approved—but to test the presenter's competence, preparation, and depth of knowledge with sometimes trivial questions.

In dealing with colleagues at all levels it is important to demonstrate competence and professionalism. Bringing a problem to another, whether boss, subordinate, or colleague, without a suggested solution and especially without all the relevant data, in the expectation that a solution will be worked out jointly, is a sign of weakness. Professionalism is demonstrated by a numerate, analytical approach to problem solving. Whatever the quality of the ultimate decision, it will not have been made without exhaustive quantitative analysis. There is an antipathy toward unsubstantiated theory and qualitative as opposed to quantitative argument. This does not mean that quantitative decisions are necessarily more effective than more conceptual or intuitive decisions, but they are ostensibly more rational.

It is also important to demonstrate "aggression," which in the American sense means the dynamic pursuit of personal and corporate goals. The single-minded corporate and personal pursuit of profit is frank and unashamed. In more participative European cultures such self-motivation is sometimes interpreted as self-centeredness. Conversely, Americans may find their European colleagues lacking in motivation and commitment.

Attitudes and behavior

Many Americans are inhibited when first coming to Europe by a belief that social conventions are more formal than in fact they are. Similarly, many Europeans are misled by the apparent informality of American ways. Lurking beneath the relaxed and familiar style, the ready use of first names, and the absence of ceremony is a subtle code of manners that can be primly Victorian.

In the work environment day-to-day interaction is energetic and open. Business discussions may be forthright to the point of being brusque. Bluntness is preferred to subtlety. Some Europeans consider American openness unseemly and brash, unaware that what they believe is their own sophisticated reserve may appear muddle-headed and devious.

At the same time, the essential assertiveness and competitiveness of business relationships are tempered by a greater degree of informal socializing and friendliness than many Europeans are used to. Monday mornings are for rerunning Sunday's ball game as well as for the weekly staff meeting. Colleagues gossip about their family life and leisure activities to an extent that many Europeans would regard as intrusive. Meanwhile, Americans may find European reserve patronizing and standoffish.

Communication

American communication is typically assertive and direct. The need to be explicit sometimes leads into a circumlocutory and pompous style in the laborious search for the right word or phrase.

Americans rarely take anything seriously unless there is a number attached to it. If it cannot be expressed as a dollar value, then some other index will do.

Informality incorporates the extensive use of humor on all formal and informal occasions. The joke is an obligatory warmup to speeches and presentations. Humor can range from the hearty to the witty and the only taboo subjects are money and the company's products.

By no means all Americans transferred to Europe will work or expect others to work the long hours associated with certain industries or cities, notably New York. Generally speaking they prefer to start work earlier than Europeans and to go home to their families for an early dinner. However, they will expect to be accessible at home in the evenings, at weekends, and on vacation. The amount of vacation time in Europe may come as a surprise. In the US two or three weeks is the usual vacation entitlement and four is a maximum for senior people after long service.

Socializing

Business life extends deep into family and social life. Colleagues and their spouses are used to meeting regularly. Americans tend to stick together overseas, not only because in many European countries there is no tradition of neighborliness but also because that is what they do at home.

Corporate status reaches outside immediate business circles. The importance given to business and the social status of business people are generally greater than in most European countries. An introduction to a stranger at a cocktail party often includes that person's employer and their title. Social standing is conferred by working for a prestigious company and diminished if that company's profitability takes a dive or its bond rating slips. At social events business is often the main topic of discussion, and despairing hosts may find the party split for the evening between those who go out to work and those who work with home and family.

> **PERSONAL COMPUTERS**
> Which country has the greatest and which the smallest number of personal computers per 100 inhabitants?
>> Portugal
>> Greece
>> Switzerland

Japanese in Europe

Japanese management methods have a pronounced indirect effect on the European competitors and suppliers of Japanese companies. There is a school of management theory inspired by and imitative of Japanese models. While Japanese business culture in its entirety is outside the scope of this book, it is relevant to look at some of the ways in which it interacts with European business cultures.

From a European perspective there are two different aspects of Japanese management: the way in which production and delivery processes are managed and how individual colleagues relate to each other. The former, "hard" element of management is relatively easy to assimilate into a European context, while the latter, the "soft" element, is so unfamiliar that accommodation can often go no further than understanding and respect.

Two examples of hard management techniques that Japanese companies are instrumental in promoting are "just-in-time" (JIT) and "total quality" systems. The aim of JIT is to match, as nearly as possible, output with market demand in a continuous process beginning at the stage of long-range planning and ending when the product reaches the end user. The aim of total quality is to eliminate error and waste at all stages of the process. This is not just on the shop floor but at every level and in every activity of the organization and every stage in the process.

As well as technical expertise, these systems demand above all the commitment of every person in the organization to carrying them out. If they are perceived as yet another tool to help management control the workers, then they fail. They will not work in a highly directive culture or one in which relations between different levels in the organization are characterized by confrontation.

Planning, in every sense including rigorous budgeting, is a vital part of the management process. Consistent with their stage of development in the European market, Japanese companies take a long-term view. They tend to concentrate on sales and market share, not profit, and on product development. Reporting on a few key variables is detailed and tightly controlled from the center.

This approach is assimilable by Europeans because it is no less intrinsic to European business culture than to Japanese. The leap forward in Japanese quality from the shoddy mimicry of 60 years ago to today's preeminence was achieved to a great extent through the adoption and elaboration of primarily American scientific management techniques. The Japanese reintroduced concepts that had been temporarily mislaid: craftsmanship, perfectionism, corporate pride, teamwork, and cooperation. These are part of a European industrial tradition too and there is no reason to think that Japan monopolizes them.

It is in the "softer" areas, such as decision making, leadership, and motivation, that the clash between European and Japanese cultures is most tangible. It is sometimes stated, for example, that the Japanese place a higher value on group norms, consensus, and the acceptance of authority. However, such a statement ignores much more fundamental differences in the underlying social context.

Signals and symbols

To many westerners Japanese ways of thought and behavior are pervaded with ambiguity, uncertainty, and relativity. Europeans have to learn to interpret hints and subtleties and work with a greater degree of indirection and lack of clarity than they are used to. Westerners and Japanese do not share the same set of communication conventions. The meaning of body language, silence, and manners as well as language gets lost in translation.

From the Japanese point of view their own behavior is perfectly clear. They in turn find confusing and ambiguous many of the subtleties of speech and behavior that Europeans take for granted. For example, the conventions of listening are different. The western way of listening is constantly to impose judgment, to filter what we see and hear through a critical faculty. While listening, the Japanese engage in a practice called *aizuchi*, a series of "yes" or "I understand" comments that serve to encourage the speaker. Westerners tend to make the mistake of interpreting *aizuchi* as agreement.

Independence vs. interdependence

Western culture values the ultimate superiority of the individual over the group. Japanese culture is the opposite. Loyalty to one's immediate group is paramount and not even self-interest overrides commitment to the welfare of the immediate community. This is a concept that westerners can accept in theory but whose everyday implications are sometimes difficult to cope with: interminable meetings, tortuous decision making, sharing responsibility, the duty to keep everyone in the group informed even about apparently trivial details. The idea of individuals sitting in their separate offices getting on with their work is an alien one for Japanese. Open-plan offices are the norm, even housing relatively senior people.

A Japanese organization chart shows only collective units, not individual titles and names. As a description of how the organization actually works it is rarely more than an approximation. More important are the paternalistic social hierarchy and the complex network of personal relationships and obligations that weave through it. The hierarchy is based on seniority and experience, as much as responsibility, and reinforced by mutual obligations that go far deeper than the expedient loyalties of the West. Significant group relationships are not between peers, as they tend to be in the West, but between people of very different status and seniority. There is a mutually supportive relationship between a senior and a junior, more akin to the working relationship that a western manager would have with a secretary than that with a subordinate.

This does not mean that a Japanese company is one big happy family, despite what its president, like his western counterpart, may claim. Individuals and groups compete strenuously and factionalism is rife. The difference is that individual success or failure is inextricable from that of the group. To westerners used to individual evaluation this can be frustrating. The corollary is that there are few personal recriminations in the case of error unless someone has consciously overstepped the rules. His or her colleagues get together and put it right. If there is a problem with that person it will be discussed within the group, and if it cannot be solved the leader will be deputed to take it to a higher level. This is in contrast with the habitual western reaction of finding someone on whom to pin the blame.

Harmony vs. conflict

Western relationships are competitive rather than consensual. Winning is very important, whether it is a decision, an argument, or a genuine conflict. Competition is valued as creative and constructive. While Japanese are certainly not averse to winning, they are even more averse to confrontation. Much of Japanese etiquette and behavior, to western eyes rigidly conformist and irritatingly elusive, is designed to avoid any hint of conflict. When the world's highest mountain was first climbed in 1953 it was referred to in the west as the "conquest" of Everest; in Japan they use the word "befriend." Extreme politeness and deference, elliptical statements, vagueness, evasiveness, and indecisiveness are disconcerting to westerners especially if they cannot read the real messages coming over. Likewise, Japanese find western clarity, assertiveness, and love of debate and argument divisive and embarrassing.

Westerners like to know where they stand. So do Japanese, but not at the cost of disturbing the peace. Few westerners have not felt at some time like having it out with someone, getting things straight, putting things on the record, making their feelings known. They are disconcerted when Japanese colleagues, especially the boss, do not respond and sidestep the issue, hoping that it will go away. When faced with conflict westerners are used to dealing with it.

Commitment and tenacity even to the point of obstinacy are prized in the West. Changing your mind and abandoning a position without a struggle are signs of weakness. Sticking to your guns in an argument, not letting go, even in trivial matters, indicates strength of character. To a Japanese it is the opposite. The ultimate "he goes or I go" threat is incomprehensible to them.

Leadership

Westerners tend to value a tough, individualistic, and dominating leadership style, including the ability to take independent decisions and have them successfully implemented. The higher a Japanese manager rises in a company, the more pains he will take to hide his ambition and capability and not to be seen as a forceful leader. Westerners who look for a decisive and charismatic boss are likely to be disappointed.

A Japanese manager concentrates on getting his group to work together. He is expected to be accessible, to work as an integral part of the group, and to share whatever information he has. Because he has spent his whole career with the company, more often than not in the same type of function, he is expected to be fully knowledgeable about his subordinates' work as well as his own.

One of the problems that Japanese managers often have with western subordinates is getting them to show initiative. Their complaint is that Europeans need to be told what to do all the time. And when they have done it, they need immediate assurance that they have done it right and a pat on the back. This would be embarrassing to the boss and personally offensive to a Japanese subordinate who expects no more than a vague indication of the job to be done. Japanese do not have personal job descriptions or performance appraisal systems. Job definition is for the group and it is assumed that everyone will do their best to fulfill it.

Their western subordinates, on the other hand, complain that they are given only vague hints of what they are supposed to do. Without defined responsibility, clear direction, and realistic goals, they may find their jobs boring and without scope. When individual descriptions are instituted in Japanese companies in Europe it is usually at the Europeans' insistence.

Europeans who discover the ground rules find that they have more scope to make their own jobs than in a circumscribed western environment. The ground rules are never do anything that is above your status, never do anything that infringes on someone else's status, and never cut across hierarchical boundaries. The way to ensure that you remain within the boundaries of your status is to keep your boss informed of the smallest detail. Among the sample of people I talked to it was those at the lower level of organization who found this the most stimulating change from a European working environment where junior people are given comparatively little scope or responsibility.

Etiquette

In the West we have seen a withdrawal from form and formality, formal etiquette and formal dress. This is probably the result of the increasing importance given to individuality and a concern for honesty and "truth" in human relationships. These are seen as being masked by uniformity of dress and behavior. We want to see others and be seen by them as who we really are and not as a cipher or dummy. Associated with this is the idea of genuineness of emotions. Rules of behavior are viewed as false or dishonest.

In Asia this is not a concern. People do not want strangers to see who they really are. In Japan only the most intimate of friends and family will call you by your first name. Even within a family an elder brother or sister will not be called by their first name but brother or sister.

Japanese in Europe have reluctantly learned to use first names, but feel more comfortable when addressed by the last name followed by *san*. Senior people may be addressed by their title plus *san* instead of their last name. First names are reserved for family and close friends.

Titles, modes of address, and language are carefully measured to indicate relative status, as are the other subtle status symbols of office life such as job titles or the positioning of desks in an open office. For example, seniors would have their backs to the windows where they could enjoy the privilege of natural light, in contrast with the fluorescent lighting pervading Japanese offices. While very sensitive to fine distinctions of rank, the western use of material goods to communicate achievement and authority is noticeably lacking in Japanese companies. Offices are workaday, cars are unostentatious, and so on.

A business card communicates the status of the owner, their title, and their name. Names are difficult to spell and remember, even for Japanese, so the card is an extension of the person's identity. It should be handled respectfully, left on the table, and put away only when the meeting is over.

More important than the actual forms of language and behavior are pervasive politeness and a concern to avoid embarrassment to oneself or others. Displays of temper or any other uncontrolled emotions are seen as a sign of weakness.

Japanese manners are based on reciprocation, a sense of mutual indebtedness. To many westerners the excessive deference of a subordinate to a superior is less surprising than the fact that it is returned in kind. Relationships between all levels are built on exchange, whether of gifts, courtesies, help, information, and so on.

Politeness is also based on apology and self-deprecation. In handing over a report one apologizes beforehand for its being a shoddy piece of work. Few westerners would offer such a hostage.

Extreme politeness does not exclude openness in relationships. Europeans, especially women, may be surprised at the personal nature of conversations. This is usually because Japanese need to know people well before they can be comfortable with them. In some European countries you don't have to trust people to work with them as long as they do their job. In a Japanese environment there is a higher tolerance of professional and human frailty, but it is compensated for by a greater demand for loyalty and trust.

Punctuality

Japanese are very punctual when politeness requires it and especially with senior people. Otherwise time is fluid. A meeting will carry on until it is finished or interrupted by the demands of a senior person outside. The working day can be very long, reflecting a demanding work ethic and a high level of commitment. Being the first to leave, even if you have no work to do, is a snub to the group and an embarrassment to your senior. As they do in Japan, Japanese in Europe may regularly work on Saturdays, rarely take more than a week's vacation or their full entitlement, and count sick days as holiday.

Humor

On informal occasions when they know everyone well, Japanese will be humorous and entertaining. At a formal meeting or among strangers they may be awkward and withdrawn and too nervous to loosen up. In presentations and speeches to westerners, many have learnt that the audience expects jokes and informality and respond accordingly. Japanese do not usually appreciate flippancy or triviality.

Social life

The most common complaint among westerners is that most major decisions seem to be made outside office hours by their Japanese colleagues. While in day-to-day activities they are kept well informed, they are kept in the dark about the overall direction of the company. For a westerner to progress in a Japanese-managed company it is essential to work late in the evening and at weekends. This can be a major impediment for women. In the workplace itself most of the women I talked to did not find Japanese more chauvinistic than their western counterparts. The difficulty was in establishing the appropriate relationships, as well as finding the time, to join in the after-hours discussions.

It is not so easy for men either. While the expatriate Japanese is considerably more flexible and adaptable to European ways than the stereotypical image of the chauvinistic and single-minded Tokyo salaryman, it is hard to break into the inner circle. As in any foreign company, a first requirement is to make an effort to speak the employer's language. As well as being practically useful, this demonstrates a commitment to career and company to which Japanese are particularly sensitive. It is this level of dedication to the organization that is probably the biggest hurdle to making any more than an averagely successful career in a Japanese company.

TEETH

Which university has the largest collection of false teeth in Europe?

      Utrecht

      Padua

      Salamanca

Euroquiz answers

p5, Coffee—Finland

p6, Murder—Luxembourg highest, Portugal lowest

p11, Birth—Turkey highest, Latvia lowest

p20, Religion—All of them

p22, Tennis—France

p30, Geography—Reunion, on the Tropic of Capricorn

p33, Food—Greece largest, Netherlands smallest

p38, Obesity—Greece

p41, Euro—Guyane

p48, Lack of ski potential—Denmark, 173mm

p52, Garbage—Switzerland

p60, Lawyers—Spain (237; Germany 125, France 60)

p69, Smoking—Greece (7.8; Russia 3.6, Romania 2.1)

p74, Languages—Sorbian, Germany; Arumanian, Greece; Friulian, Italy

p80, Literature—France

p84, Penguins—Edinburgh

p90, Phones—Germany

p95, Golf—Corfu

p98, Christians—Lithuania

p101, Police—Finland

p104, Divorce—Finland highest, Greece lowest

p110, Work—Turkey most, France least

p121, Votes for women—1906 Finland, 1945 Italy, 1971 Switzerland

p127, AIDS—Portugal highest, Finland lowest

p130, Furniture—Luzembourg biggest, Finland smallest

p139, Medical care—Switzerland most, Estonia least

p145, Pollution—Norway

p159, Aid—Denmark

p163, Jailbirds—Russia

p168, Dog lovers—Poland

p171, Men of war—Turkey

p175, Jews—France

p178, Nudists—Netherlands

p181, Libraries—Moscow (Lenin Library)

p195, Death on the road—Greece (20.1; Italy 12.1; Germany 8.7)

About the Author

John Mole was educated at Oxford University and INSEAD. After a 15-year career with an American bank in the US, the Middle East, and Europe, he now divides his time between entrepreneurship and consulting on international management. He offers advice on the development of a global business culture and training in negotiation, communication, and team building in a range of activities from conference presentations to in-house workshops He can be contacted by email through his web site www.johnmole.com.